Apache Iceberg:
The Definitive Guide

*Data Lakehouse Functionality, Performance,
and Scalability on the Data Lake*

Tomer Shiran, Jason Hughes, and Alex Merced
Forewords by Gerrit Kazmaier, Raghu Ramakrishnan, and Rick Sears

Beijing · Boston · Farnham · Sebastopol · Tokyo

Apache Iceberg: The Definitive Guide

by Tomer Shiran, Jason Hughes, and Alex Merced

Copyright © 2024 O'Reilly Media Inc. All rights reserved.

Published by O'Reilly Media, Inc., 1005 Gravenstein Highway North, Sebastopol, CA 95472.

O'Reilly books may be purchased for educational, business, or sales promotional use. Online editions are also available for most titles (*https://oreilly.com*). For more information, contact our corporate/institutional sales department: 800-998-9938 or *corporate@oreilly.com*.

Acquisitions Editor: Aaron Black	**Indexer:** Potomac Indexing, LLC
Development Editor: Gary O'Brien	**Interior Designer:** David Futato
Production Editor: Elizabeth Faerm	**Cover Designer:** Karen Montgomery
Copyeditor: Audrey Doyle	**Illustrator:** Kate Dullea
Proofreader: Kim Wimpsett	

May 2024:   First Edition

Revision History for the First Edition

2024-05-02:   First Release

See *https://oreilly.com/catalog/errata.csp?isbn=9781098148621* for release details.

The O'Reilly logo is a registered trademark of O'Reilly Media, Inc. *Apache Iceberg: The Definitive Guide*, the cover image, and related trade dress are trademarks of O'Reilly Media, Inc.

This work is part of a collaboration between O'Reilly and Dremio. See our statement of editorial independence (*https://oreil.ly/editorial-independence*).

978-1-098-14862-1

[LSI]

Praise for *Apache Iceberg: The Definitive Guide*

This book is a fantastic learning resource and reference guide for
Apache Iceberg internals. My team finds it invaluable.

—Kaashif Hymabaccus, senior software engineer,
Bloomberg

Apache Iceberg is on track to become the de facto table format for
the next generation of data platforms. This book is an indispensable
guide to navigate through its core concepts and components, a journey
that most data engineers will have to take in the upcoming years.

—Mahdi Karabiben, staff data engineer,
Zendesk

Since the introduction of the data lakehouse, Apache Iceberg has
been on the rise. This book equips you with the core concepts of
Iceberg as a table format, gives you everything you need to run
it in production, and will still be your reference material months
after getting started. Well done, Tomer, Jason, and Alex!

—Max Schultze, associate director of data engineering,
HelloFresh

A comprehensive overview of Apache Iceberg from architecture
to design and implementation solutions.

—Simeon Schwarz, director, data and analytics,
OMS National Insurance Company

Table of Contents

Part III.   Apache Iceberg in Practice

Foreword by Gerrit Kazmaier

As someone deeply invested in the evolution of data management, I am thrilled to introduce this pivotal book on Apache Iceberg at a time when the industry is encountering complex challenges in managing data. Apache Iceberg, with its groundbreaking open table format, is not just a technological advancement; it represents a significant shift in how organizations can approach managing data in the AI era.

My involvement in the data community has allowed me to witness firsthand the growing curiosity and demand for knowledge about data lakehouses and Apache Iceberg. This book, therefore, arrives not just as an informative resource but as a necessary guide for those eager to understand and apply this technology in their work. It delves into the architecture of Apache Iceberg and extends to its practical applications and best practices, serving as an indispensable tool for data architects and engineers.

This book is more than just a compendium of information; it is a testament to the evolving landscape of data management and a beacon for those navigating its complexities. I am confident that it will be a valuable asset to anyone seeking to leverage Apache Iceberg in the data architectures.

— Gerrit Kazmaier
Vice President and General Manager
Data analytics, Google Cloud

Foreword by Raghu Ramakrishnan

Apache Iceberg is one of the leading open formats for updatable Parquet-based tables, which are emerging as the new data storage standard for analytics. Historically, relational databases have stored data row-by-row, packed into physical pages for efficient I/O. Columnar table formats, however, have proven far more efficient for query-intensive workloads. Data lakes began by supporting queries over columnar formats such as Parquet, but of course, transactional updates must also be supported efficiently to address traditional warehouse scenarios. Iceberg is emerging as a popular choice of table format supporting scenarios that require query-intensive workloads mixed with updates, and bulk ingests.

This timely and well-written book does an excellent job of presenting Iceberg, starting from the basics and extending to the architecture and how to get the best performance for a wide range of workloads, including SQL queries in Apache Spark and Dremio, as well as stream processing in Apache Flink. It also includes a chapter examining Iceberg in production settings, including the use of metadata tables and features like branching, partitioning, and snapshots to handle complex scenarios at scale. It should prove valuable to readers interested in Iceberg system development and application developers using Iceberg (or a system based on Iceberg).

— Raghu Ramakrishnan
CTO for data, Microsoft
Technical fellow

Foreword by Rick Sears

Data has become a central part of building modern software applications and growing modern data-driven organizations. Data engineers, data administrators, data analysts, and data scientists are among the individuals in these organizations who want to make more use of their data. Many of these data practitioners choose to build their data-driven applications on Amazon Web Services (AWS), often choosing to store their data in a data lake based on Amazon Simple Storage Service (S3).

These customers may want to change and manipulate their data over time while still making use of the data while it's changing and, therefore, build their applications with support for transactional data lake technologies. Apache Iceberg is a key technology used by AWS customers building transactional data lakes because it is fast, efficient, and reliable at scale while also offering simple integrations with popular data processing frameworks running on AWS such as Apache Spark, Apache Flink, Apache Hive, Presto, Trino, Dremio, and more, as well as supported by AWS services such as Amazon EMR, Amazon Redshift, Amazon Athena, AWS Glue, and others.

Apache Iceberg: The Definitive Guide has a focus on practical applications and scenarios useful for data practitioners using Apache Iceberg and has hands-on exercises that include using Iceberg with key AWS technologies, such as Amazon EMR and AWS Glue, supporting Iceberg-specific optimizations that make it simple to build and scale applications using Iceberg. The book covers the full gamut needed by these practitioners, from the problems it aims to solve and the architecture powering data-driven applications to best practices and real-world usages in AWS, so readers can not only understand and experiment with Apache Iceberg but also get up and running in production in very little time.

The content in this book is based on discussions with AWS customers as well as the broader community. As Apache Iceberg becomes more and more important to AWS customers, I am excited for everyone to have this important reference to build, scale, and optimize their applications using Iceberg.

— Rick Sears
General Manager, Amazon Web Services
Amazon EMR, Amazon Athena, AWS Lake
Formation, and AWS Glue Data Catalog

Preface

Welcome to *Apache Iceberg: The Definitive Guide*! We're delighted you have embarked on this learning journey with us. In this preface, we provide an overview of this book, why we wrote it, and how you can make the most of it.

About This Book

In these pages, you'll learn what Apache Iceberg is, why it exists, how it works, and how to harness its power. Designed for data engineers, architects, scientists, and analysts working with large datasets across various use cases from BI dashboards to AI/ML, this book explores the core concepts, inner workings, and practical applications of Apache Iceberg. By the time you reach the end, you will have grasped the essentials and possess the practical knowledge to implement Apache Iceberg effectively in your data projects. Whether you are a newcomer or an experienced practitioner, *Apache Iceberg: The Definitive Guide* will be your trusted companion on this enlightening journey into Apache Iceberg.

Why We Wrote This Book

As we observed the rapid growth and adoption of the Apache Iceberg ecosystem, it became evident that a growing knowledge gap needed to be addressed. Initially, we began by sharing insights through a series of blog posts on the Dremio platform to provide valuable information to the burgeoning Iceberg community. However, it soon became clear that a comprehensive and centralized resource was essential to meet the increasing demand for a definitive Iceberg reference. This realization was the driving force behind the creation of *Apache Iceberg: The Definitive Guide*. Our goal is to provide readers with a single authoritative source that bridges the knowledge gap and empowers individuals and organizations to make the most of Apache Iceberg's capabilities in their data-related endeavors.

What You Will Find Inside

In the following chapters, you will learn what Apache Iceberg is and how it works, how you can take advantage of the format with a variety of tools, and best practices to manage the quality and governance of the data in Apache Iceberg tables. Here is a summary of each chapter's content:

Chapter 1, "Introduction to Apache Iceberg"
Exploration of the historical context of data lakehouses and the essential concepts underlying Apache Iceberg.

Chapter 2, "The Architecture of Apache Iceberg"
Deep dive into the intricate design of Apache Iceberg, examining how its various components function together.

Chapter 3, "Lifecycle of Write and Read Queries"
Examination of the step-by-step process involved in Apache Iceberg transactions, highlighting updates, reads, and time-travel queries.

Chapter 4, "Optimizing the Performance of Iceberg Tables"
Discussions on maintaining optimized performance in Apache Iceberg tables through techniques such as compaction and sorting.

Chapter 5, "Iceberg Catalogs"
In-depth explanation of the role of Apache Iceberg catalogs, exploring the different catalog options available.

Chapter 6, "Apache Spark"
Practical sessions using Apache Spark to manage and interact with Apache Iceberg tables.

Chapter 7, "Dremio's SQL Query Engine"
Exploration of the Dremio lakehouse platform, focusing on DDL, DML, and table optimization for Apache Iceberg tables.

Chapter 8, "AWS Glue"
Demonstration of the use of AWS Glue Catalog and AWS Glue Studio for working with Apache Iceberg tables.

Chapter 9, "Apache Flink"
Practical exercises in using Apache Flink for streaming data processing with Apache Iceberg tables.

Chapter 10, "Apache Iceberg in Production"
Insights into managing data quality in production, using metadata tables for table health monitoring and employing table and catalog versioning for various operational needs.

Chapter 11, "Streaming with Apache Iceberg"
> Use of tools such as Apache Spark, Flink, and AWS Glue for streaming data processing into Iceberg tables.

Chapter 12, "Governance and Security"
> Exploration of the application of governance and security at various levels in Apache Iceberg tables, such as storage, semantic layers, and catalogs.

Chapter 13, "Migrating to Apache Iceberg"
> Guidelines on transforming existing datasets from different file types and databases into Apache Iceberg tables.

Chapter 14, "Real-World Use Cases of Apache Iceberg"
> A look at real-world applications of Apache Iceberg, including business intelligence dashboards and implementing change data capture.

How to Use This Book

This book is meticulously crafted to enhance your understanding and practical skills in Apache Iceberg, whether you're a beginner or an advanced user. While the book is structured in a sequential manner, enabling you to build a comprehensive knowledge base from start to finish, its design also accommodates flexible reading. Each chapter is self-contained, allowing you to dive directly into specific topics or use cases of interest without having to read the preceding chapters. This approach makes this book an invaluable resource for both systematic learning and targeted, just-in-time knowledge acquisition.

Throughout the book, you'll find references to code snippets and practical examples. To support your learning experience, we have established a dedicated GitHub repository for the book (*https://oreil.ly/supp-guide-apache-iceberg*). This repository is organized by chapter, ensuring that you have easy access to all the necessary reference materials, code snippets, and examples pertinent to each chapter's content. Whether you are looking to understand the architectural nuances of Apache Iceberg or seeking to implement specific functionalities, the repository serves as a complementary tool to enhance your learning and application of concepts discussed in the book. For even more content, including a bonus chapter on the Iceberg Java/Python APIs and additional Iceberg use case overviews, visit this supplemental repository (*https://oreil.ly/apache-ice_more-content*).

Whether you choose to read this guide cover to cover or focus on individual chapters based on your immediate needs, this book is designed to be a comprehensive and accessible resource on Apache Iceberg, enriched by practical, hands-on components accessible through our accompanying GitHub repository.

Feedback and Questions

We value your feedback and questions. If you have any issues, have suggestions for improvement, or simply want to reach out to us, please don't hesitate to email us at *tech-advocacy@dremio.com*. We also invite you to follow and connect with us on LinkedIn.

Following is a list of additional resources for you to learn about Apache Iceberg and get involved in the Apache Iceberg community:

- "Apache Iceberg 101" article and resource directory (*https://oreil.ly/hDv4H*)
- Apache Iceberg documentation (*https://iceberg.apache.org*)
- Apache Iceberg GitHub repository (*https://github.com/apache/iceberg*)
- Iceberg Slack channel (see the Iceberg documentation for invitation)
- Iceberg mailing list (see the Iceberg documentation to sign up)
- Apache Iceberg Workshops LinkedIn page (*https://oreil.ly/WghwD*)
- The Apache Iceberg Blog Directory (*https://iceberg.apache.org/blogs*)

Conventions Used in This Book

The following typographical conventions are used in this book:

Italic
> Indicates new terms, URLs, email addresses, filenames, and file extensions.

`Constant width`
> Used for program listings, as well as within paragraphs to refer to program elements such as variable or function names, databases, data types, environment variables, statements, and keywords.

`Constant width bold`
> Shows commands or other text that should be typed literally by the user.

`Constant width italic`
> Shows text that should be replaced with user-supplied values or by values determined by context.

This element signifies a tip or suggestion.

 This element signifies a general note.

Using Code Examples

Supplemental material (code examples, exercises, etc.) is available for download at *https://oreil.ly/supp-guide-apache-iceberg*. For even more content, including a bonus chapter on the Iceberg Java/Python APIs and additional Iceberg use case overviews, visit *https://oreil.ly/apache-ice_more-content*.

If you have a technical question or a problem using the code examples, please send email to *support@oreilly.com*.

This book is here to help you get your job done. In general, if example code is offered with this book, you may use it in your programs and documentation. You do not need to contact us for permission unless you're reproducing a significant portion of the code. For example, writing a program that uses several chunks of code from this book does not require permission. Selling or distributing examples from O'Reilly books does require permission. Answering a question by citing this book and quoting example code does not require permission. Incorporating a significant amount of example code from this book into your product's documentation does require permission.

We appreciate, but generally do not require, attribution. An attribution usually includes the title, author, publisher, and ISBN. For example: "*Apache Iceberg: The Definitive Guide* by Tomer Shiran, Jason Hughes, and Alex Merced (O'Reilly). Copyright 2024 O'Reilly Media Inc., 978-1-098-14863-8."

If you feel your use of code examples falls outside fair use or the permission given above, feel free to contact us at *permissions@oreilly.com*.

O'Reilly Online Learning

O'REILLY® For more than 40 years, *O'Reilly Media* has provided technology and business training, knowledge, and insight to help companies succeed.

Our unique network of experts and innovators share their knowledge and expertise through books, articles, and our online learning platform. O'Reilly's online learning platform gives you on-demand access to live training courses, in-depth learning paths, interactive coding environments, and a vast collection of text and video from O'Reilly and 200+ other publishers. For more information, visit *https://oreilly.com*.

How to Contact Us

Please address comments and questions concerning this book to the publisher:

O'Reilly Media, Inc.
1005 Gravenstein Highway North
Sebastopol, CA 95472
800-889-8969 (in the United States or Canada)
707-827-7019 (international or local)
707-829-0104 (fax)
support@oreilly.com
https://www.oreilly.com/about/contact.html

We have a web page for this book, where we list errata, examples, and any additional information. You can access this page at *https://oreil.ly/apache-iceberg*.

For news and information about our books and courses, visit *https://oreilly.com*.

Find us on LinkedIn: *https://linkedin.com/company/oreilly-media*.

Watch us on YouTube: *https://youtube.com/oreillymedia*.

Acknowledgments

We would like to express our deepest gratitude to Dremio and O'Reilly Media for providing us the opportunity to write this book. We would especially like to extend our gratitude to our O'Reilly editor, Gary O'Brien, who always helped keep us on the right track during the writing process. Thank you to our tech reviewers, who held us accountable at every turn, making sure the book was accurate and complete: Kamran Ali, Jai Balani, Michal Gancarski, Mahdi Karabiben, Kevin Kho, Marc Laforet, Max Schultze, and Simeon Schwarz. Also, thanks for the contributions of Dipankar Mazumdar.

We also sincerely thank our families, who were patient with us during long nights writing and editing this book. Finally, we'd like to thank the Apache Iceberg community for developing one of the most exciting and transformative projects in data.

Thank you for choosing *Apache Iceberg: The Definitive Guide*. We hope you find it both informative and enjoyable. Let's dive into the exciting world of Apache Iceberg together!

Happy reading!

## PART I

Fundamentals of Apache Iceberg

The first part of the book will cover the fundamentals of Apache Iceberg, including topics such as the architecture of Iceberg tables, the lifecycle of read and write queries, and Iceberg catalogs. The goal is to establish a solid foundation of understanding to build on for the subsequent parts of the book.

## CHAPTER 1

Introduction to Apache Iceberg

Data is a primary asset from which organizations curate the information and insights needed to make critical business decisions. Whether it is used to analyze trends in annual sales of a particular product or to predict future market opportunities, data shapes the direction for organizations to follow to be successful. Further, today data isn't just a nice-to-have. It is a requirement, not just for winning in the market but for competing in it. With such a massive demand for information, there has been an enormous effort to accumulate the data generated by the various systems within an organization to derive insights.

At the same time, the rate at which operational and analytical systems have been generating data has skyrocketed. While more data has presented enterprises the opportunity to make better-informed decisions, there is also a dire need to have a platform that stores and analyzes all this data so that it can be used to build analytical products such as business intelligence (BI) reports and machine learning (ML) models to support decision making. Lakehouse architecture, which we will elaborate on in this chapter, decouples how we store our data from how we process it for more flexibility. This chapter will walk you through the history and evolution of data platforms from a practical point of view and present the benefits of a lakehouse architecture with Apache Iceberg open table formats.

How Did We Get Here? A Brief History

In terms of storage and processing systems, relational database management systems (RDBMSs) have long been a standard option for organizations to keep a record of all their transactional data. For example, say you run a transportation company and you wanted to maintain information about new bookings made by your customers. In this case, each new booking would be a new row in an RDBMS. RDBMSs used for this purpose support a specific data processing category called *online transaction processing* (OLTP). Examples of OLTP-optimized RDBMSs are PostgreSQL, MySQL, and Microsoft SQL Server. These systems are designed and optimized to enable you to interact very quickly with one or a few rows of data at a time and are a good choice for supporting a business's day-to-day operations.

But say you wanted to understand the average profit you made on all your new bookings from the preceding quarter. In that case, using the data stored in an OLTP-optimized RDBMS would have led to significant performance problems once your data got large enough. Some of the reasons for this include the following:

- Transactional systems are focused on inserting, updating, and reading a small subset of rows in a table, so storing the data in a row-based format is ideal. However, analytics systems usually focus on aggregating certain columns or working with all the rows in a table, making a columnar structure more advantageous.

- Running transactional and analytics workloads on the same infrastructure can result in a competition for resources.

- Transactional workloads benefit from normalizing the data into several related tables that are joined if needed, while analytics workloads may perform better when the data is denormalized into the same table to avoid large-scale join operations.

Now imagine that your organization had a large number of operational systems that generated a vast amount of data and your analytics team wanted to build dashboards that relied on aggregations of the data from these different data sources (i.e., application databases). Unfortunately, OLTP systems are not designed to deal with complex aggregate queries involving a large number of historical records. These workloads are known as *online analytical processing* (OLAP) workloads. To address this limitation, you would need a different kind of system optimized for OLAP workloads. It was this need that prompted the development of the lakehouse architecture.

Foundational Components of a System Designed for OLAP Workloads

A system designed for OLAP workloads is composed of a set of technological components that enable supporting modern-day analytical workloads, as showcased in Figure 1-1 and described in the following subsections.

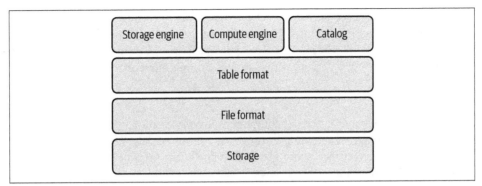

Figure 1-1. Technical components supporting analytical workloads

Storage

To analyze historical data coming in from a variety of sources, you need to have a system that allows you to store large to significant amounts of data. Therefore, storage is the first component you would need in a system that can deal with analytical queries on large datasets. There are many options for storage, including a local filesystem on direct-attached storage (DAS); a distributed filesystem on a set of nodes that you operate, such as the Hadoop Distributed File System (HDFS); and object storage provided as a service by cloud providers, such as Amazon Simple Storage Service (Amazon S3).

Regarding the types of storage, you could use row-oriented databases or columnar databases, or you could mix the two in some systems. In recent years, columnar databases have enjoyed tremendous adoption as they have proven to be more efficient when dealing with vast volumes of data.

File format

For storage purposes, your raw data needs to be organized in a particular file format. Your choice of file format impacts things such as the compression of the files, the data structure, and the performance of a given workload.

File formats generally fall into three high-level categories: structured (CSV), semistructured (JSON), and unstructured (text files). In the structured and semistructured categories, file formats can be row oriented or column oriented (columnar). Row-oriented file formats store all the columns of a given row together, while column-oriented file formats store all the rows of a given column together. Two common examples of row-oriented file formats are comma-separated values (CSV) and Apache Avro. Examples of columnar file formats are Apache Parquet and Apache ORC.

Depending on the use case, certain file formats can be more advantageous than others. For example, row-oriented file formats are generally better if you are dealing with a small number of records at a time. In comparison, columnar file formats are generally better if you are dealing with a sizable number of records at a time.

Table format

The table format is another critical component for a system that can support analytical workloads with aggregated queries on a vast volume of data. The table format acts like a metadata layer on top of the file format and is responsible for specifying how the datafiles should be laid out in storage.

Ultimately, the goal of a table format is to abstract the complexity of the physical data structure and facilitate capabilities such as Data Manipulation Language (DML) operations (e.g., doing inserts, updates, and deletes) and changing a table's schema. Modern table formats also bring in the atomicity and consistency guarantees required for the safe execution of DML operations on the data.

Storage engine

The storage engine is the system responsible for actually doing the work of laying out the data in the form specified by the table format and keeping all the files and data structures up-to-date with the new data. Storage engines handle some of the critical tasks, such as physical optimization of the data, index maintenance, and getting rid of old data.

Catalog

When dealing with data from various sources and on a larger scale, it is important to quickly identify the data you might need for your analysis. A catalog's role is to tackle this problem by leveraging metadata to identify datasets. The catalog is the central location where compute engines and users can go to find out about the existence of a table, as well as additional information such as the table name, table schema, and where the table data is stored on the storage system. Some catalogs are internal to a system and can only be directly interacted with via that system's engine; examples of these catalogs include Postgres and Snowflake. Other catalogs, such as Hive and Project Nessie, are open for any system to use. Keep in mind that these metadata catalogs aren't the same as catalogs for human data discovery, such as Colibra, Atlan, and the Dremio Software internal catalog.

Compute engine

The compute engine is the final component needed to efficiently deal with a massive amount of data persisted in a storage system. A compute engine's role in such a system would be to run user workloads to process the data. Depending on the volume of data, computation load, and type of workload, you can utilize one or more compute engines for this task. When dealing with a large dataset and/or heavy computational requirements, you might need to use a distributed compute engine in a processing paradigm called massively parallel processing (MPP). A few examples of MPP-based compute engines are Apache Spark, Snowflake, and Dremio.

Bringing It All Together

Traditionally for OLAP workloads, these technical components have all been tightly coupled into a single system known as a *data warehouse*. Data warehouses allow organizations to store data coming in from a variety of sources and run analytical workloads on top of the data. In the next section, we will discuss in detail the capabilities of a data warehouse, how the technical components are integrated, and the pros and cons of using such a system.

The Data Warehouse

A data warehouse or OLAP database is a centralized repository that supports storing large volumes of data ingested from various sources such as operational systems, application databases, and logs. Figure 1-2 presents an architectural overview of the technical components of a data warehouse.

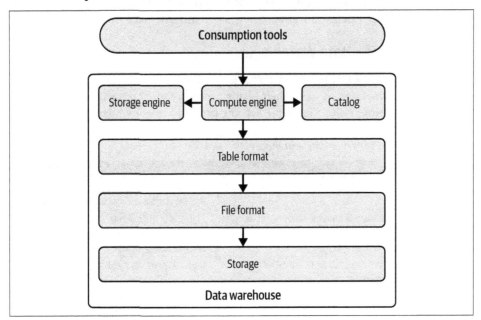

Figure 1-2. Technical components of a data warehouse

A data warehouse owns all the technical components in a single system. In other words, all the data is stored in its proprietary file and table formats on its proprietary storage system. This data is then managed exclusively by the data warehouse's storage engine, is registered in its catalog, and can be accessed only by the user or analytical engines through its compute engine.

A Brief History

Up until about 2015, most data warehouses had the storage and compute components tightly coupled on the same nodes, since most were designed and run on premises. However, this resulted in a lot of problems. Scaling became a big issue because datasets grew in volume at an accelerating pace while the number and intensity of workloads (i.e., compute tasks running on the warehouse) also increased. Specifically, there was no way to independently increase the compute and storage resources depending on your tasks. If your storage needs grew more quickly than your compute needs, it didn't matter. You still had to pay for additional compute even though you didn't need it.

This led to the next generation of data warehouses being built with a big focus on the cloud. These data warehouses began gaining traction around 2015 as cloud-native computing burst onto the scene, allowing you to separate the compute and storage components and scale these resources to suit your tasks. They even allowed you to shut down compute when you weren't using it and not lose your storage.

Pros and Cons of a Data Warehouse

While data warehouses, whether on premises or cloud based, make it easy for enterprises to quickly make sense of all their historical data, there are certain areas where a warehouse still causes issues. Table 1-1 lists the pros and cons of a data warehouse.

Table 1-1. Pros and cons of a data warehouse

Pros	Cons
Serves as the single source of truth as it allows storing and querying data from various sources	Locks the data into a vendor-specific system that only the warehouse's compute engine can use
Supports querying vast amounts of historical data, enabling analytical workloads to run quickly	Expensive in terms of both storage and computation; as the workload increases, the cost becomes hard to manage
Provides effective data governance policies to ensure that data is available, usable, and aligned with security policies	Mainly supports structured data
Organizes the data layout for you, ensuring that it's optimized for querying	Does not enable organizations to natively run advanced analytical workloads such as ML
Ensures that data written to a table conforms to the technical schema	

A data warehouse acts as a centralized repository for organizations to store all their data coming in from a multitude of sources, allowing data consumers such as analysts and BI engineers to access data easily and quickly from one single source to start their analysis. In addition, the technological components powering a data warehouse enable you to access vast volumes of data while supporting BI workloads to run on top of it.

Although data warehouses have been elemental in the democratization of data and allowed businesses to derive historical insights from varied data sources, they are primarily limited to relational workloads. For example, returning to the transportation company example from earlier, say that you wanted to derive insights into how much you will make in total sales in the next quarter. In this case, you would need to build a forecasting model using historical data. However, you cannot achieve this capability natively with a data warehouse as the compute engine, and the other technical components are not designed for ML-based tasks. So your main viable option would be to move or export the data from the warehouse to other platforms supporting ML workloads. This means you would have data in multiple copies, and having to create pipelines for each data movement can lead to critical issues such as data drift and model decay when pipelines move data incorrectly or inconsistently.

Another hindrance to running advanced analytical workloads on top of a data warehouse is that a data warehouse only supports structured data. But the rapid generation and availability of other types of data, such as semistructured and unstructured data (JSON, images, text, etc.), has allowed ML models to reveal interesting insights. For our example, this could be understanding the sentiments of all the new booking reviews made in the preceding quarter. This ultimately would impact an organization's ability to make future-oriented decisions.

There are also specific design challenges in a data warehouse. Returning to Figure 1-2, you can see that all six technical components are tightly coupled in a data warehouse. Before you understand what that implies, an essential thing to observe is that both file and table formats are *internal* to a particular data warehouse. This design pattern leads to a *closed form* of data architecture. It means that the actual data is accessible only using the data warehouse's compute engine, which is specifically designed to interact with the warehouse's table and file formats. This type of architecture leaves organizations with a massive concern about locked-in data. With the increase in workloads and the vast volumes of data ingested to a warehouse over time, you are bound to that particular platform. And that means your analytical workloads, such as BI and any future tools you plan to onboard, can only run on top of this particular data warehouse. This also prevents you from migrating to another data platform that can cater specifically to your requirements.

Additionally, a significant cost factor is associated with storing data in a data warehouse and using the compute engines to process the data. This cost only increases with time as you increase the number of workloads in your environment, thereby invoking more compute resources. In addition to the monetary costs, there are other overheads, such as the need for engineering teams to build and manage numerous pipelines to move data from operational systems, and delayed time-to-insight on the part of data consumers. These challenges have prompted organizations to seek alternative data platforms that allow data to be within their control and stored in open file formats, thereby allowing downstream applications such as BI and ML to run in parallel with much-reduced costs. This led to the emergence of data lakes.

The Data Lake

While data warehouses provided a mechanism for running analytics on structured data, they still had several issues:

- A data warehouse could only store structured data.
- Storage in a data warehouse is generally more expensive than on-prem Hadoop clusters or cloud object storage.
- Storage and compute in traditional on-prem data warehouses are often commingled and therefore cannot be scaled separately. More storage costs came with more compute costs whether you needed the compute power or not.

Addressing these issues required an alternative storage solution that was cheaper and could store all your data without the need to conform to a fixed schema. This alternative solution was the data lake.

A Brief History

Originally, you'd use Hadoop, an open source, distributed computing framework, and its HDFS filesystem component to store and process large amounts of structured and unstructured datasets across clusters of inexpensive computers. But it wasn't enough to just be able to store all this data. You'd want to run analytics on it too.

The Hadoop ecosystem included MapReduce, an analytics framework from which you'd write analytics jobs in Java and run them on the Hadoop cluster. Writing MapReduce jobs was verbose and complex, and many analysts are more comfortable writing SQL than Java, so Hive was created to convert SQL statements into MapReduce jobs.

To write SQL, a mechanism to distinguish which files in your storage are part of a particular dataset or table was needed. This resulted in the birth of the Hive table format, which recognized a directory and the files inside it as a table.

Over time, people moved away from using Hadoop clusters to using cloud object storage (e.g., Amazon S3, Minio, Azure Blob Storage), as it was easier to manage and cheaper to use. MapReduce also fell out of use in favor of other distributed query engines such as Apache Spark, Presto, and Dremio. What did stick around was the Hive table format, which became the standard in the space for recognizing files in your storage as singular tables on which you can run analytics. However, cloud storage required more network costs in accessing those files, which the Hive format architecture didn't anticipate and which led to excessive network calls due to Hive's dependence on the table's folder structure.

A feature that distinguishes a data lake from a data warehouse is the ability to leverage different compute engines for different workloads. This is important because there has never been a silver-bullet compute engine that is best for every workload and that can scale compute independently of storage. This is just inherent to the nature of computing, since there are always trade-offs, and what you decide to trade off determines what a given system is good for and what it is not as well suited for.

Note that in data lakes, there isn't really any service that fulfills the needs of the storage engine function. Generally, the compute engine decides how to write the data, and then the data is usually never revisited and optimized, unless entire tables or partitions are rewritten, which is usually done on an ad hoc basis. Figure 1-3 depicts how the components of a data lake interact with one another.

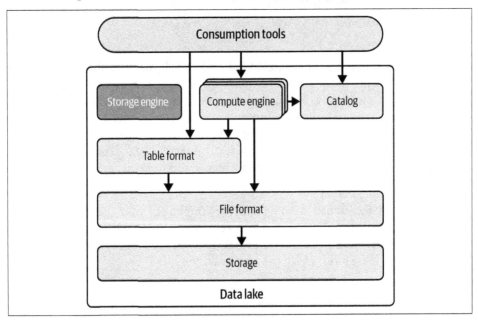

Figure 1-3. Technical components of a data lake

Pros and Cons of a Data Lake

Of course, no architectural pattern is perfect, and that applies to data lakes. While data lakes have a lot of benefits, they also have several limitations. The following are the benefits:

Lower cost

The costs of storing data and executing queries on a data lake are much lower than in a data warehouse. This makes a data lake particularly useful for enabling analytics on data whose priority isn't high enough to justify the cost of a data warehouse, enabling a wider analytical reach.

Stores data in open formats

In a data lake, you can store the data in any file format you like, whereas in a data warehouse, you have no say in how the data is stored, which would typically be a proprietary format built for that particular data warehouse. This allows you to have more control over the data and consume the data in a greater variety of tools that can support these open formats.

Handles unstructured data

Data warehouses can't handle unstructured data such as sensor data, email attachments, and logfiles, so if you wanted to run analytics on unstructured data, the data lake was the only option.

These are the limitations:

Performance

Since each component of a data lake is decoupled, many of the optimizations that can exist in tightly coupled systems are absent, such as indexes and ACID (Atomicity, Consistency, Isolation, Durability) guarantees. While they can be re-created, it requires a lot of effort and engineering to cobble the components (storage, file format, table format, engines) in a way that results in performance comparable to that of a data warehouse. This made data lakes undesirable for high-priority data analytics where performance and time mattered.

Requires lots of configuration

As previously mentioned, creating a tighter coupling of your chosen components with the level of optimizations you'd expect from a data warehouse would require significant engineering. This would result in a need for lots of data engineers to configure all these tools, which can also be costly.

Lack of ACID transactions

One notable drawback of data lakes is the absence of built-in ACID transaction guarantees that are common in traditional relational databases. In data lakes, data is often ingested in a *schema-on-read* fashion, meaning that schema validation and consistency checks occur during data processing rather than at the time of ingestion. This can pose challenges for applications that require strong transactional integrity, such as financial systems or applications dealing with sensitive data. Achieving similar transactional guarantees in a data lake typically involves implementing complex data processing pipelines and coordination mechanisms, adding to the engineering effort required for critical use cases. While data lakes excel at scalability and flexibility, they may not be the ideal choice when strict ACID compliance is a primary requirement.

Table 1-2 summarizes these pros and cons.

Table 1-2. Pros and cons of a data lake

Pros	Cons
Lower cost	Performance
Stores data in open formats	Lack of ACID guarantees
Handles unstructured data	Lots of configuration required
Supports ML use cases	

Should I Run Analytics on a Data Lake or a Data Warehouse?

While data lakes provided a great place to land all your structured and unstructured data, there were still imperfections. After running ETL (extract, transform, and load) to land your data in your data lake, you'd generally take one of two tracks when running analytics.

For instance, you could set up an additional ETL pipeline to create a copy of a curated subset of data that is for high-priority analytics and store it in the warehouse to get the performance and flexibility of the data warehouse.

However, this results in a few issues:

- Additional costs in the compute for the additional ETL work and in the cost to store a copy of data you are already storing in a data warehouse where the storage costs are often greater

- Additional copies of the data, which may be needed to populate data marts for different business lines and even more copies as analysts create physical copies of data subsets in the form of BI extracts to speed up dashboards, leading to a web of data copies that are hard to govern, track, and keep in sync

Alternatively, you could use query engines that support data lake workloads, such as Dremio, Presto, Apache Spark, Trino, and Apache Impala, to execute queries on the data lake. These engines are generally well suited for read-only workloads. However, due to the limitations of the Hive table format, they run into complexity when trying to update the data safely from the data lake.

As you can see, data lakes and data warehouses have their own unique benefits and limitations. This necessitated the need to develop a new architecture that offers their benefits while minimizing their faults, and that architecture is called a data lakehouse.

The Data Lakehouse

While using a data warehouse gave us performance and ease of use, analytics on data lakes gave us lower costs, flexibility by using open formats, the ability to use unstructured data, and more. The desire to thread the needle leads to great strides and innovation, which leads to what we now know as the data lakehouse.

The data lakehouse architecture decouples the storage and compute from data lakes and brings in mechanisms that allow for more data warehouse–like functionality (ACID transactions, better performance, consistency, etc.). Enabling this functionality are data lake table formats that eliminate all the previous issues with the Hive table format. You store the data in the same places you would store it with a data lake, you use the query engines you would use with a data lake, and your data is stored in the same formats it would be stored in on a data lake. What truly transforms your world from "read-only" data to a "center of my data world" data lakehouse is the table format providing a metadata/abstraction layer between the engine and storage for them to interact more intelligently (see Figure 1-4).

Table formats create an abstraction layer on top of file storage that enables better consistency, performance, and ACID guarantees when working with data directly on data lake storage, leading to several value propositions:

Fewer copies = less drift
> With ACID guarantees and better performance you can now move workloads typically saved for the data warehouse–like updates and other data manipulation to the data lakehouse for reduced costs and data movement. If you move your data to the lakehouse, you can have a more streamlined architecture with fewer copies. Fewer copies means lower storage costs, lower compute costs from moving data to a data warehouse, less drift (the data model changes/breaking across different versions of the same data), and better governance of your data to maintain compliance with regulations and internal controls.

Faster queries = fast insights
> The end goal is always to get business value through quality insights from our data. Everything else is just steps to that end. If you can make faster queries, that means you can get insights more quickly. Data lakehouses enable faster-performing queries over data lakes and comparable data warehouses by using optimizations at the query engine (cost-based optimizers, caching), table format (better file skipping and query planning using metadata), and file format (sorting and compression).

Historical data snapshots = mistakes that don't hurt

Data lakehouse table formats maintain historical data snapshots, enabling the possibility of querying and restoring tables to their previous snapshots. You can work with your data and not have to be up at night wondering whether a mistake will lead to hours of auditing, repairing, and then backfilling.

Affordable architecture = business value

There are two ways to increase profits: increase revenue and decrease costs. And data lakehouses not only help you get business insights to drive up revenue, but they also can help you decrease costs. This means you can reduce storage costs by avoiding duplication of your data, avoid additional compute costs from additional ETL work to move data, and enjoy lower prices for the storage and compute you are using relative to typical data warehouse rates.

Open architecture = peace of mind

Data lakehouses are built on open formats, such as Apache Iceberg as a table format and Apache Parquet as a file format. Many tools can read and write to these formats, which allows you to avoid vendor lock-in. Vendor lock-in results in cost creep and tool lock-out, where your data sits in formats that tools can't access. By using open formats, you can rest easy, knowing that your data won't be siloed into a narrow set of tools.

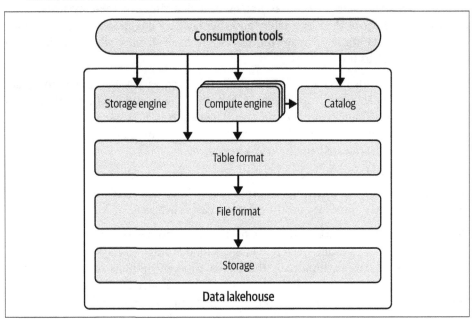

Figure 1-4. Technical components of a data lakehouse

To summarize, with modern innovations from the open standards previously discussed, the best of all worlds can exist by operating strictly on the data lake, and this architectural pattern is the data lakehouse. The key component that makes all this possible is the table format that enables engines to have the guarantees and improved performance over data lakes when working with data that just didn't exist before. Now let's turn the discussion to the Apache Iceberg table format.

What Is a Table Format?

A *table format* is a method of structuring a dataset's files to present them as a unified "table." From the user's perspective, it can be defined as the answer to the question "what data is in this table?"

This simple answer enables multiple individuals, teams, and tools to interact with the data in the table concurrently, whether they are reading from it or writing to it. The main purpose of a table format is to provide an abstraction of the table to users and tools, making it easier for them to interact with the underlying data in an efficient manner.

Table formats have been around since the inception of RDBMSs such as System R, Multics, and Oracle, which first implemented Edgar Codd's relational model, although the term *table format* was not used at that time. In these systems, users could refer to a set of data as a table, and the database engine was responsible for managing the dataset's byte layout on disk in the form of files, while also handling complexities such as transactions.

All interactions with the data in these RDBMSs, such as reading and writing, are managed by the database's storage engine. No other engine can interact with the files directly without risking system corruption. The details of how the data is stored are abstracted away, and users take for granted that the platform knows where the data for a specific table is located and how to access it.

However, in today's big data world, relying on a single closed engine to manage all access to the underlying data is no longer practical. Your data needs access to a variety of compute engines optimized for different use cases such as BI or ML.

In a data lake, all your data is stored as files in some storage solution (e.g., Amazon S3, Azure Data Lake Storage [ADLS], Google Cloud Storage [GCS]), so a single table may be made of dozens, hundreds, thousands, or even millions of individual files on that storage. When using SQL with our favorite analytical tools or writing ad hoc scripts in languages such as Java, Scala, Python, and Rust, we wouldn't want to constantly define which of these files are in the table and which of them aren't. Not only would this be tedious, but it would also likely lead to inconsistency across different uses of the data.

So the solution was to create a standard method of understanding "what data is in this table" for data lakes, as illustrated in Figure 1-5.

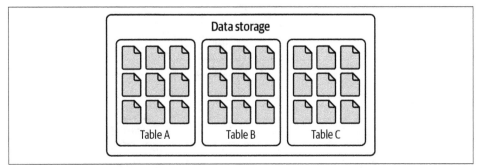

Figure 1-5. Datafiles organized into tables using a table format

Hive: The Original Table Format

When it came to the world of running analytics on Hadoop data lakes, the Map-Reduce framework was used, which required users to write complex and tedious Java jobs, which wasn't accessible to many analysts. Facebook, feeling the pain of this situation, developed a framework called Hive in 2009. Hive provided a key benefit to make analytics on Hadoop much easier: the ability to write SQL instead of MapReduce jobs directly.

The Hive framework would take SQL statements and then convert them into Map-Reduce jobs that could be executed. To write SQL statements, there had to be a mechanism for understanding what data on your Hadoop storage represented a unique table, and the Hive table format and Hive Metastore for tracking these tables were born.

The Hive table format took the approach of defining a table as any and all files within a specified directory (or prefixes for object storage). The partitions of those tables would be the subdirectories. These directory paths defining the table are tracked by a service called the *Hive Metastore*, which query engines can access to know where to find the data applicable to their query. This is illustrated in Figure 1-6.

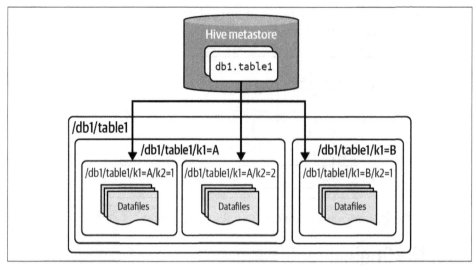

Figure 1-6. The architecture of a table stored using the Hive table format

The Hive table format had several benefits:

- It enabled more efficient query patterns than full table scans, so techniques such as partitioning (dividing the data based on a partitioning key) and bucketing (an approach to partitioning or clustering/sorting that uses a hash function to evenly distribute values) made it possible to avoid scanning every file for faster queries.

- It was file format agnostic, so it allowed the data community over time to develop better file formats, such as Apache Parquet, and use them in their Hive tables. It also did not require transformation prior to making the data available in a Hive table (e.g., Avro, CSV/TSV).

- Through atomic swaps of the listed directory in the Hive Metastore, you can make all-or-nothing (atomic) changes to an individual partition in the table.

- Over time, this became the de facto standard, working with most data tools and providing a uniform answer to "what data is in this table?"

While these benefits were significant, there were also many limitations that became apparent as time passed:

- File-level changes are inefficient, since there was no mechanism to atomically swap a file in the same way the Hive Metastore could be used to swap a partition directory. You are essentially left making swaps at the partition level to update a single file atomically.

- While you could atomically swap a partition, there wasn't a mechanism for atomically updating multiple partitions as one transaction. This opens up the possibility for end users seeing inconsistent data between transactions updating multiple partitions.

- There really aren't good mechanisms to enable concurrent simultaneous updates, especially with tools beyond Hive itself.

- An engine listing files and directories was time-consuming and slowed down queries. Having to read and list files and directories that may not need scanning in the resulting query comes at a cost.

- Partition columns were often derived from other columns, such as deriving a month column from a timestamp. Partitioning helped only if you filtered by the partition column, and someone who has a filter on the timestamp column may not intuitively know to also filter on the derived month column, leading to a full table scan since partitioning was not taken advantage of.

- Table statistics would be gathered through asynchronous jobs, often resulting in state table statistics, if any statistics were available at all. This made it difficult for query engines to further optimize queries.

- Since object storage often throttles requests against the same prefix (think of an object storage prefix as analogous to a file directory), queries on tables with large numbers of files in a single partition (so that all the files would be in one prefix) can have performance issues.

The larger the scale of the datasets and use cases, the more these problems would be amplified. This resulted in significant pain in need of a new solution, so newer table formats were created.

Modern Data Lake Table Formats

In seeking to address the limitations of the Hive table format, a new generation of table formats arose with different approaches in solving the problems with Hive.

Creators of modern table formats realized the flaw that led to challenges with the Hive table format was that the definition of the table was based on the contents of directories, not on the individual datafiles. Modern table formats such as Apache Iceberg, Apache Hudi, and Delta Lake all took this approach of defining tables as a canonical list of files, providing metadata for engines informing which *files* make up the table, not which *directories*. This more granular approach to defining "what is a table" unlocked the door to features such as ACID transactions, time travel, and more.

Modern table formats all aim to bring a core set of major benefits over the Hive table format:

- They allow for ACID transactions, which are safe transactions that either complete in full or are canceled. In legacy formats such as the Hive table format, many transactions could not have these guarantees.
- They enable safe transactions when there are multiple writers. If two or more writers write to a table, there is a mechanism to make sure the writer that completes their write second is aware of and considers what the other writer(s) have done to keep the data consistent.
- They offer better collection of table statistics and metadata that can allow a query engine to plan scans more efficiently so that it will need to scan fewer files.

Let's explore what Apache Iceberg is and how it came to be.

What Is Apache Iceberg?

Apache Iceberg is a table format created in 2017 by Netflix's Ryan Blue and Daniel Weeks. It arose from the need to overcome challenges with performance, consistency, and many of the challenges previously stated with the Hive table format. In 2018, the project was made open source and was donated to the Apache Software Foundation, where many other organizations started getting involved with it, including Apple, Dremio, AWS, Tencent, LinkedIn, and Stripe. Many additional organizations have contributed to the project since then.

How Apache Iceberg Came to Be

Netflix, in the creation of what became the Apache Iceberg format, concluded that many of the problems with the Hive format stemmed from one simple but fundamental flaw: each table is tracked as directories and subdirectories, limiting the granularity that is necessary to provide consistency guarantees, better concurrency, and several of the features that often are available in data warehouses.

With this in mind, Netflix set out to create a new table format with several goals in mind:

Consistency
> If updates to a table occur over multiple partitions, it must not be possible for end users to experience inconsistency in the data they are viewing. An update to a table across multiple partitions should be done quickly and atomically so that the data is consistent to end users. They see the data either before the update or after the update, and not in between.

Performance

With Hive's file/directory listing bottleneck, query planning would take excessively long to complete before actually executing the query. The table should provide metadata and avoid excessive file listing so that not only can query planning be a faster process, but also the resulting plans can be executed more quickly since they scan only the files necessary to satisfy the query.

Easy to use

To get the benefits of techniques such as partitioning, end users should not have to be aware of the physical structure of the table. The table should be able to give users the benefits of partitioning based on naturally intuitive queries and not depend on filtering extra partition columns derived from a column they are already filtering by (e.g., filtering by a month column when you've already filtered the timestamp it is derived from).

Evolvability

Updating schemas of Hive tables could result in unsafe transactions, and updating how a table is partitioned would result in a need to rewrite the entire table. A table should be able to evolve its schema and partitioning scheme safely and without the need for rewriting.

Scalability

All the preceding goals should be able to be accomplished at the petabyte scale of Netflix's data.

So the team began creating the Iceberg format, which focuses on defining a table as a canonical list of files instead of tracking a table as a list of directories and subdirectories. The Apache Iceberg project is a specification, or a standard of how metadata defining a data lakehouse table should be written across several files. To support the adoption of this standard, Apache Iceberg has many support libraries to help individuals work with the format or compute engines to implement support. Along with these libraries, the project has created implementations for open source compute engines such as Apache Spark and Apache Flink.

Apache Iceberg aims for existing tools to embrace the standard and is designed to take advantage of existing, popular storage solutions and compute engines in the hope that existing options will support working with the standard. The purpose of this approach is to let the ecosystem of existing data tools build out support for Apache Iceberg tables and let Iceberg become the standard for how engines can recognize and work with tables on the data lake. The goal is for Apache Iceberg to become so ubiquitous in the ecosystem that it becomes another implementation detail that many users don't have to think about. They just know they are working with tables and don't need to think about it beyond that, regardless of which tool they are using to interact with the table. This is already becoming a reality as many tools allow end users to work with Apache Iceberg tables so easily that they don't need to understand the underlying Iceberg format. Eventually, with automated table optimization and ingestion tools, even more technical users such as data engineers won't have to think as much about the underlying format and will be able to work with their data lake storage in the way they've worked with data warehouses, without ever dealing directly with the storage layer.

The Apache Iceberg Architecture

Apache Iceberg tracks a table's partitioning, sorting, schema over time, and so much more using a tree of metadata that an engine can use to plan queries at a fraction of the time it would take with legacy data lake patterns. Figure 1-7 depicts this tree of metadata.

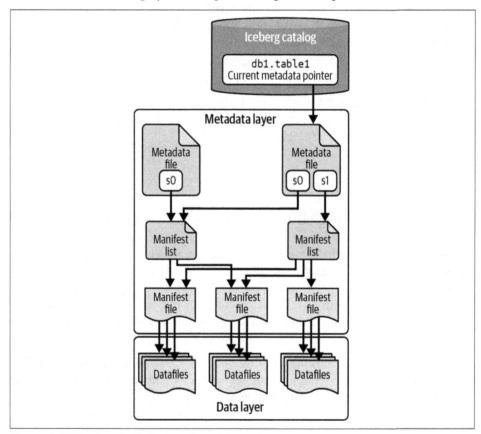

Figure 1-7. The Apache Iceberg architecture

This metadata tree breaks down the metadata of the table into four components:

Manifest file
A list of datafiles, containing each datafile's location/path and key metadata about those datafiles, which allows for creating more efficient execution plans.

Manifest list
Files that define a single snapshot of the table as a list of manifest files along with stats on those manifests that allow for creating more efficient execution plans.

Metadata file
Files that define a table's structure, including its schema, partitioning scheme, and a listing of snapshots.

Catalog
Tracks the table location (similar to the Hive Metastore), but instead of containing a mapping of table name -> set of directories, it contains a mapping of table name -> location of the table's most recent metadata file. Several tools, including a Hive Metastore, can be used as a catalog, and we have dedicated Chapter 5 to this subject.

Each of these files will be covered in more depth in Chapter 2.

Key Features of Apache Iceberg

Apache Iceberg's unique architecture enables an ever-growing number of features that go beyond just solving the challenges with Hive and instead unlock entirely new functionality for data lakes and data lakehouse workloads. In this section, we provide a high-level overview of key features of Apache Iceberg. We'll go into more depth on these features in later chapters.

ACID transactions

Apache Iceberg uses optimistic concurrency control to enable ACID guarantees, even when you have transactions being handled by multiple readers and writers. Optimistic concurrency assumes transactions won't conflict and checks for conflicts only when necessary, aiming to minimize locking and improve performance. This way, you can run transactions on your data lakehouse that either commit or fail and nothing in between. A pessimistic concurrency model, which uses locks to prevent conflicts between transactions, assuming conflicts are likely to occur, was unavailable in Apache Iceberg at the time of this writing but may be coming in the future.

Concurrency guarantees are handled by the catalog, as it is typically a mechanism that has built-in ACID guarantees. This is what allows transactions on Iceberg tables to be atomic and provide correctness guarantees. If this didn't exist, two different systems could have conflicting updates, resulting in data loss.

Partition evolution

A big headache with data lakes prior to Apache Iceberg was dealing with the need to change the table's physical optimization. Too often, when your partitioning needs to change, the only choice you have is to rewrite the entire table, and at scale this can get very expensive. The alternative is to just live with the existing partitioning scheme and sacrifice the performance improvements a better partitioning scheme can provide.

With Apache Iceberg you can update how the table is partitioned at any time without the need to rewrite the table and all its data. Since partitioning has everything to do with the metadata, the operations needed to make this change to your table's structure are quick and cheap.

Figure 1-8 depicts a table that was initially partitioned by month and then evolved to partition based on day going forward. The previously written data remains in month partitions while new data is written in day partitions, and in a query, the engine makes a plan for each partition based on the partition scheme applied to it.

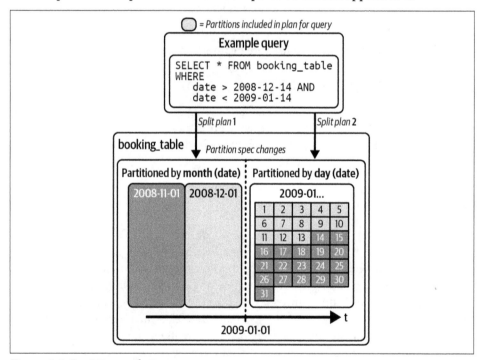

Figure 1-8. Partition evolution

Hidden partitioning

Sometimes users don't know how a table is physically partitioned, and frankly, they shouldn't have to care. Often a table is partitioned by some timestamp field and a user wants to query by that field (e.g., get average revenue by day for the last 90 days). To a user, the most intuitive way to do that is to include a filter of event_time stamp >= DATE_SUB(CURRENT_DATE, INTERVAL 90 DAY). However, this will result in a full table scan because the table is actually partitioned by separate fields called event_year, event_month, and event_day. This occurs because partitioning on a timestamp results in tiny partitions since the values are at second, millisecond, or lower granularity.

This problem is resolved by how Apache Iceberg handles partitioning. In Iceberg, partitioning occurs in two parts: the column, which physical partitioning should be based on; and an optional transform to that value including functions such as bucket, truncate, year, month, day, and hour. The ability to apply a transform eliminates the need to create new columns just for partitioning. This results in more intuitive queries benefiting from partitioning as consumers will not need to add extra filter predicates to their queries on additional partitioning columns.

In Figure 1-9, let's assume the table is using day partitioning. The query depicted in the figure would result in a full table scan in Hive since another "day" column was probably created for partitioning, while in Iceberg the metadata would track the partitioning as "the transformed value of CURRENT_DATE" and therefore would use the partitioning when filtering by CURRENT_DATE (we will discuss this in more detail later in the book).

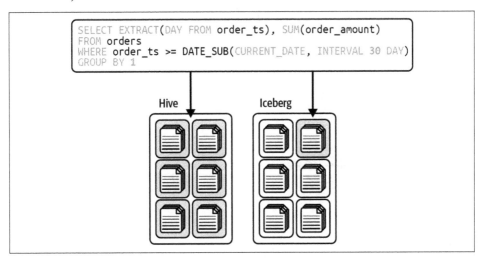

Figure 1-9. The benefits of partitioning in Apache Iceberg

Row-level table operations

You can optimize the table's row-level update patterns to take one of two forms: copy-on-write (COW) or merge-on-read (MOR). When using COW, for a change of any row in a given datafile, the entire file is rewritten (with the row-level change made in the new file) even if a single record in it is updated. When using MOR, for any row-level updates, only a new file that contains the changes to the affected row that is reconciled on reads is written. This gives flexibility to speed up heavy update and delete workloads.

Time travel

Apache Iceberg provides immutable snapshots, so the information for the table's historical state is accessible, allowing you to run queries on the state of the table at a given point in time in the past, or what's commonly known as *time travel*. This can help you in situations such as doing end-of-quarter reporting without the need for duplicating the table's data to a separate location or for reproducing the output of an ML model as of a certain point in time. This is depicted in Figure 1-10.

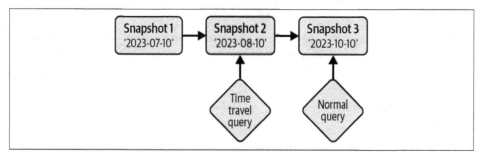

Figure 1-10. Querying the table as it was using time travel

Version rollback

Not only does Iceberg's snapshot isolation allow you to query the data as it is, but it also reverts the table's current state to any of those previous snapshots. Therefore, undoing mistakes is as easy as rolling back (see Figure 1-11).

ID	Name	Age	Date		ID	Name	Age	Date
1	Bob	46	Jan. 1st, 2023		1	Bob	46	Jan. 1st, 2023
2	Josie	65	Jan. 10th, 2023	*Rollback*	2	Josie	65	Jan. 10th, 2023
3	Gene	30	Jan. 20th, 2023		3	Gene	30	Jan. 20th, 2023
4	Alex	37	Feb. 2nd, 2023					
5	Tony	34	Feb. 15th, 2023					

Figure 1-11. Moving the table's state to a previous point in time by rolling back

Schema evolution

Tables change, whether that means adding/removing a column, renaming a column, or changing a column's data type. Regardless of how your table needs to evolve, Apache Iceberg gives you robust schema evolution features—for example, updating an int column to a long column as values in the column get larger.

Conclusion

In this chapter, you learned that Apache Iceberg is a data lakehouse table format built to improve upon many of the areas where Hive tables were lacking. By decoupling from relying on the physical structure of files along with its multilevel metadata tree, Iceberg is able to provide Hive transactions, ACID guarantees, schema evolution, partition evolution, and several other features enabling the data lakehouse. The Apache Iceberg project is able to do this by building a specification and supporting libraries that let existing data tools build support for the open table format.

In Chapter 2, we'll take a deep dive into Apache Iceberg's architecture that makes all this possible.

The Architecture of Apache Iceberg

In this chapter, we'll discuss the architecture and specification that enable Apache Iceberg to resolve the problems inherent in the Hive table format by looking under the covers of an Iceberg table. We'll cover the different structures of an Iceberg table and what each structure provides and enables so that you can understand what's happening under the hood as well as best architect your Apache Iceberg–based lakehouse.

As mentioned in Chapter 1, there are three different layers of an Apache Iceberg table: the catalog layer, the metadata layer, and the data layer. Figure 2-1 shows the different components that make up each layer.

In the following sections, we'll go through each of these components in detail. Since it can be easier to understand concepts new to you by starting with a familiar one, we'll work from the bottom up, starting with the data layer.

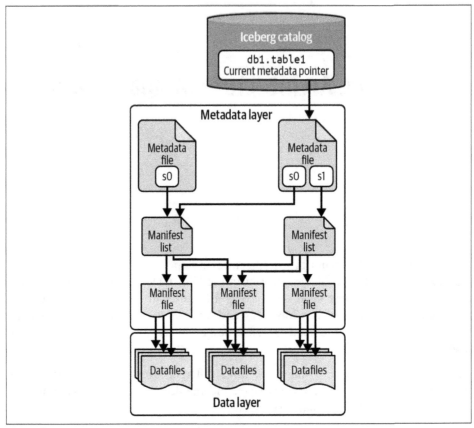

Figure 2-1. The architecture of an Apache Iceberg table

The Data Layer

The data layer of an Apache Iceberg table is what stores the actual data of the table and is primarily made up of the datafiles themselves, although delete files are also included. The data layer is what provides the user with the data needed for their query. While there are some exceptions where structures in the metadata layer can provide a result (e.g., get me the max value for column X), most commonly the data layer is involved in providing results to user queries. The files in the data layer make up the leaves of the tree structure of an Apache Iceberg table.

In real-world usage, the data layer is backed by a distributed filesystem (e.g., Hadoop Distributed File System [HDFS]) or something that looks like a distributed filesystem, such as object storage (e.g., Amazon Simple Storage Service [Amazon S3], Azure Data Lake Storage [ADLS], Google Cloud Storage [GCS]). This enables data lakehouse architectures to be built on and benefit from these extremely scalable and low-cost storage systems.

Datafiles

Datafiles store the data itself. Apache Iceberg is file format agnostic and currently supports Apache Parquet, Apache ORC, and Apache Avro. This is important for the following reasons:

- Many organizations store data in multiple file formats because different groups are able to, or were able to, choose which file format they wanted to use on their own. This is also true of companies that have grown and changed the file format they use based on changes in scale and needs.
- It provides the flexibility to choose different formats depending on what is best suited for a given workload. For example, Parquet might be used for large-scale online analytical processing (OLAP) analytics, whereas Avro might be used for low-latency streaming analytics tables.
- It future-proofs an organization's choice of file format. If a new file format is developed that is better suited for a set of workloads, that file format could be used in an Apache Iceberg table.

While Apache Iceberg is file format agnostic, in the real world the file format most commonly used is Apache Parquet. Parquet is most common because its columnar structure provides large performance gains for OLAP workloads over row-based file formats, and it has become the de facto standard in the industry, meaning basically every engine and tool supports Parquet. Its columnar structure lays the foundation for performance features such as the ability for a single file to be split multiple ways for increased parallelism, statistics for each of these split points, and increased compression, which provides lower storage volume and higher read throughput.

In Figure 2-2, you can see how a given Parquet file has a set of rows ("Row group 0" in the figure) that are then broken down so that all the rows' values for a given column are stored together ("Column a" in the figure). All the rows' values for a given column are further broken down into subsets of the rows' values for this column, which are called pages ("Page 0 in the figure). Each of these levels can be read independently by engines and tools, and therefore each can be read in parallel by a given engine or tool. In addition, Parquet stores statistics (e.g., minimum and maximum values for a given column for a given row group) that enable engines and tools to decide whether it needs to read all the data or whether it can prune row groups that don't fit the query.

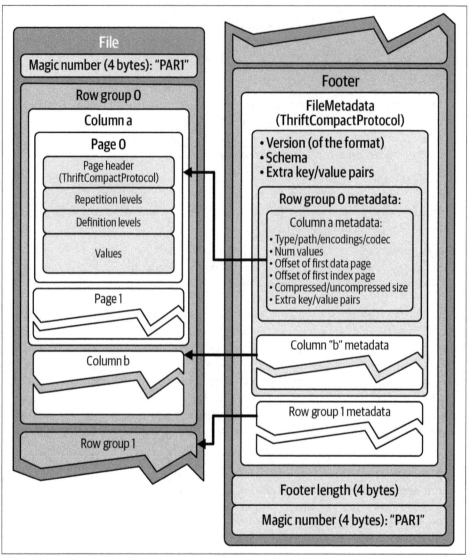

Figure 2-2. The architecture of a Parquet file

Delete Files

Delete files track which records in the dataset have been deleted. Since it's a best practice to treat data lake storage as immutable, you can't update rows in a file in place. Instead, you need to write a new file. This new file can be a copy of the old file with the changes reflected in a new copy of it (called *copy-on-write* [COW]), or it can be a new file that only has the changes written, which engines reading the data then coalesce (called *merge-on-read* [MOR]). Delete files enable the MOR strategy for performing updates and deletes to Iceberg tables. That is, delete files only apply to MOR tables (we'll go into more depth as to why in Chapter 4). Note that delete files are only supported in the Iceberg v2 format, which at the time of this writing is widely adopted by almost every tool supporting Iceberg but is still something to be aware of. Figure 2-3 is a simplified diagram showing a MOR table's datafiles before and after a delete operation is run on it.

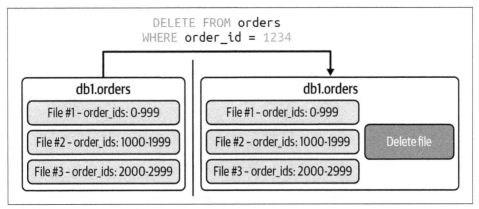

Figure 2-3. A diagram showing a MOR table before and after a DELETE is run on it

There are two ways to identify a given row that needs to be removed from the logical dataset when an engine reads the dataset: either identify the row by its exact position in the dataset or identify the row by the values of one or more fields of the row. Therefore, there are two types of delete files. The former is addressed by what are called positional delete files, and the latter is addressed by what are called equality delete files.

These two approaches have different pros and cons and therefore different situations where one is preferred over the other. We'll go into more depth as to these considerations and situations in Chapter 4 when we discuss COW versus MOR, but following is a high-level description.

Positional delete files

Positional delete files denote what rows have been logically deleted, and therefore the engine reading the data removes them from its representation of the table when it uses the table, by identifying the exact position in the table where the row is located. It does this by specifying the file path of the specific file that contains the row and the row number within that file.

Figure 2-4 shows deleting the row with the order_id of 1234. Assuming the data in the file is sorted by order_id ascending, this row is in file #2 and is row #234 (note that the row referencing is zero indexed, so row #0 in file #2 is order_id = 1000, and therefore row #234 in file #2 is order_id = 1234).

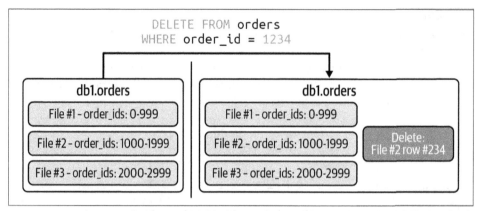

Figure 2-4. A diagram showing a MOR table configured for positional deletes before and after a DELETE is run on it

Equality delete files

Equality delete files denote what rows have been logically deleted and therefore the rows that the engine reading the data needs to remove from its representation of the table when it uses the table, by identifying the row by the values of one or more of the fields for the row. This is best done when there is a unique identifier for each row in the table (aka primary key) so that a single field's value can uniquely identify a row (e.g., "delete the row where the row has a value for order_id of 1234"). However, multiple rows can also be deleted via this method (e.g., "delete all rows where interaction_customer_id = 5678").

Figure 2-5 shows deleting the row with the order_id of 1234 using an equality delete file. An engine writes a delete file that says "delete any rows where order_id = 1234," which any engine reading it then adheres to. Note that in contrast to positional delete files, there is no reference to where these rows are located within the table.

Note also that there is a situation that can occur where an equality delete file deletes a record via column values, and then in a subsequent commit, a record is added back to the dataset that matches the delete file's column values. In that situation, you don't want to have query engines remove the newly added record from the logical table when reading it. The solution to this in Apache Iceberg is sequence numbers. For example, covering the situation in Figure 2-5, the manifest file would note that the datafiles on the left of Figure 2-5 all have a sequence number of 1. Then the manifest file tracking the delete file on the right would have a sequence number of 2. Then the datafile created in the subsequent insert of a new row with order_id of 1234 would have a sequence number of 3. So when an engine reads the table, it knows to apply the delete file to all datafiles that have a sequence number of less than 2 (the delete file's sequence number), but not to the datafiles that have a sequence number of 2 or higher. Via this method, the correct state of the table is maintained as changes are made over time.

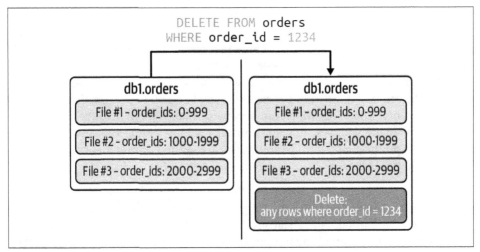

Figure 2-5. A diagram showing a MOR table configured for equality deletes before and after a DELETE is run on it

The Metadata Layer

The metadata layer is an integral part of an Iceberg table's architecture and contains all the metadata files for an Iceberg table. It's a tree structure that tracks the datafiles and metadata about them as well as the operations that resulted in their creation. This tree structure is made up of three file types, all of which are colocated with the datafiles: manifest files, manifest lists, and metadata files. The metadata layer is essential for efficiently managing large datasets and enabling core features such as time travel and schema evolution.

Manifest Files

Manifest files keep track of files in the data layer (i.e., datafiles and delete files) as well as additional details and statistics about each file, such as the minimum and maximum values for a datafile's columns. As mentioned in Chapter 1, the primary difference that allows Iceberg to address the problems of the Hive table format is tracking what data is in a table at the file level. Manifest files are the files that do this tracking at the leaf level of the metadata tree.

> While manifest files track datafiles as well as delete files, a separate set of manifest files are used for each of them (i.e., a single manifest file will contain only datafiles or delete files), though the manifest file schemas are identical.

Each manifest file keeps track of a subset of the datafiles. They contain information such as details about partition membership, record counts, and lower and upper bounds of columns that are used to improve efficiency and performance while reading the data from these datafiles. While some of these statistics are also stored in the datafiles themselves, a single manifest file stores these statistics for multiple datafiles, meaning the pruning done from the stats in a single manifest file greatly reduces the need to open many datafiles, which can hurt performance (even if you're just opening the footer of many datafiles, this still can take a long time). This process will be covered in depth in Chapter 3. These statistics are written during the write operation by the engine/tool for each subset of datafiles a manifest file tracks.

Because these statistics are written in smaller batches by each engine for their subset of the datafiles written, it is much more lightweight to write these statistics compared to the Hive table format, where statistics are collected and stored as part of a long and expensive read job requiring the engine to read an entire partition or entire table, compute the statistics for all that data, and then write the stats for that partition/table. This is because the writer of the data has already processed all the data it is writing, and therefore it is more lightweight for this writer to add a step to collect statistics for this data as it processes it for writing. In practice, this means the statistics collection jobs when using the Hive table format are not rerun very often (if at all), resulting in poorer query performance since engines do not have the information necessary to make informed decisions about how to execute a given query. As a result, Iceberg tables are much more likely to have up-to-date and accurate statistics, allowing engines to make better decisions when processing them, resulting in higher job performance.

You can find an example of the full contents of a manifest file (*Chapter_2/manifest-file.json*) in the book's GitHub repository (*https://oreil.ly/supp-guide-apache-iceberg*). Note that in Iceberg, manifest files are in Avro format, though for viewing convenience, we have converted the Avro contents to JSON format.

Manifest Lists

A manifest list is a snapshot of an Iceberg table at a given point in time. For the table at that point in time, it contains a list of all the manifest files, including the location, the partitions it belongs to, and the upper and lower bounds for partition columns for the datafiles it tracks.

A manifest list contains an array of structs, with each struct keeping track of a single manifest file. The struct's schema is detailed in Table 2-1, which has been adapted from the public Iceberg docs. Also note that this is for Iceberg v2 tables.

Table 2-1. Schema of an Iceberg manifest file

Always present?	Field name	Data type	Description
Yes	`manifest_path`	`string`	Location of the manifest file
Yes	`manifest_length`	`long`	Length of the manifest file in bytes
Yes	`partition_spec_id`	`int`	ID of a partition spec used to write the manifest; refers to an entry listed in `partition-specs` in the table's metadata file
Yes	`content`	`int` with meaning: 0: data, 1: `deletes`	Types of files tracked by the manifest, either datafiles or delete files
Yes	`sequence_number`	`long`	Sequence number when the manifest was added to the table
Yes	`min_sequence_number`	`long`	Minimum data sequence number of all live datafiles or delete files in the manifest
Yes	`added_snapshot_id`	`long`	ID of the snapshot where the manifest file was added
Yes	`added_files_count`	`int`	Number of entries in the manifest file that have ADDED (1) as the value for the `status` field
Yes	`existing_files_count`	`int`	Number of entries in the manifest file that have EXISTING (0) as the value for the `status` field
Yes	`deleted_files_count`	`int`	Number of entries in the manifest file that have DELETED (2) as the value for the `status` field
Yes	`added_rows_count`	`long`	Sum of the number of rows in all files in the manifest that have ADDED as the value for the `status` field
Yes	`existing_rows_count`	`long`	Sum of the number of rows in all files in the manifest that have EXISTING as the value for the `status` field
Yes	`deleted_rows_count`	`long`	Sum of the number of rows in all files in the manifest that have DELETED as the value for the `status` field
No	`partitions`	`array<field_summary>` (see Table 2-2)	List of field summaries for each partition field in the spec; each field in the list corresponds to a field in the manifest file's partition spec
No	`key_metadata`	`binary`	Implementation-specific key metadata for encryption

As referenced in the second-to-last row in Table 2-1, `field_summary` is a struct with the schema shown in Table 2-2.

Table 2-2. Schema of `field_summary`

Always present?	Field name	Data type	Description
Yes	`contains_null`	`boolean`	Whether the manifest contains at least one partition with a null value for the field
No	`contains_nan`	`boolean`	Whether the manifest contains at least one partition with a NaN value for the field
No	`lower_bound`	`bytes`	Lower bound for the non-null, non-NaN values in the partition field, or null if all values are null or NaN; the value is serialized to bytes
No	`upper_bound`	`bytes`	Upper bound for the non-null, non-NaN values in the partition field, or null if all values are null or NaN; the value is serialized to bytes

You can find an example of the full contents of a manifest list (*Chapter_2/manifest-list.json*) in the book's GitHub repository (*https://oreil.ly/supp-guide-apache-iceberg*). Note that in Iceberg, manifest lists are in Avro format, though for viewing convenience, we have converted the Avro contents to JSON format.

Metadata Files

Manifest lists are tracked by metadata files. Another aptly named file, metadata files store metadata about an Iceberg table at a certain point in time. This includes information about the table's schema, partition information, snapshots, and which snapshot is the current one.

Each time a change is made to an Iceberg table, a new metadata file is created and is registered as the latest version of the metadata file atomically via the catalog, which we'll cover in the next section. This ensures that a linear history of the table commits and helps during scenarios such as concurrent writes, that is, multiple engines writing data simultaneously. Also, this way, engines will always see the latest version of the table during read operations.

The metadata file's schema is detailed in Table 2-3, which has been adapted from the public Iceberg docs.

Table 2-3. Metadata file schema

Always present?	Field name	Data type	Description
Yes	`format-version`	`integer`	An integer version number for the format. Currently, this can be 1 or 2 based on the spec. Implementations must throw an exception if a table's version is higher than the supported version. The default at the time of this writing is 2.
Yes	`table-uuid`	`string`	A UUID that identifies the table and is generated when the table is created. Implementations must throw an exception if a table's UUID does not match the expected UUID after refreshing metadata.
Yes	`location`	`string`	The table's base location. This is used by writers to determine where to store datafiles, manifest files, and table metadata files.
Yes	`last-sequence-number`	`64-bit signed integer`	The table's highest assigned sequence number. This is a monotonically increasing `long` that tracks the order of snapshots in a table.
Yes	`last-updated-ms`	`64-bit signed integer`	Timestamp in milliseconds from the Unix epoch when the table was last updated. Each table metadata file should update this field just before writing.
Yes	`last-column-id`	`integer`	The highest assigned column ID for the table. This is used to ensure that columns are always assigned an unused ID when evolving schemas.
Yes	`schemas`	`array`	A list of schemas, stored as objects with `schema-id`.
Yes	`current-schema-id`	`integer`	ID of the table's current schema.
Yes	`partition-specs`	`array`	A list of partition specs, stored as full partition spec objects.
Yes	`default-spec-id`	`integer`	ID of the "current" spec that writers should use by default.
Yes	`last-partition-id`	`integer`	The highest assigned partition field ID across all partition specs for the table. This is used to ensure that partition fields are always assigned an unused ID when evolving specs.
No	`properties`	`map`	A string-to-string map of table properties. This is used to control settings that affect reading and writing and is not intended to be used for arbitrary metadata. For example, `commit.retry.num-retries` is used to control the number of commit retries.
No	`current-snapshot-id`	`64-bit signed integer`	ID of the current table snapshot. This must be the same as the current ID of the `main` branch in `refs`.
No	`snapshots`	`array`	A list of valid snapshots. Valid snapshots are snapshots for which all datafiles exist in the filesystem. A datafile must not be deleted from the filesystem until the last snapshot in which it was listed is garbage collected.
No	`snapshot-log`	`array`	A list of timestamp and snapshot ID pairs that encodes changes to the current snapshot for the table. Each time the `current-snapshot-id` is changed, a new entry should be added with the `last-updated-ms` and the new `current-snapshot-id`. When snapshots are expired from the list of valid snapshots, all entries before a snapshot that has expired should be removed.

Always present?	Field name	Data type	Description
No	metadata-log	array	A list of timestamp and metadata file location pairs that encodes changes to the previous metadata files for the table. Each time a new metadata file is created, a new entry of the previous metadata file location should be added to the list. Tables can be configured to remove the oldest metadata log entries and keep a fixed-size log of the most recent entries after a commit.
Yes	sort-orders	array	A list of sort orders, stored as full sort order objects.
Yes	default-sort-order-id	integer	Default sort order ID of the table. Note that this could be used by writers, but it is not used when reading because reads use the specs stored in manifest files.
No	refs	map	A map of snapshot references. The map keys are the unique snapshot reference names in the table, and the map values are snapshot reference objects. There is always a main branch reference pointing to the current-snapshot-id even if the refs map is null.
No	statistics	array	A list (optional) of table statistics.

You can find an example of the full contents of a metadata file (*Chapter_2/metadata-file.json*) in the book's GitHub repository (*https://oreil.ly/supp-guide-apache-iceberg*).

Puffin Files

While there are structures in datafiles and delete files to enhance the performance of interacting with the data in an Iceberg table, sometimes you need more advanced structures to enhance the performance of specific types of queries.

For example, say you wanted to know how many unique people placed an order with you in the past 30 days. The statistics in the datafiles, not in the metadata files, as we'll see shortly, cover this kind of use case. Certainly you could use those statistics to improve performance by some amount (e.g., pruning out only the data for the last 30 days), but you would still have to read every order in those 30 days and do aggregations in the engine, which can take too long depending on factors such as the size of the data, resources allocated to the engine, and cardinality of the fields.

Enter the puffin file format. A *puffin file* stores statistics and indexes about the data in the table that improve the performance of an even broader range of queries, such as the aforementioned example, than the statistics stored in the datafiles and metadata files.

The file contains sets of arbitrary byte sequences called *blobs*, along with the associated metadata required to analyze the blobs. Figure 2-6 shows the structure of a puffin file.

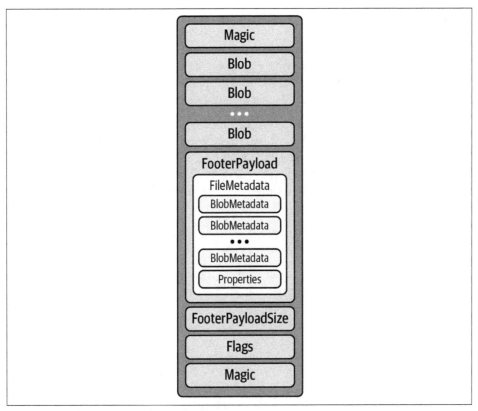

Figure 2-6. The structure of a puffin file

While this structure enables statistics and index structures of any type (e.g., bloom filters), currently the only type supported is the Theta sketch (*https://oreil.ly/YLM8A*) from the Apache DataSketches library. This structure enables computing the *approximate* number of distinct values of a column for a given set of rows, enabling the computation to be much faster and use much fewer resources, often orders of magnitude fewer. This can be valuable when an operation needs to know the number of distinct values for a column (e.g., the number of users per region), but it's too cost or time intensive to find the exact number. It can also be valuable when the use case allows for an approximation, especially when the operation is run repeatedly, such as for dashboards.

The Catalog

Anyone reading from a table (let alone tens, hundreds, or thousands of tables) needs to know where to go first; somewhere they can go to find out where to read/write data for a given table. The first step for anyone looking to interact with the table is to find the location of the metadata file that is the current metadata pointer.

This central place where you go to find the current location of the current metadata pointer is the Iceberg *catalog*. The primary requirement for an Iceberg catalog is that it must support atomic operations for updating the current metadata pointer. This support for atomic operations is required so that all readers and writers see the same state of the table at a given point in time.

Within the catalog, there is a reference or pointer for each table to that table's current metadata file. For example, in Figure 2-1 there are two metadata files. The value for the table's current metadata pointer in the catalog is the location of the metadata file.

Because the only requirements for an Iceberg catalog are that it needs to store the current metadata pointer and provide atomic guarantees, there are many different backends that can serve as an Iceberg catalog. However, different catalogs store the current metadata pointer differently. Following are a few examples:

- With Amazon S3 as the catalog, there's a file called *version-hint.text* in the table's metadata folder whose contents is the version number of the current metadata file. Note that anytime you use a distributed filesystem (or something that looks like one) to store the current metadata pointer, the catalog used is actually called the *hadoop* catalog.

- With Hive Metastore as the catalog, the table entry in the Hive Metastore has a table property called `location` that stores the location of the current metadata file.

- With Nessie as the catalog, the table entry in Nessie has a table property called `metadataLocation` that stores the location of the current metadata file for the table.

In the preceding examples of the manifest files, manifest lists, and metadata files, we were using the AWS Glue Catalog. Leveraging Iceberg metadata about the table, we can see what the catalog is saying the current metadata file is. Running the following query gives us the details about the current state of the table, most notably the current metadata file location:

```
SELECT *
FROM my_catalog.iceberg_book.orders.metadata_log_entries
ORDER BY timestamp DESC
LIMIT 1
```

Timestamp	Metadata File	Latest Snapshot ID	Latest Schema ID	Latest Sequence Number
2023-03-21 22:55:31.868	s3://jason-dremio-product-us-west-2/iceberg-book/iceberg_book.db/orders/metadata/00002-509f0747-4dc4-4965-b354-ce5fb747c2f5.metadata.json	8619686881304977663	0	2

So, if we want to read data from this table that is using the Glue Catalog, we know that we then need to go ahead and retrieve the metadata file at the path *s3://jason-dremio-product-us-west-2/iceberg-book/iceberg_book.db/orders/metadata/00002-509f0747-4dc4-4965-b354-ce5fb747c2f5.metadata.json.*

Conclusion

In this chapter, we discussed the architecture and format of Apache Iceberg tables that enable them to resolve the Hive table format's problems and achieve capabilities such as ACID transactions on the data lake. The three layers we covered—the data layer, the metadata layer, and the catalog—and their file types and structures are leveraged by engines and tools to read and write data efficiently, as well as achieve more advanced capabilities such as time travel and schema evolution.

In Chapter 3, we'll discuss the lifecycle of queries run in these engines and tools to see exactly how these file types and structures are leveraged.

Lifecycle of Write and Read Queries

The Apache Iceberg table format provides high-performance queries during reads and writes, allowing you to run online analytical processing (OLAP) workloads directly on the data lake. What facilitates this performance is the way the various components of the Iceberg table format are designed. It is therefore critical to understand the structure of these components so that query engines can effectively use them for faster query planning and execution. We discussed these architectural components in detail in Chapter 2. At a high level, all these components can be segregated into three different layers, as presented in Figure 3-1.

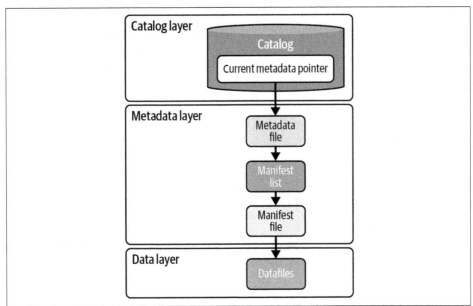

Figure 3-1. Apache Iceberg's components

Let's quickly review how a query engine interacts with these components for reads and writes:

Catalog layer

As you learned in Chapter 2, a catalog holds the references to the current metadata pointer, that is, the latest metadata file for each table. Irrespective of whether you are doing a read operation or a write operation, the catalog is the first component that a query engine interacts with. In the case of reads, the engine reaches out to the catalog to learn about the current state of the table, and for writes, the catalog is used to adhere to the schema defined and to know about the table's partitioning scheme.

Metadata layer

The metadata layer in Apache Iceberg consists of three components: metadata files, manifest lists, and manifest files. Each time a query engine writes something to an Iceberg table, a new metadata file is created atomically and is defined as the latest version of the metadata file. This ensures that a linear history of the table commits, and it helps during scenarios such as concurrent writes (i.e., multiple engines writing data simultaneously). Also, during read operations, engines will always see the latest version of the table. Query engines interact with the manifest lists to get information about partition specifications that help them skip the nonrequired manifest files for faster performance. Finally, information from the manifest files, such as upper and lower bounds for a specific column, null value counts, and partition-specific data, is used by the engine for file pruning.

Data layer

Query engines filter through the metadata files to read the datafiles required by a particular query efficiently. On the write side, datafiles get written on the file storage, and the related metadata files are created and updated accordingly.

In the following sections, you will learn about the lifecycle of the various write and read operations in Apache Iceberg and how each operation interacts with the components just described to bring about the best query performance. Note that, throughout this chapter, we will present queries using Spark SQL and Dremio's SQL Query Engine as the compute engines.

Writing Queries in Apache Iceberg

The write process in Apache Iceberg involves a series of steps that enable query engines to efficiently insert and update data. When a write query is initiated, it is sent to the engine for parsing. The catalog is then consulted to ensure consistency and integrity in the data and to write the data as per the defined partition strategies. The datafiles and metadata files are then written based on the query. Finally, the catalog file is updated to reflect the latest metadata, enabling subsequent read operations to access the most up-to-date version of the data. Figure 3-2 depicts a high-level overview of the process.

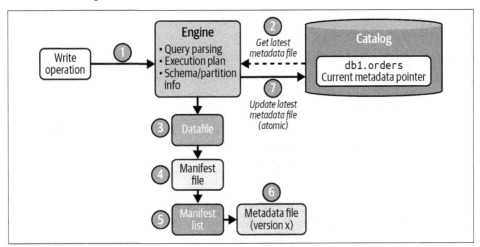

Figure 3-2. Overview of the Apache Iceberg write process

Create the Table

We'll start by creating an Iceberg table so that you can understand the underlying process. The example query will create a table called `orders` with four columns. While the syntax to do this in Spark and Dremio's SQL Query Engine is very similar, it is shown separately in the rest of this chapter so that the code can be run directly in each system and you can follow along. These code samples are also provided in the book's GitHub repository (*https://oreil.ly/supp-guide-apache-iceberg*). This table is partitioned at the hour granularity of the `order_ts` field. Note how you don't have to add an explicit column for partitioning with Iceberg tables. This feature is called *hidden partitioning*, as we discussed in Chapter 1.

```
# Spark SQL
CREATE TABLE orders (
    order_id BIGINT,
    customer_id BIGINT,
    order_amount DECIMAL(10, 2),
    order_ts TIMESTAMP
)
USING iceberg
PARTITIONED BY (HOUR(order_ts))

# Dremio
CREATE TABLE orders (
  order_id BIGINT,
  customer_id BIGINT,
  order_amount DECIMAL(10, 2),
```

```
    order_ts TIMESTAMP
)
PARTITION BY (HOUR(order_ts))
```

Send the query to the engine

First, the query is sent to the query engine for parsing. Then, since it is a CREATE statement, the engine will start creating and defining the table.

Write the metadata file

At this point, the engine starts creating a metadata file named *v1.metadata.json* in the data lake filesystem to store information about the table. A generic form of the URL of the path looks something like this: *s3://path/to/warehouse/db1/table1/metadata/ v1.metadata.json*.

Based on the information on the table path, */path/to/warehouse/db1/table1*, the engine writes the metadata file. It then defines the schema of the table orders by specifying the columns and data types and stores it in the metadata file. Finally, it assigns a unique identifier to the table: table-uuid. Once the query executes successfully, the metadata file *v1.metadata.json* is written to the data lake file storage:

```
s3://datalake/db1/orders/metadata/v1.metadata.json
```

If you inspect the metadata file, you will see the schema of the defined table along with the partition specification:

```
{
  "table-uuid" : "072db680-d810-49ac-935c-56e901cad686",
  "schema" : {
    "type" : "struct",
    "schema-id" : 0,
    "fields" : [ {
      "id" : 1,
      "name" : "order_id",
      "required" : false,
      "type" : "long"
    }, {
      "id" : 2,
      "name" : "customer_id",
      "required" : false,
      "type" : "long"
    }, {
      "id" : 3,
      "name" : "order_amount",
      "required" : false,
      "type" : "decimal(10, 2)"
    }, {
      "id" : 4,
      "name" : "order_ts",
      "required" : false,
```

```
        "type" : "timestamptz"
      }
  },
  "partition-spec" : [ {
      "name" : "order_ts_hour",
      "transform" : "hour",
      "source-id" : 4,
      "field-id" : 1000
    } ]
  }
```

This is the current state of the table; you have created a table, but it is an empty table with no records. In Iceberg terms, this is called a *snapshot* (refer to Chapter 2 for details). An important thing to note here is that since you haven't inserted any records yet, there is no actual data in the table, so there are no datafiles in your data lake. Therefore, the snapshot doesn't point to any manifest list; hence, there are no manifest files.

Update the catalog file to commit changes

Finally, the engine updates the current metadata pointer to point to the *v1.metadata. json* file in the catalog file *version-hint.text*, as this is the present state of the table. Note that the name of the catalog file, *version-hint.text*, is specific to the catalog choice. For this demonstration, we have leveraged the filesystem-based Hadoop catalog. In Chapter 5, we'll compare and contrast the different Iceberg catalog choices you have. Figure 3-3 illustrates the hierarchy of the Iceberg components after the table is created.

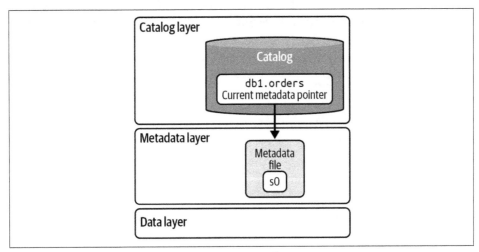

Figure 3-3. Hierarchy of the Iceberg components after executing CREATE

Insert the Query

Now let's insert some records into the table and understand how things work. We have created a table called orders with four columns. For this demonstration, we will input the following values into the table: an order_id of 123, a customer_id of 456, an order_amount of 36.17, and an order_ts of 2023-03-07 08:10:23. Here is the query:

```
# Spark SQL/Dremio's SQL Query Engine
INSERT INTO orders VALUES (
    123,
    456,
    36.17,
    '2023-03-07 08:10:23'
)
```

Send the query to the engine

The query is sent to the query engine for parsing. Since this is an INSERT statement, the engine needs information about the table, such as its schema, to start with query planning.

Check the catalog

First, the query engine makes a request of the catalog to determine the location of the current metadata file and then reads it. Because we are using the Hadoop catalog, the engine will read the */orders/metadata/version-hint.txt* file and see that the content of the file is a single integer: 1. Because of this, and leveraging logic from the catalog implementation, the engine knows the current metadata file location is */orders/metadata/v1.metadata.json*, which is the file our previous CREATE TABLE operation created. So the engine will read this file. Although the engine's motivation in this case is to insert new datafiles, it still interacts with the catalog, primarily for two reasons:

- The engine needs to understand the current schema of the table to adhere to it.
- The engine needs to learn about the partitioning scheme to organize data accordingly while writing.

Write the datafiles and metadata files

After the engine learns about the table schema and the partitioning scheme, it starts writing the new datafiles and the related metadata files. Here's what happens in this process.

The engine first writes the records as a Parquet datafile (Parquet is the default, but this can be changed) based on the hourly defined partitioning scheme of the table.

Additionally, if a sort order is defined for the table, records will be sorted before being written into the datafile. This is what it might look like in the filesystem:

```
s3://datalake/db1/orders/data/order_ts_hour=2023-03-07-08/0_0_0.parquet
```

After writing the datafile, the engine creates a manifest file. This manifest file is given information about the path of the actual datafile the engine created. In addition, the engine writes statistical information, such as the upper and lower bounds of a column and the null value counts, in the manifest file, which is highly beneficial for the query engine to prune files and provide the best performance. The engine computes this information while processing the data it's going to write, so this is a relatively lightweight operation, at least compared to a process that starts from scratch and has to compute the statistics. The manifest file is written as a *.avro* file in the storage system:

```
s3://datalake/db1/orders/metadata/62acb3d7-e992-4cbc-8e41-58809fcacb3e.avro
```

Here is a JSON representation of a manifest file's content. Please note that this is not the full content of the manifest file, but rather, an excerpt with some of the key information pertaining to our topic:

```
{
"data_file" : {
    "file_path" :
    "s3://datalake/db1/orders/data/order_ts_hour=2023-03-07-08/0_0_0.parquet",
"file_format" : "PARQUET",
        "block_size_in_bytes" : 67108864,
        "null_value_counts" : [],
        "lower_bounds" : {
        "array": [{
"key": 1,
        "value": 123
}],
}
        "upper_bounds" : {
        "array": [{
"key": 1,
        "value": 123
}],
},
    }
}
```

Next, the engine creates a manifest list to keep track of the manifest file. If existing manifest files are associated with this snapshot, those will also be added to this new manifest list. The engine writes this file to the data lake with information such as the manifest file's path, the number of datafiles/rows added or deleted, and statistics about partitions, such as the lower and upper bounds of the partition columns. Again, the engine already has all this information, so it's a lightweight operation to have these statistics. This information helps read queries exclude any nonrequired manifest files, facilitating faster queries:

```
s3://datalake/db1/orders/metadata/
snap-8333017788700497002-1-4010cc03-5585-458c-9fdc-188de318c3e6.avro
```

Here is a snippet of the content of a manifest list:

```
{
  "manifest_path":
  "s3://datalake/db1/orders/metadata/62acb3d7-e992-4cbc-8e41-58809fcacb3e.avro",
  "manifest_length": 6152,
  "added_snapshot_id": 8333017788700497002,
  "added_data_files_count": 1,
  "added_rows_count": 1,
  "deleted_rows_count": 0,
  "partitions": {
        "array": [ {
            "contains_null": false,
            "lower_bound": {
                "bytes": "¹Ô\\u0006\\u0000"
            },
            "upper_bound": {
                "bytes": "¹Ô\\u0006\\u0000"
            }
        } ]
    }
}
```

Finally, the engine creates a new metadata file, *v2.metadata.json*, with a new snapshot, s1, by considering the existing metadata file, *v1.metadata.json* (previously current), while keeping track of the previous snapshot, s0. This new metadata file includes information about the manifest list created by the engine, with details such as the manifest list filepath, snapshot ID, and summary of the operation. Also, the engine makes a reference that this manifest list (or snapshot) is now the current one:

```
s3://datalake/db1/orders/metadata/v2.metadata.json
```

Here is what the content of this new metadata file looks like (this is an excerpt of the metadata file):

```
        "current-snapshot-id" : 8333017788700497002,
          "refs" : {
            "main" :  {
              "snapshot-id" : 8333017788700497002,
              "type" : "branch"
}
},
"snapshots" : [ {
    "snapshot-id" : 8333017788700497002,
    "summary" : {
      "operation" : "append",
      "added-data-files" : "1",
```

```
        "added-records" : "1",
    },
        "manifest-list" : "s3://datalake/db1/orders/metadata/
snap-8333017788700497002-1-4010cc03-5585-458c-9fdc-188de318c3e6.avro",
    } ],
```

Update the catalog file to commit changes

Now the engine goes to the catalog again to ensure that no other snapshots were committed while this INSERT operation was being run. By doing this validation, Iceberg guarantees no interference in operations in a scenario where multiple writers write data concurrently. With any write operation, Iceberg creates metadata files optimistically, assuming that the current version will remain unchanged until the writer commits. Upon completing the write, the engine commits atomically by switching the table's metadata file pointer from the existing base version to the new version, *v2.metadata.json*, which now becomes the current metadata file.

A visual representation of what the Iceberg component hierarchy looks like at this stage is presented in Figure 3-4.

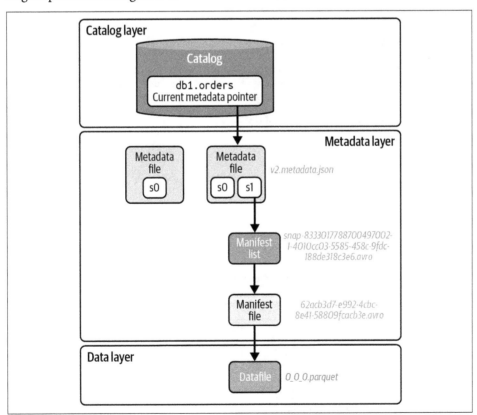

Figure 3-4. Iceberg component's hierarchy after executing INSERT

Merge Query

For our next write operation, we will do an UPSERT/MERGE INTO. Such queries are usually run when you want to update an existing row if a specific value exists in the table, and if not, you just insert the new row.

So, for our example, let's say there is a stage table, orders_staging, that consists of two records: one that has an update for the existing order_id (order_id=123) and another that is an entirely new order. We want to keep the orders table updated with the latest details for each order, and therefore we will update the order_amount if the order_id already exists in the destination table (orders). If not, we will just insert the new record. Here is the query:

```
# Spark SQL
MERGE INTO orders o
USING (SELECT * FROM orders_staging) s
ON o.order_id = s.order_id
WHEN MATCHED THEN UPDATE SET order_amount = s.order_amount
WHEN NOT MATCHED THEN INSERT *;

# Dremio
MERGE INTO orders o
USING (SELECT * FROM orders_staging) s
ON o.order_id = s.order_id
WHEN MATCHED THEN UPDATE SET order_amount = s.order_amount
WHEN NOT MATCHED THEN INSERT (order_id, customer_id, order_amount, order_ts)
    VALUES (s.order_id, s.customer_id, s.order_amount, s.order_ts)
```

This query would merge the following datasets:

orders:

order_id	customer_id	order_amount	order_ts
123	456	36.17	2023-03-07 08:10:23

orders_staging:

order_id	customer_id	order_amount	order_ts
123	456	50.5	2023-03-07 08:10:23
124	326	60	2023-01-27 10:05:03

Send the query to the engine

The query is first parsed by the query engine. In this case, since two tables are involved (stage and destination), the engine needs the data for both tables to start with the query planning.

Check the catalog

Similar to the INSERT operation discussed in the previous section, the query engine first makes a request to the catalog to determine the current metadata file location and then reads it. Because the catalog used for this exercise is Hadoop, the engine will read the */orders/metadata/version-hint.txt* file and retrieve its content, which is the integer 2. After getting this information and using the catalog logic, the engine learns that the current metadata file location is */orders/metadata/v2.metadata.json*. This is the file that our previous INSERT operation generated, so the engine will read this file. It will then look at the current schema of the table so that the write operations can adhere to it. Finally, the engine will learn how datafiles are organized based on the partitioning strategy and start writing the new datafiles.

Write datafiles and metadata files

First, the query engine will read and load data in memory from both the orders_staging and orders tables to determine the matching records. Note that we will go over the READ process in detail in the next section. The engine will traverse through each record in both tables based on the order_id field and find out the records that match.

One important thing to note here is that as the engine is determining the matches, what gets tracked in memory will be based on the two strategies defined by the Iceberg table properties: copy-on-write (COW) and merge-on-read (MOR).

While we will go into more depth on these two strategies in Chapter 4, in short, with the COW strategy, whenever the Iceberg table is updated, any associated datafiles with the relevant records will be rewritten as a new datafile. However, with MOR, the datafiles will not be rewritten; instead, new *delete* files will be generated to keep track of the changes.

In our case, we'll use the COW strategy. So the datafile *0_0_0.parquet*, which contains the record with order_id = 123 from the orders table, will be read into memory. Then the order_amount field for this order_id will be updated with the new order_amount from the order_staging table in the in-memory copy of this data. Finally, these modified details are then written to a new Parquet datafile:

```
s3://datalake/db1/orders/data/order_ts_hour=2023-03-07-08/0_0_1.parquet
```

Note that we just had one record in the orders table in this specific example. However, even if there were other records in this table that didn't match the condition specified in the query, the engine would still make a copy of all these records and only the matching rows would have been updated, whereas the nonmatching ones are written into an independent file. This is due to the write strategy, COW. You will learn more about these writing strategies in Chapter 4.

Now the record in the `order_staging` table that didn't match the condition will be treated as a regular INSERT and will be written as a new datafile in a different partition as the hour(`order_ts`) value is different for this one:

```
s3://datalake/db1/orders/data/order_ts_hour=2023-01-27-10/0_0_0.parquet
```

After writing the datafiles, the engine creates a new manifest file that holds a reference to the filepath of these two datafiles. Additionally, various statistics about these datafiles, such as the lower and upper bounds of a column and the value counts, are included in the manifest file:

```
s3://datalake/db1/orders/metadata/faf71ac0-3aee-4910-9080-c2e688148066.avro
```

You can see an example of what the resulting manifest file may look like in the book's GitHub repository (*https://oreil.ly/supp-guide-apache-iceberg*).

The engine then generates a new manifest list that points to the manifest file created in the previous step. It also tracks any existing manifest files and writes the manifest list to the data lake:

```
s3://datalake/db1/orders/metadata/snap-5139476312242609518-1-e22ff753-2738-4d7d-
a810-d65dcc1abe63.avro
```

Upon inspecting the manifest list (refer to the book's GitHub repository (*https://oreil.ly/supp-guide-apache-iceberg*)), you can also see things such as partition statistics and the number of added and deleted files.

After that, the engine goes on to create a new metadata file, *v3.metadata.json*, with a new snapshot, s2, based on the previously current metadata file, *v2.metadata.json*, and the snapshots included as part of that, s0 and s1 (in the book's GitHub repository (*https://oreil.ly/supp-guide-apache-iceberg*), you can see an example of how this would look):

```
s3://datalake/db1/orders/metadata/v3.metadata.json
```

Update the catalog file to commit changes

Finally, the engine runs a check at this point to ensure that there are no write conflicts and then updates the catalog with the value of the latest metadata file, which is *v3.metadata.json*. Visually, the Iceberg components would look like Figure 3-5 at this stage of the UPSERT operation.

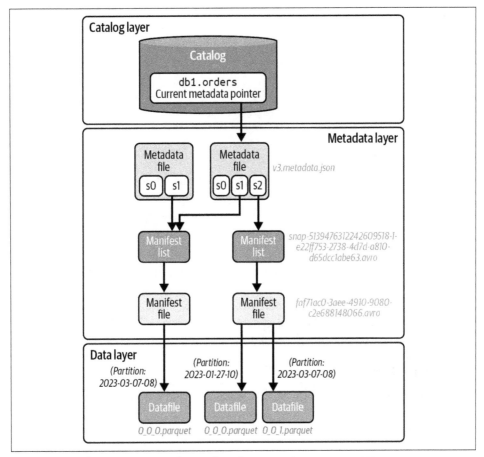

Figure 3-5. Iceberg components hierarchy after executing MERGE INTO

Reading Queries in Apache Iceberg

Reading data from Apache Iceberg tables follows a well-defined sequence of actions, seamlessly allowing queries to be transformed into actionable insights. When a read query is initiated, it is sent to the query engine first. The engine leverages the catalog to retrieve the latest metadata file location, which contains critical information about the table's schema and other metadata files, such as the manifest list that ultimately leads to the actual datafiles. Statistical information about columns is used in this process to limit the number of files being read, which helps improve query performance.

The SELECT Query

In this section, we will cover how the various components of Apache Iceberg work together when a READ query is executed. Here is the query that we will run:

```
# Spark SQL/Dremio Sonar
SELECT *
FROM orders
WHERE order_ts BETWEEN '2023-01-01' AND '2023-01-31'
```

Send the query to the engine

At this stage, the engine will start planning the query based on the metadata files.

Check the catalog

The query engine requests the catalog for the current *metadata file* path for the orders table and then reads it. As discussed in the previous two sections, the engine will read the */orders/metadata/version-hint.txt* file as we are using a Hadoop catalog here. The content of this file is a single integer: 3. Based on this information and the logic implemented for catalog implementation, the engine knows that the current metadata file location is */orders/metadata/v3.metadata.json*. This is the file that our previous MERGE INTO operation generated.

Get information from the metadata file

The engine then opens and reads the metadata file, *v3.metadata.json*, to get information about a couple of things. First it determines the table's schema to prepare its internal memory structures for reading the data. See examples of the data in the *metadata.json* file in the book's GitHub repository (*https://oreil.ly/supp-guide-apache-iceberg*). Then it learns about the table's partitioning scheme to understand how the data is organized. The query engine can later leverage this to skip irrelevant datafiles.

One of the most important pieces of information that the engine retrieves from the metadata file is the current-snapshot-id. This is what signifies the current state of the table. Based on the current-snapshot-id, the engine will locate the *manifest list* filepath from the snapshots array to traverse further and scan the relevant files.

Get information from the manifest list

After getting the location of the manifest list filepath from the metadata file, the query engine reads the file *snap-5139476312242609518-1-e22ff753-2738-4d7d-a810-d65dcc1abe63.avro* to derive further details (see examples in the book's GitHub repository (*https://oreil.ly/supp-guide-apache-iceberg*)). The most critical piece of information that the engine gets from this file is the *manifest file* path location for each snapshot within that manifest list. The engine needs this information to get the relevant datafiles for a specific query.

The manifest list also contains critical information on partitions, such as the partition-spec-id. This tells the engine about the partition scheme used to write a particular snapshot. Currently, the value of this field is 0 (see the book's GitHub repository (*https://oreil.ly/supp-guide-apache-iceberg*)), which implies that this is the only partition defined for the table.

There are also other partition-specific statistics, such as the lower and upper bounds of the partition columns for a manifest. This information is beneficial when the engine determines which manifest files to skip for better file pruning. Other details, such as the total number of datafiles added/deleted and the number of rows added/deleted for each snapshot, are also found in this file.

Get information from the manifest file

The engine then opens the manifest file *faf71ac0-3aee-4910-9080-c2e688148066.avro* that wasn't pruned (i.e., relevant to the query). It reads the file to get the details (view examples in the book's GitHub repository (*https://oreil.ly/supp-guide-apache-iceberg*)). First, the query engine scans every entry, each representing a datafile tracked by this manifest file. It compares the partition values that each of these datafiles belongs to, to the values used in our query filters.

In the query, we requested to get all the order details between '2023-01-01' and '2023-01-31'. Therefore, the engine would ignore the partition value, 2023-03-07-08, as it doesn't match the filter value range. When the filter values match the partition value, the engine will check for all the records in this partition.

Based on the partition value, the engine looks for the corresponding datafile, *0_0_0.parquet*. The engine also gathers other statistical information, such as the lower and upper bounds of each column and the null value counts, to skip any irrelevant files.

Data and file optimization techniques such as partitioning and metrics-based filtering (upper/lower bounds of columns) that are available by default in Apache Iceberg allow the engine to avoid full table scans, as seen in this example, thereby facilitating significant performance guarantees. Finally, the record is returned to the user:

order_id	customer_id	order_amount	order_ts
1 125	321	20.50	2023-01-27 10:30:05 +00:00

Visually, this entire READ process looks like Figure 3-6.

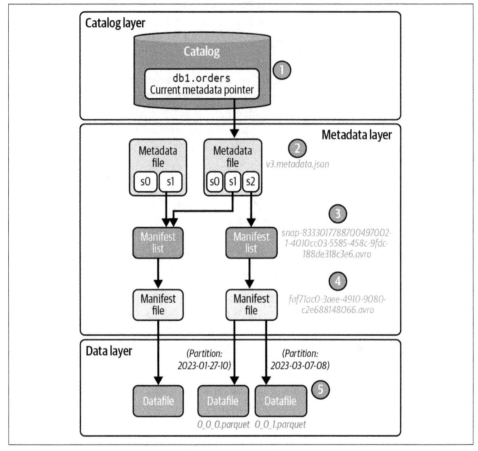

Figure 3-6. How a READ query works in Apache Iceberg

Referring to Figure 3-6, note the following:

1. The query engine interacts with the catalog to get the current metadata file (*v3.metadata.json*).

2. It then gets the current-snapshot-id (S2 in this case) and the manifest list location for that snapshot.

3. The manifest file path is then retrieved from the manifest list.

4. The engine determines the datafile path based on the partition filter (2023-03-07-08) from the manifest file.

5. The matching data from the required datafile is then returned to the user.

The Time-Travel Query

An important capability in the world of databases and data warehouses is the ability to go back in time to a particular state of the table to query historical data (i.e., data that has been changed or deleted). Apache Iceberg brings a similar time-travel capability to a data lakehouse architecture. This can be particularly useful for scenarios such as analyzing your organization's data from previous quarters, restoring accidentally deleted rows, or reproducing analysis results. Apache Iceberg provides two ways to run time-travel queries: using a timestamp and using a snapshot ID.

In this section, you will learn how to run time-travel queries for an Apache Iceberg table. For the purpose of this demonstration, let's say we needed to travel back to the state before we executed the MERGE INTO query (i.e., when we just ran our INSERT statement). So, given those assumptions, the first thing we need to understand is the history of the Iceberg table. One of the best things about Apache Iceberg is that it allows you to analyze various table-specific metadata information via system tables called *metadata tables*. You will learn about metadata tables in detail in Chapter 10. To analyze our order table's history, we will query the history metadata table (available in the book's GitHub repository (*https://oreil.ly/supp-guide-apache-iceberg*) are examples of metadata throughout this section):

```
# Spark SQL
SELECT * FROM catalog.db.orders.history;
# Dremio
SELECT * FROM TABLE (table_history('orders'))
```

This gives us a list of all the transactions that have occurred in this table:

made_current_at	snapshot_id	parent_id	is_current_ancestor
2023-03-06 21:28:35.360	7327164675870333694	null	true
2023-03-07 20:45:08.914	8333017788700497002	7327164675870333694	true
2023-03-09 19:58:40.448	5139476312242609518	8333017788700497002	true

To summarize the `history` metadata table:

- The first snapshot, with ID `7327164675870333694`, was generated after we ran the `CREATE` statement.

- The second snapshot, `8333017788700497002`, was created after we inserted a new record using the `INSERT` statement.

- Finally, our `MERGE INTO` query created the third snapshot, `5139476312242609518`.

Since our requirement is to time-travel to the state prior to the final transaction (i.e., `MERGE`), the timestamp or the snapshot ID we will be targeting is the second one. This is the query that we will run:

```
# Spark SQL
SELECT * FROM orders
TIMESTAMP AS OF '2023-03-07 20:45:08.914'
# Dremio Sonar
SELECT * FROM orders
AT TIMESTAMP '2023-03-07 20:45:08.914'
```

 If we don't provide the exact timestamp value, Iceberg will look for snapshots older than the specified value and return the results. If no older snapshots exist, Iceberg will throw an exception such as this:

```
IllegalArgumentException: Cannot find a snapshot older
than 2023-03-06T21:28:35+00:00.
```

If we want to use the snapshot ID to time-travel, the query would look like this:

```
# Spark SQL
SELECT *
FROM orders
VERSION AS OF 8333017788700497002
# Dremio
SELECT *
FROM orders
AT SNAPSHOT 8333017788700497002
```

Now let's quickly cover what happens behind the scenes with the Iceberg components when the time-travel query is run and how the relevant datafile is returned to the user.

Send the query to the engine

As with any `SELECT` statement, the query is first sent to the engine, which parses it. The engine will leverage the table metadata to start planning the query.

Check the catalog

In this step, the query engine requests the catalog to know the location of the current metadata file and reads it. Since we have leveraged the Hadoop catalog in this exercise, the engine will read the content of the */orders/metadata/version-hint.txt* file, which is the integer 3. With this information, and following the catalog's implementation logic, the engine determines that the location of the current metadata file is */orders/metadata/v3.metadata.json*. The engine will finally read this file to understand the table schema and things such as partitioning strategy.

Get information from the metadata file

Next, the engine reads the metadata file to get the table information. The current metadata file keeps track of all the snapshots generated for our Iceberg table, unless they were intentionally expired as part of the metadata maintenance strategies (more about this in Chapter 4). From the available list of snapshots, the engine will determine the particular snapshot specified in the time-travel query based on either the timestamp value or the snapshot ID.

The engine also learns about the table's schema and the partitioning scheme to use later for file pruning. Finally, it gets the location of the corresponding manifest list path for that particular snapshot:

```
s3://datalake/db1/orders/metadata/
snap-8333017788700497002-1-4010cc03-5585-458c-9fdc-188de318c3e6.avro
```

Get information from the manifest list

Based on the manifest list path, the engine opens and reads the specified *.avro* file containing data about our snapshot. The engine derives a couple of important pieces of information from the manifest list:

- The manifest file path location, which holds references to the actual datafiles: *s3://datalake/db1/orders/metadata/62acb3d7-e992-4cbc-8e41-58809fcacb3e.avro*
- Information such as the number of datafiles added/deleted and statistical information about partitions

Get information from the manifest file

Finally, the engine reads any manifest files that match our query and gets details. The most important information in the manifest file is the *datafile path*, which contains the path to the file with the records for a query. The engine would go through each datafile in the manifest to determine whether it should be read or not. Besides the datafile path location, the engine also gathers statistical information on the columns discussed in the previous sections.

In the end, the engine reads the datafile *0_0_0.parquet*, and the following output is returned to the user:

```
order id  customer_id  order_amount  order_ts
```

| 123 | 456 | 36.17 | 2023-03-07 08:10:23 +00:00 |

This is the record we inserted into the table before running the MERGE INTO query. Figure 3-7 provides a visual summary of the process.

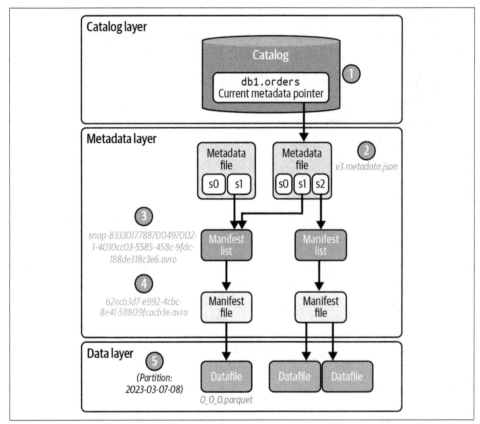

Figure 3-7. How the time-travel query works in Iceberg

Referring to Figure 3-7, note the following:

1. The query engine interacts with the catalog to get the current metadata file (*v3.metadata.json*).

2. It then selects the snapshot (S1 in this case) based on either the timestamp or the version ID supplied in the time-travel query and gets the manifest list location for that snapshot.

3. The manifest file path is then retrieved from the manifest list.

4. The engine determines the datafile path based on the partition filter (2023-03-07-08) from the manifest file.

5. The matching data from the required datafile is then returned to the user.

Conclusion

In this chapter, we discussed the internal workings of various read and write queries, such as creating tables and inserting and updating records, to understand how different architectural components of Apache Iceberg are leveraged by compute engines.

In Chapter 4, we will cover the out-of-the-box optimization techniques available in Apache Iceberg to ensure high performance when reading and writing data to tables.

Optimizing the Performance of Iceberg Tables

As you saw in Chapter 3, Apache Iceberg tables provide a layer of metadata that allows the query engine to create smarter query plans for better performance. However, this metadata is only the beginning of how you can optimize the performance of your data.

You have various optimization levers at your disposal, including reducing the number of datafiles, data sorting, table partitioning, row-level update handling, metrics collection, and external factors. These levers play a vital role in enhancing data performance, and this chapter explores each of them, addressing potential slowdowns and providing acceleration insights. Implementing robust monitoring with preferred tools is crucial for identifying optimization needs, including the use of Apache Iceberg metadata tables, which we will cover in Chapter 10.

Compaction

Every procedure or process comes at a cost in terms of time, meaning longer queries and higher compute costs. Stated differently, the more steps you need to take to do something, the longer it will take for you to do it. When you are querying your Apache Iceberg tables, you need to open and scan each file and then close the file when you're done. The more files you have to scan for a query, the greater the cost these file operations will put on your query. This problem is magnified in the world of streaming or "real-time" data, where data is ingested as it is created, generating lots of files with only a few records in each.

In contrast, batch ingestion, where you may ingest a whole day's worth or a week's worth of records in one job, allows you to more efficiently plan how to write the data as better-organized files. Even with batch ingestion, it is possible to run into the "small files problem," where too many small files have an impact on the speed and performance of your scans because you're doing more file operations, have a lot more metadata to read (there is metadata on each file), and have to delete more files when doing cleanup and maintenance operations. Figure 4-1 depicts both of these scenarios.

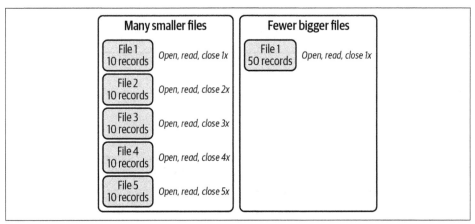

Figure 4-1. Many smaller files are slower to read than the same data in fewer larger files

Essentially, when it comes to reading data, there are fixed costs you can't avoid and variable costs you can avoid using different strategies. Fixed costs include reading the particular data relevant to your query; you can't avoid having to read the data to process it. Although variable costs would include file operations to access the data, using many of the strategies we will discuss throughout this chapter you can reduce those variable costs as much as possible. After using these strategies, you'll be using only the necessary compute to get your job done more cheaply and more quickly (getting the job done more quickly has the benefit of being able to terminate compute clusters earlier, reducing their costs).

The solution to this problem is to periodically take the data in all these small files and rewrite it into fewer larger files (you may also want to rewrite manifests if there are too many manifests relative to the number of datafiles you have). This process is called *compaction*, as you are compacting many files into a few. Compaction is illustrated in Figure 4-2.

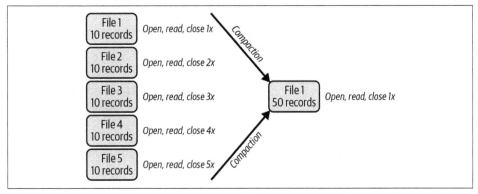

Figure 4-2. Compaction takes many smaller files and processes them into fewer bigger files

Hands-on with Compaction

You may be thinking that while the solution sounds simple, it will involve you having to write some extensive code in Java or Python. Fortunately, Apache Iceberg's Actions package includes several maintenance procedures (the Actions package is specifically for Apache Spark, but other engines can create their own maintenance operation implementation). This package is used from within Spark either by writing SparkSQL as shown through most of this chapter or by writing imperative code such as the following (keep in mind that these actions still maintain the same ACID guarantees as normal Iceberg transactions):

```
Table table = catalog.loadTable("myTable");
SparkActions
    .get()
    .rewriteDataFiles(table)
    .option("rewrite-job-order", "files-desc")
    .execute();
```

In this snippet, we initiated a new instance of our table and then triggered `rewrite DataFiles`, which is the Spark action for compaction. The builder pattern used by `SparkActions` allows us to chain methods together to fine-tune the compaction job to express not only that we want compaction to be done, but also how we want it to be done.

There are several methods you can chain between the call to `rewriteDataFiles` and the `execute` method that begins the job:

binPack
    Sets the compaction strategy to binpack (discussed later), which is the default and doesn't need to be explicitly supplied

Sort

> Changes the compaction strategy to sort the data rewritten by one or more fields in a priority order, further discussed in "Compaction Strategies" on page 74

zOrder

> Changes the compaction strategy to z-order–sort the data based on multiple fields with equal weighting, further discussed in "Sorting" on page 76

filter

> Enables you to pass an expression used to limit which files are rewritten

option

> Changes a single option

options

> Takes a map of several option configurations

There are several possible options you can pass to configure the job; here are a few important ones:

target-file-size-bytes

> This will set the intended size of the output files. By default, this will use the write.target.file-size-bytes property of the table, which defaults to 512 MB.

max-concurrent-file-group-rewrites

> This is the ceiling for the number of file groups to write simultaneously.

max-file-group-size-bytes

> The maximum size of a file group is not one single file. This setting should be used when dealing with partitions larger than the memory available to the worker writing a particular file group so that it can split that partition into multiple file groups to be written concurrently.

partial-progress-enabled

> This allows commits to occur while file groups are compacted. Therefore, for long-running compaction, this can allow concurrent queries to benefit from already compacted files.

partial-progress-max-commits

> If partial progress is enabled, this setting sets the maximum number of commits allowed to complete the job.

rewrite-job-order

> The order to write file groups, which can matter when using partial progress to make sure the higher-priority file groups are committed sooner rather than later, can be based on the groups ordered by byte size or number of files in a group (bytes-asc, bytes-desc, files-asc, files-desc, none).

File Size and Row Group Size

For Apache Parquet files, there is row group size and a file size. The row group size is the size of one group of rows in a Parquet file, and each file can have multiple groups. Therefore, an Iceberg table's default configuration would allow for a 128 MB row group size and a 512 MB file size (four row groups per file). You'll always want to make sure these two settings are aligned (i.e., that the row size is evenly divided by the file size). Fewer row groups results in a smaller file size, as there are fewer groups to have group metadata written for, while more row groups improves predicate pushdown because the row group metadata can have more fine-grained ranges, making it possible for the query engine to eliminate reading more row groups that don't contain data relevant to the current query.

Another example is that you may want to increase the file size to 1 GB per file but keep row groups to 128 MB (eight row groups per file); that way, there are fewer files to open and close. Although the types of queries you're running often require reading most of the data, you'd prefer fewer row groups since predicate pushdown will not speed up the process of getting all the data.

Row group size and file size can both be set as table properties (`write.parquet.row-group-size-bytes` and `write.target-file-size-bytes`, respectively), but the file size can be set for individual compaction jobs using the `options` settings.

As the engine plans the new files to be written in the compaction job, it will begin grouping these files into file groups that will be written in parallel (meaning one file from each group can be written concurrently). In your compaction jobs, you can configure options on how big these file groups can be and how many should be written simultaneously to help prevent memory issues.

Partial Progress

Partial progress allows new snapshots to be created as file groups are completed. This allows queries to benefit from the already compacted files as others are completed. It also helps prevent out-of-memory (OOM) situations for large compaction jobs because progress is saved as it completes the job, and less data needs to be retained in memory.

Keep in mind that more snapshots means more metadata files taking up storage in your table location. But if you want your readers to benefit from a compaction job sooner rather than later, this can be a useful feature. If you want to balance out the cost of additional snapshots with the benefits of partial progress, you can adjust the `max-commits` to limit the number of total commits a single compaction job will make.

The following code snippet uses several of the possible table options in practice:

```
Table table = catalog.loadTable("myTable");
SparkActions
    .get()
    .rewriteDataFiles(table)
    .sort()
    .filter(Expressions.and(
    Expressions.greaterThanOrEqual("date", "2023-01-01"),
    Expressions.lessThanOrEqual("date", "2023-01-31")))
    .option("rewrite-job-order", "files-desc")
    .execute();
```

In the preceding example, we implemented a sort strategy that, by default, adheres to the sort order specified in the table's properties. Additionally, we incorporated a filter to exclusively rewrite data from the month of January. It's important to note that this filter requires creation of an expression using Apache Iceberg's internal expression-building interface. Furthermore, we configured the `rewrite-job-order` to prioritize the rewriting of larger groups of files first. This means a file that is being rewritten from a group of five files will be processed before one that consolidates from just two files.

 The Expressions library is designed to facilitate creating expressions around Apache Iceberg's metadata structures. The library provides APIs to build and manipulate these expressions, which can then be used to filter data in tables and read operations. Iceberg's expressions can also be used in manifest files to summarize the data in each datafile, which allows Iceberg to skip files that do not contain rows that could match a filter. This mechanism is essential for Iceberg's scalable metadata architecture.

While this is all well and good, it can be done more easily using the Spark SQL extensions, which include call procedures that can be called using the following syntax from Spark SQL:

```
-- using positional arguments
CALL catalog.system.procedure(arg1, arg2, arg3)

-- using named arguments
CALL catalog.system.procedure(argkey1 => argval1, argkey2 => argval2)
```

Using the `rewriteDataFiles` procedure in this syntax would look like Example 4-1.

Example 4-1. Using the `rewrite_data_files` procedure to run compaction jobs

```
-- Rewrite Data Files CALL Procedure in SparkSQL
CALL catalog.system.rewrite_data_files(
  table => 'musicians',
```

```
  strategy => 'binpack',
  where => 'genre = "rock"',
  options => map(
    'rewrite-job-order','bytes-asc',
    'target-file-size-bytes','1073741824', -- 1GB
    'max-file-group-size-bytes','10737418240' -- 10GB
  )
)
```

In this scenario, we may have been streaming some data into our musicians table and noticed that a lot of small files were generated for rock bands, so instead of running compaction on the whole table, which can be time-consuming, we targeted just the data that was problematic. We also tell Spark to prioritize file groups that are larger in bytes and to keep files that are around 1 GB each with each file group of around 10 GB. You can see what the result of these settings would be in Figure 4-3.

 Notice in Example 4-1 the use of double quotation marks in our where filter. Because we had to use single quotes around the filter, we use double quotes in the string, even if SQL would normally use single quotes for "rock". The where option is essentially equivalent to the filter method mentioned earlier. Without it, the whole table would possibly be rewritten.

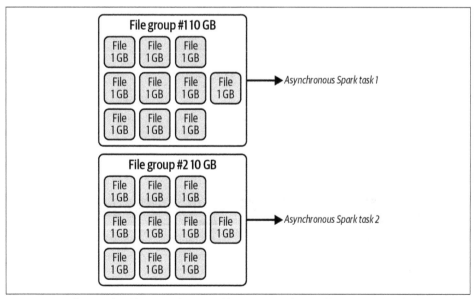

Figure 4-3. The result of having the max file group and max file size set to 10 GB and 1 GB, respectively

Other engines can implement their own custom compaction tools. For example, Dremio has its own Iceberg table management feature via its `OPTIMIZE` command, which is a unique implementation but follows many of the APIs from the `Rewrite DataFiles` action:

```
OPTIMIZE TABLE catalog.MyTable
```

The preceding command would achieve your basic binpack compaction by compacting all the files into fewer, more optimal files. But like the `rewriteDataFiles` procedure in Spark, we can get more granular.

For example, here we are compacting only a particular partition:

```
OPTIMIZE TABLE catalog.MyTable
    FOR PARTITIONS sales_year IN (2022, 2023) AND sales_month IN ('JAN', 'FEB',
'MAR')
```

And here we are compacting with particular file size parameters:

```
OPTIMIZE TABLE catalog.MyTable
    REWRITE DATA (MIN_FILE_SIZE_MB=100, MAX_FILE_SIZE_MB=1000,
TARGET_FILE_SIZE_MB=512)
```

In this code snippet, we are rewriting only the manifests:

```
OPTIMIZE TABLE catalog.MyTable
    REWRITE MANIFESTS
```

As you can see, you can use Spark or Dremio to achieve compaction of your Apache Iceberg tables.

Compaction Strategies

As mentioned earlier, there are several compaction strategies that you can use when using the `rewriteDataFiles` procedure. Table 4-1 summarizes these strategies, including their pros and cons. In this section, we will discuss binpack compaction; standard sorting and z-order sorting will be covered later in the book.

Table 4-1. Pros and cons of compaction strategies

Strategy	What it does	Pros	Cons
Binpack	Combines files only; no global sorting (will do local sorting within tasks)	This offers the fastest compaction jobs.	Data is not clustered.
Sort	Sorts by one or more fields sequentially prior to allocating tasks (e.g., sort by field a, then within that, sort by field b)	Data clustered by often queried fields can lead to much faster read times.	This results in longer compaction jobs compared to binpack.
z-order	Sorts by multiple fields that are equally weighted, prior to allocating tasks (X and Y values in this range are in one grouping; those in another range are in another grouping)	If queries often rely on filters on multiple fields, this can improve read times even further.	This results in longer-running compaction jobs compared to binpack.

The binpack strategy is essentially pure compaction with no other considerations for how the data is organized beyond the size of the files. Of the three strategies, binpack is the fastest as it can just write the contents of the smaller files to a larger file of your target size, whereas sort and z-order must sort the data before they can allocate file groups for writing. This is particularly useful when you have streaming data and need compaction to run at a speed that meets your service level agreements (SLAs).

 If an Apache Iceberg table has a sort order set within its settings, even if you use binpack, this sort order will be used for sorting data within a single task (local sort). Using the sort and z-order strategies will sort the data before the query engine allocates the records into different tasks, optimizing the clustering of data across tasks.

If you were ingesting streaming data, you may need to run a quick compaction on data that is ingested after every hour. You could do something like this:

```
CALL catalog.system.rewrite_data_files(
    table => 'streamingtable',
    strategy => 'binpack',
    where => 'created_at between "2023-01-26 09:00:00" and "2023-01-26 09:59:59" ',
    options => map(
      'rewrite-job-order','bytes-asc',
      'target-file-size-bytes','1073741824',
      'max-file-group-size-bytes','10737418240',
      'partial-progress-enabled', 'true'
    )
)
```

In this compaction job, the binpack strategy is employed for faster alignment with streaming SLA requirements. It specifically targets data ingestion within a one-hour time frame, which can dynamically adjust to the most recent hour. The use of partial progress commits ensures that as file groups are written, they are immediately committed, leading to immediate performance enhancements for readers. Importantly, this compaction process focuses solely on previously written data, isolating it from any concurrent writes coming from streaming operations that would introduce new datafiles.

Using a faster strategy on a limited scope of data can make your compaction jobs much faster. Of course, you could probably compact the data even more if you allowed compaction beyond one hour, but you have to balance out the need to run the compaction job quickly with the need for optimization. You may have an additional compaction job for a day's worth of data overnight and a compaction job for a week's worth of data over the weekend to keep optimizing in continuous intervals while interfering as little as possible with other operations. Keep in mind that compaction always honors the current partition spec, so if data from an old partition spec is rewritten, it will have the new partitioning rules applied.

Automating Compaction

It would be a little tricky to meet all your SLAs if you have to manually run these compaction jobs, so looking into how to automate these processes could be a real benefit. Here are a couple of approaches you can take to automate these jobs:

- You can use an orchestration tool such as Airflow, Dagster, Prefect, Argo, or Luigi to send the proper SQL to an engine such as Spark or Dremio after an ingestion job completes or at a certain time or periodic interval.

- You can use serverless functions to trigger the job after data lands in cloud object storage.

- You can set up cron jobs to run the appropriate jobs at specific times.

These approaches require you to script out and deploy these services manually. However, there is also a class of managed Apache Iceberg catalog services that features automated table maintenance and includes compaction. Examples of these kinds of services include Dremio Arctic and Tabular.

Sorting

Before we get into the details of the sort compaction strategy, let's understand sorting as it relates to optimizing a table.

Sorting or "clustering" your data has a very particular benefit when it comes to your queries: it helps limit the number of files that need to be scanned to get the data needed for a query. Sorting the data allows data with similar values to be concentrated into fewer files, allowing for more efficient query planning.

For example, suppose you have a dataset representing every player on every NFL team across 100 Parquet files that aren't sorted in any particular way. If you did a query just for players on the Detroit Lions, even if a file of 100 records has only one record of a Detroit Lions player, that file must be added to the query plan and be scanned. This means you may need to scan up to 53 files (the maximum number of players that can be on an NFL team). If you sorted the data alphabetically by team name, all the Detroit Lions players should be in about four files (100 files divided by 32 NFL teams equals 3.125), which would probably include a handful of players from the Green Bay Packers and the Denver Broncos. So, by having the data sorted, you've reduced the number of files you have to scan from possibly 53 to 4, which, as we discussed in "Compaction Strategies" on page 74, greatly improves the performance of the query. Figure 4-4 depicts the benefits of scanning sorted datasets.

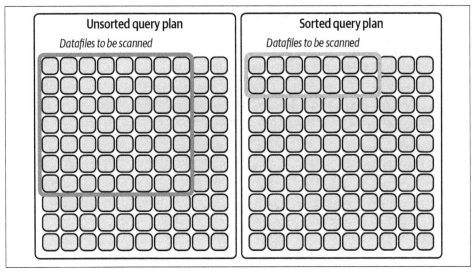

Figure 4-4. Sorted datasets results in scanning fewer datafiles

Sorted data can be quite useful if how the data is sorted leans into typical query patterns such as in this example, where you may regularly query the NFL data based on a particular team. Sorting data in Apache Iceberg can happen at many different points, so you want to make sure you leverage all these points.

There are two main ways to create a table. One way is with a standard CREATE TABLE statement:

```
-- Spark Syntax
CREATE TABLE catalog.nfl_players (
    id bigint ,
    player_name varchar,
    team varchar,
    num_of_touchdowns int,
    num_of_yards int,
      player_position varchar,
      player_number int,
)

-- Dremio Syntax
CREATE TABLE catalog.nfl_players (
    id bigint ,
    player_name varchar,
    team varchar,
    num_of_touchdowns int,
    num_of_yards int,
      player_position varchar,
      player_number int,
)
```

The other way is with a CREATE TABLE...AS SELECT (CTAS) statement:

```
-- Spark SQL & Dremio Syntax
CREATE TABLE catalog.nfl_players
    AS (SELECT * FROM non_iceberg_teams_table);
```

After creating the table, you set the sort order of the table, which any engine that supports the property will use to sort the data before writing and will also be the default sort field when using the sort compaction strategy:

```
ALTER TABLE catalog.nfl_teams WRITE ORDERED BY team;
```

If doing a CTAS, sort the data in your AS query:

```
CREATE TABLE catalog.nfl_teams
    AS (SELECT * FROM non_iceberg_teams_table ORDER BY team);

ALTER TABLE catalog.nfl_teams WRITE ORDERED BY team;
```

The ALTER TABLE statement sets a global sort order that will be used for all future writes by engines that honor the sort order. You could also specify it with INSERT INTO, like so:

```
INSERT INTO catalog.nfl_teams
    SELECT *
        FROM staging_table
        ORDER BY team
```

This will ensure that the data is sorted as you write it, but it isn't perfect. Going back to the previous example, if the NFL dataset was updated each year for changes in the teams' rosters, you may end up having many files splitting Lions and Packers players from multiple writes. This is because you'd now need to write a new file with the new Lions players for the current year. This is where the sort compaction strategy comes into play.

The sort compaction strategy will sort the data across all the files targeted by the job. So, for example, if you wanted to rewrite the entire dataset with all players sorted by team globally, you could run the following statement:

```
CALL catalog.system.rewrite_data_files(
  table => 'nfl_teams',
  strategy => 'sort',
  sort_order => 'team ASC NULLS LAST'
)
```

Here is a breakdown of the string that was passed for the sort order:

team
    Will sort the data by the team field

ASC
    Will sort the data in ascending order (DESC would sort in descending order)

NULLS LAST

Will put all players with a null value at the end of the sort, after the Washington Commanders (NULLS FIRST would put all players before the Arizona Cardinals)

Figure 4-5 shows the result of the sort.

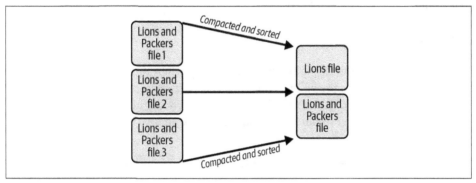

Figure 4-5. Compacting and sorting the data into fewer files

You can sort by additional fields as well. For example, you may want the data sorted by team, but then within each team you may want it sorted alphabetically by name. You can achieve this by running a job with these parameters:

```
CALL catalog.system.rewrite_data_files(
  table => 'nfl_teams',
  strategy => 'sort',
  sort_order => 'team ASC NULLS LAST, name ASC NULLS FIRST'
)
```

Sorting by team will have the highest weight, followed by sorting by name. You'll probably see players in this order in the file where the Lions roster ends and the Packers roster begins, as shown in Figure 4-6.

Figure 4-6. Sorted list of players across files

If end users regularly asked questions such as "Who are all the Lions players whose name starts with A," this dual sort would accelerate the query even further. However, if end users asked "Who are all the NFL players whose name starts with A," this wouldn't be as helpful, as all the "A" players are stretched across more files than if you had just sorted by name alone. This is where z-ordering can be useful.

The bottom line is that to get the best advantage of sorting, you need to understand the types of questions your end users are asking so that you can have the data sorted to lean into their questions effectively.

Z-order

There are times when multiple fields are a priority when querying a table, and this is where a z-order sort may be quite helpful. With a z-order sort you are sorting the data by multiple data points, which allows engines a greater ability to reduce the files scanned in the final query plan. Let's imagine we're trying to locate item Z in a 4 × 4 grid (Figure 4-7).

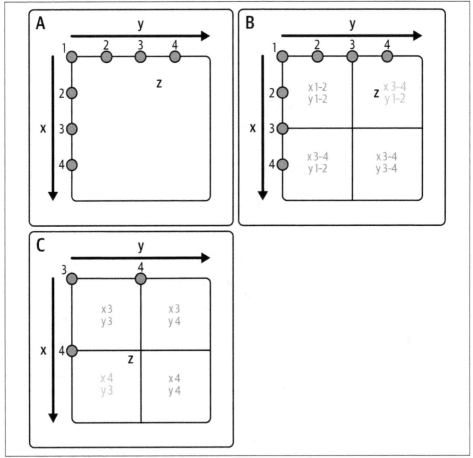

Figure 4-7. Understanding the basics of z-ordering

Referring to "A" in Figure 4-7, we have a value (z), which we can say equals 3.5, and we want to narrow the area we want to search within our data. We can narrow down our search by breaking the field into four quadrants based on ranges of X and Y values, as shown in "B" in the figure.

So if we know what data we are looking for based on fields we z-ordered by, we can possibly avoid searching large portions of the data since it's sorted by both fields. We can then take that quadrant and break it down even further and apply another z-order sort to the data in the quadrant, as shown in "C" in the figure. Since our search is based on multiple factors (X and Y), we could eliminate 75% of the searchable area by taking this approach.

You can sort and cluster your data in the datafiles in a similar way. For example, let's say you have a dataset of all people involved in a medical cohort study, and you are trying to organize outcomes in the cohort by age and height; z-ordering the data may be quite worthwhile. You can see this in action in Figure 4-8.

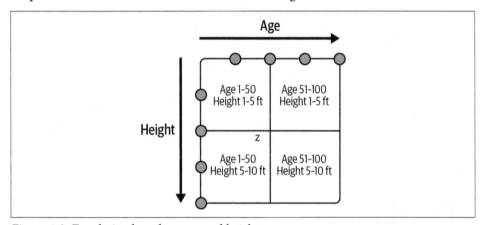

Figure 4-8. Z-ordering based on age and height

Data that falls into a particular quadrant will be in the same datafiles, which can really slim down files to scan as you try to run analytics on different age/height groups. If you are searching for people with a height of 6 feet and an age of 60, you could immediately eliminate the datafiles that have data that belongs in the other three quadrants.

This works because the datafiles will fall into four categories:

- A: File with records containing Age 1–50 and Height 1–5
- B: File with records containing Age 51–100 and Height 1–5
- C: File with records containing Age 1–50 and Height 5–10
- D: File with records containing Age 51–100 and Height 5–10

If the engine knows you are searching for someone who is 60 years of age and is 6 feet tall, as it uses the Apache Iceberg metadata to plan the query, all the datafiles in categories A, B, and C will be eliminated and will never be scanned. Keep in mind that even if you only searched by age, you'd see a benefit from clustering by being able to eliminate at least two of the four quadrants.

Achieving this would involve running a compaction job:

```
CALL catalog.system.rewrite_data_files(
  table => 'people',
  strategy => 'sort',
  sort_order => 'zorder(age,height)'
)
```

Using the sort and z-order compaction strategies not only allows you to reduce the number of files your data exists in, but also makes sure the order of the data in those files enables even more efficient query planning.

While sorting is effective, it comes with some challenges. First, as new data is ingested, it becomes unsorted, and until the next compaction job, the data remains somewhat scattered across multiple files. This occurs because new data is added to a new file and is potentially sorted within that file but not in the context of all previous records. Second, files may still contain data for multiple values of the sorted field, which can be inefficient for queries that only require data with a specific value. For instance, in the earlier example, files contained data for both Lions and Packers players, making it inefficient to scan Packers records when you were only interested in Lions players.

To deal with this, we have partitioning.

Partitioning

If you know a particular field is pivotal to how the data is accessed, you may want to go beyond sorting and into partitioning. When a table is partitioned, instead of just sorting the order based on a field, it will write records with distinct values of the target field into their own datafiles.

For example, in politics, you'll likely often query voter data based on a voter's party affiliation, making this a good partition field. This would mean all voters in the "Blue" party will be listed in distinct files from those in the "Red," "Yellow," and "Green" parties. If you were to query for voters in the "Yellow" party, none of the datafiles you scan would include anyone from any other parties. You can see this illustrated in Figure 4-9.

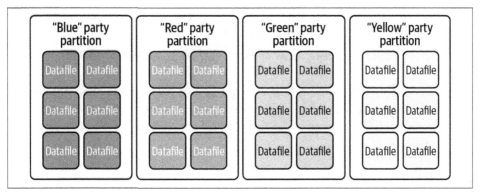

Figure 4-9. Partitioning and grouping data into groups of files

Traditionally, partitioning a table based on derived values of a particular field required creating an additional field that had to be maintained separately and required users to have knowledge of that separate field when querying. For example:

- Partitioning by day, month, or year on a timestamp column required you to create an additional column based on the timestamp expressing the year, month, or day in isolation.
- Partitioning by the first letter of a text value required you to create an additional column that only had that letter.
- Partitioning into buckets (a set number of divisions to evenly distribute records into based on a hash function) required you to create an additional column that stated which bucket the record belonged in.

You'd then set the partitioning at table creation to be based on the derived fields, and the files would be organized into subdirectories based on their partition:

```
--Spark SQL
CREATE TABLE MyHiveTable (...) PARTITIONED BY month;
```

You'd have to manually transform the value every time you inserted records:

```
INSERT INTO MyTable (SELECT MONTH(time) AS month, ... FROM data_source);
```

When querying the table, the engine would have no awareness of the relationship between the original field and the derived field. This would mean that the following query would benefit from partitioning:

```
SELECT * FROM MYTABLE WHERE time BETWEEN '2022-07-01 00:00:00' AND '2022-07-31
00:00:00' AND month = 7;
```

However, users often aren't aware of this workaround column (and they shouldn't have to be). This means that most of the time, users would issue a query similar to the following, which would result in a full table scan, making the query take much longer to complete and consume far more resources:

```
SELECT * FROM MYTABLE WHERE time BETWEEN '2022-07-01 00:00:00' AND '2022-07-31 00:00:00';
```

The preceding query is more intuitive for a business user or data analyst using the data, as they may not be as aware of the internal engineering of the table, resulting in many accidental full table scans. This is where Iceberg's hidden partitioning capability comes in.

Hidden Partitioning

Apache Iceberg handles partitioning quite differently, addressing many of these pain points when optimizing your tables with partitioning. One resulting feature of this approach is called *hidden partitioning*.

It starts with how Apache Iceberg tracks partitioning. Instead of tracking it by relying on how files are physically laid out, Iceberg tracks the range of partition values at the snapshot and manifest levels, allowing for many levels of new flexibility:

- Instead of having to generate additional columns to partition based on transform values, you can use built-in transforms that engines and tools can apply when planning queries from the metadata.
- Since you don't need an additional column when using these transforms, you store less in your datafiles.
- Since the metadata allows the engine to be aware of the transform on the original column, you can filter solely on the original column and get the benefit of partitioning.

That means if you create a table partitioned by month:

```
CREATE TABLE catalog.MyTable (...) PARTITIONED BY months(time) USING iceberg;
```

the following query would benefit from partitioning:

```
SELECT * FROM MYTABLE WHERE time BETWEEN '2022-07-01 00:00:00' AND '2022-07-31 00:00:00';
```

As you may have seen in the prior CREATE TABLE statement, you apply transforms like a function on the target column being transformed. Several transforms are available when planning your partitioning:

- year (just the year)
- month (month and year)
- day (day, month, and year

- hour (hours, day, month, and year)
- truncate
- bucket

The year, month, day, and hour transforms work on a timestamp column. Keep in mind that if you specify month, the partition values as tracked in the metadata will reflect the month and year of the timestamp, and if you use day, they will reflect the year, month, and day of the timestamp, so there is no need to use multiple transforms for more granular partitioning.

The truncate transform partitions the table based on the truncated value of a column. For example, if you wanted to partition a table based on the first letter of a person's name, you could create a table like so:

```
CREATE TABLE catalog.MyTable (...) PARTITIONED BY truncate(name, 1) USING iceberg;
```

The bucket transform is perfect for partitioning based on a field with high cardinality (lots of unique values). The bucket transform will use a hash function to distribute the records across a specified number of buckets. So, for example, maybe you want to partition voter data based on zip codes, but there are so many possible zip codes that you would end up with too many partitions with small datafiles. You could run something like the following:

```
CREATE TABLE catalog.voters (...) PARTITIONED BY bucket(24, zip) USING iceberg;
```

Any bucket will have several zip codes included, but at least if you look for a particular zip code, you are not doing a full table scan, just a scan of the bucket that includes the zip code you're searching for. So, with Apache Iceberg's hidden partitioning, you have a more expressive way to express common partitioning patterns. Taking advantage of them requires no additional thought from the end user than to filter by the fields they'd naturally filter by.

Partition Evolution

Another challenge with traditional partitioning is that since it relied on the physical structure of the files being laid out into subdirectories, changing how the table was partitioned required you to rewrite the entire table. This becomes an inevitable problem as data and query patterns evolve, necessitating that we rethink how we partition and sort the data.

Apache Iceberg solves this problem with its metadata-tracked partitioning as well, because the metadata tracks not only partition values but also historical partition schemes, allowing the partition schemes to evolve. So, if the data in two different files were written based on two different partition schemes, the Iceberg metadata would make the engine aware so that it could create a plan with partition scheme A separately from partition scheme B, creating an overall scan plan at the end.

For example, let's say you have a table of membership records partitioned by the year in which members registered:

```
CREATE TABLE catalog.members (...) PARTITIONED BY years(registration_ts) USING
iceberg;
```

Then, several years later, the pace of membership growth made it worthwhile to start breaking the records down by month. You could alter the table to adjust the partitioning like so:

```
ALTER TABLE catalog.members ADD PARTITION FIELD months(registration_ts)
```

The neat thing about Apache Iceberg's date-related partition transforms is that if you evolve to something granular, there is no need to remove the less granular partitioning rule. However, if you are using bucket or truncate and you decide you no longer want to partition the table by a particular field, you can update your partition scheme like so:

```
ALTER TABLE catalog.members DROP PARTITION FIELD bucket(24, id);
```

When a partitioning scheme is updated, it applies only to new data written to the table going forward, so there is no need to rewrite the existing data. Also, keep in mind that any data rewritten by the rewriteDataFiles procedure will be rewritten using the new partitioning scheme, so if you want to keep older data in the old scheme, make sure to use the proper filters in your compaction jobs to not rewrite it.

Other Partitioning Considerations

Say you migrate a Hive table using the migrate procedure (discussed in Chapter 13). It may currently be partitioned on a derived column (e.g., a month column based on a timestamp column in the same table), but you want to express to Apache Iceberg that it should use an Iceberg transform instead. There is a REPLACE PARTITION command for just this purpose:

```
ALTER TABLE catalog.members REPLACE PARTITION FIELD registration_day WITH
days(registration_ts) AS day_of_registration;
```

This will not alter any datafiles, but it will allow the metadata to track the partition values using Iceberg transforms.

You can optimize tables in many ways. For example, using partitioning to write data with unique values to unique files, sorting the data in those files, and then making sure to compact those files into fewer larger files will keep your table performance nice and crisp. Although it's not always about general use optimization, there are particular use cases, such as row-level updates and deletes, that you can optimize for as well using copy-on-write and merge-on-read.

Copy-on-Write Versus Merge-on-Read

Another consideration when it comes to the speed of your workloads is how you handle row-level updates. When you are adding new data, it just gets added to a new datafile, but when you want to update preexisting rows to either update or delete them, there are some considerations you need to be aware of:

- In data lakes, and therefore in Apache Iceberg, datafiles are immutable, meaning they can't be changed. This provides lots of benefits, such as the ability to achieve snapshot isolation (since files that old snapshots refer to will have consistent data).

- If you're updating 10 rows, there is no guarantee they are in the same file, so you may have to rewrite 10 files and every row of data in them to update 10 rows for the new snapshot.

There are three approaches to dealing with row-level updates, covered in detail throughout this section and summarized in Table 4-2.

Table 4-2. Row-level update modes in Apache Iceberg

Update style	Read speed	Write speed	Best practice
Copy-on-write	Fastest reads	Slowest updates/deletes	
Merge-on-read (position deletes)	Fast reads	Fast updates/deletes	Use regular compaction to minimize read costs.
Merge-on-read (equality deletes)	Slow reads	Fastest updates/deletes	Use more frequent compaction to minimize read costs.

Copy-on-Write

The default approach is referred to as copy-on-write (COW). In this approach, if even a single row in a datafile is updated or deleted, that datafile is rewritten, and the new file takes its place in the new snapshot. You can see this exemplified in Figure 4-10.

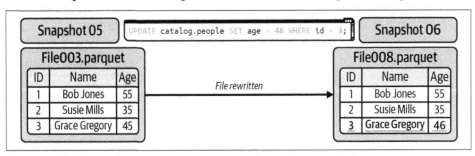

Figure 4-10. The results of using copy-on-write for updating a single row

This is ideal if you're optimizing for reads because read queries can just read the data without having to reconcile any deleted or updated files. However, if your workloads consist of very regular row-level updates, rewriting entire datafiles for those updates may slow down your updates beyond what your SLAs allow. The pros of this approach include faster reads, while the cons involve slower row-level updates and deletes.

Merge-on-Read

The alternative to copy-on-write is merge-on-read (MOR), where instead of rewriting an entire datafile, you capture in a delete file the records to be updated in the existing file, with the delete file tracking which records should be ignored.

If you are deleting a record:

- The record is listed in a delete file.
- When a reader reads the table, it will reconcile the datafile with the delete file.

If you are updating a record:

- The record to be updated is tracked in a delete file.
- A new datafile is created with only the updated record.
- When a reader reads the table, it will ignore the old version of the record because of the delete file and use the new version in the new datafile.

This is depicted in Figure 4-11.

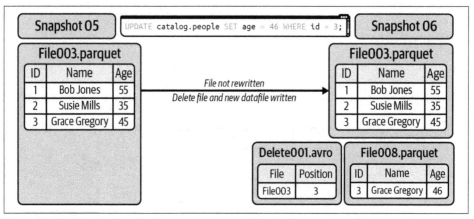

Figure 4-11. The results of using merge-on-read for updating a single row

This avoids the need to rewrite unchanged records to new files just because they exist in a datafile with a record to be updated, speeding up the write transaction. But it comes at the cost of slower reads, as queries will have to scan the delete files to know which records to ignore in the proper datafiles.

To minimize the cost of reads, you'll want to run regular compaction jobs, and to keep those compaction jobs running efficiently, you'll want to take advantage of some of the properties you learned before:

- Use a `filter/where` clause to only run compaction on the files ingested in the last time frame (hour, day).
- Use partial progress mode to make commits as file groups are rewritten so that readers can start seeing marginal improvements sooner rather than later.

Using these techniques, you can speed up the write side of heavy update workloads while minimizing the costs to read performance. The advantage of this approach includes faster row-level updates, but this comes with the drawback of slower reads due to the need to reconcile delete files.

When doing MOR writes, delete files enable you to track which records need to be ignored in existing datafiles for future reads. We'll use an analogy to help you understand the high-level concept between the different types of delete files. (Keep in mind which types of delete files are written, as this is usually decided by the engine for particular use cases, not typically by table settings.)

When you have a ton of data and you want to kick out a specific row, you have a couple of options:

- You can look for the row data based on where it's sitting in the dataset, kind of like finding your friend in a movie theater by their seat number.
- You can look for the row data based on what it's made of, like picking out your friend in a crowd because they're wearing a bright red hat.

If you use the first option, you'll use what are called *positional delete files*. But if you use the second option, you'll need equality delete files. Each method has its own strengths and weaknesses. This means that depending on the situation, you might want to pick one over the other. It's all about what works best for you!

Let's explore these two types of delete files. Position deletes track which rows in which files should be ignored. The following table is an example of how this data is laid out in a position delete file:

Row to delete (position deletes)	
Filepath	Position
001.parquet	0
001.parquet	5
006.parquet	5

When reading the specified files, the position delete file will skip the row at the specified position. This requires a much smaller cost at read time since it has a pretty specific point at which it must skip a row. However, this has write time costs, since the writer of the delete file will need to know the position of the deleted record, which requires it to read the file with the deleted records to identify those positions.

Equality deletes instead specify values that, if a record matches, should be ignored. The following table shows how the data in an equality delete file may be laid out:

Rows to delete (equality deletes)	
Team	State
Yellow	NY
Green	MA

This requires no write time costs since you don't need to open and read files to track the targeted values, but it has much greater read time costs. The read time costs exist because there is no information where records with matching values exist, so when reading the data, there has to be a comparison with every record that could possibly contain a matching record. Equality deletes are great if you need the highest write speed possible, but aggressive compaction should be planned to reconcile those equality deletes to reduce the impact on your reads.

Configuring COW and MOR

Whether a table is configured to handle row-level updates via COW or MOR depends on the following:

- The table properties
- Whether the engine you use to write to Apache Iceberg supports MOR writes

The following table properties determine whether a particular transaction is handled via COW or MOR:

`write.delete.mode`
    Approach to use for delete transactions

`write.update.mode`
    Approach to use for update transactions

`write.merge.mode`
    Approach to use for merge transactions

Keep in mind that for this and all Apache Iceberg table properties, while many are part of the specification, it is still on the specific compute engine to honor the specification. You may run into different behavior, so read up on which table properties are honored by engines you use for particular jobs that use those properties. Query engine developers will have every intention of honoring all Apache Iceberg table properties, but this does require implementations for the specific engine's architecture. Over time, engines should have all these properties honored so that you get the same behavior across all engines.

Since Apache Spark support for Apache Iceberg is handled from within the Apache Iceberg project, all these properties are honored from within Spark, and they can be set at the creation of a table in Spark like so:

```
CREATE TABLE catalog.people (
    id int,
    first_name string,
    last_name string
) TBLPROPERTIES (
    'write.delete.mode'='copy-on-write',
    'write.update.mode'='merge-on-read',
    'write.merge.mode'='merge-on-read'
) USING iceberg;
```

This property can also be set after the table is created using an ALTER TABLE statement:

```
ALTER TABLE catalog.people SET TBLPROPERTIES (
    'write.delete.mode'='merge-on-read',
    'write.update.mode'='copy-on-write',
    'write.merge.mode'='copy-on-write'
);
```

It's as simple as that. But remember the following when working with non–Apache Spark engines:

- Table properties may or may not be honored. It's up to the engine to implement support.
- When using MOR, make sure the engines you use to query your data can read delete files.

Other Considerations

Beyond your datafiles and how they are organized, there are many levers for improving performance. We will discuss many of them in the following sections.

Metrics Collection

As discussed in Chapter 2, the manifest for each group of datafiles is tracking metrics for each field in the table to help with min/max filtering and other optimizations. The types of column-level metrics that are tracked include:

- Counts of values, null values, and distinct values
- Upper and lower bound values

If you have very wide tables (i.e., tables with lots of fields; e.g., 100+), the number of metrics being tracked can start to become a burden on reading your metadata. Fortunately, using Apache Iceberg's table properties, you can fine-tune which columns have their metrics tracked and which columns don't. This way, you can track metrics on columns that are often used in query filters and not capture metrics on ones that aren't, so their metrics data doesn't bloat your metadata.

You can tailor the level of metrics collection for the columns you want (you don't need to specify all of them) using table properties, like so:

```
ALTER TABLE catalog.db.students SET TBLPROPERTIES (
    'write.metadata.metrics.column.col1'='none',
    'write.metadata.metrics.column.col2'='full',
    'write.metadata.metrics.column.col3'='counts',
    'write.metadata.metrics.column.col4'='truncate(16)',
);
```

As you can see, you can set how the metrics are collected for each individual column to several potential values:

none
: Don't collect any metrics.

counts
: Only collect counts (values, distinct values, null values).

truncate(XX)
: Count and truncate the value to a certain number of characters, and base the upper/lower bounds on that. So, for example, a string column may be truncated to 16 characters and have its metadata value ranges be based on the abbreviated string values.

full
: Base the counts and upper/lower bounds on the full value.

You don't need to set this explicitly for every column as, by default, Iceberg sets this to truncate(16).

Rewriting Manifests

Sometimes the issue isn't your datafiles, as they are well sized with well-sorted data. It's that they've been written across several snapshots, so an individual manifest could be listing more datafiles. While manifests are more lightweight, more manifests still means more file operations. There is a separate rewriteManifests procedure to rewrite only the manifest files so that you have a smaller total number of manifest files, and those manifest files list a large number of datafiles:

```
CALL catalog.system.rewrite_manifests('MyTable')
```

If you run into any memory issues while running this operation, you can turn off Spark caching by passing a second argument: `false`. If you are rewriting lots of manifests and they are being cached by Spark, it could result in issues with individual executor nodes:

```
CALL catalog.system.rewrite_manifests('MyTable', false)
```

When it would be good to run this operation is a matter of when your datafile sizes are optimal but the number of manifest files isn't. For example, if you have 5 GB of data in one partition split among 10 datafiles but these files are listed within five manifest files, you don't need to rewrite the datafiles, but you can probably consolidate listing the 10 files into one manifest.

Optimizing Storage

As you make updates to the table or run compaction jobs, new files are created, but old files aren't being deleted since those files are associated with historical snapshots of the table. To prevent storing a bunch of unneeded data, you should periodically expire snapshots. Keep in mind that you cannot time-travel to an expired snapshot. During expiration, any datafiles not associated with still-valid snapshots will get deleted.

You can expire snapshots that were created on or before a particular timestamp:

```
CALL catalog.system.expire_snapshots('MyTable', TIMESTAMP '2023-02-01
00:00:00.000', 100)
```

The second argument is a minimum number of snapshots to retain (by default, it will retain the last five days of snapshots), so it will only expire snapshots that are on or before the timestamp. But if the snapshot falls within the 100 most recent snapshots, it will not expire.

You can also expire particular snapshot IDs:

```
CALL catalog.system.expire_snapshots(table => 'MyTable', snapshot_ids =>
ARRAY(53))
```

In this example, a snapshot with the ID of 53 is expired. We can look up the snapshot ID by opening the *metadata.json* file and examining its contents or by using the metadata tables detailed in Chapter 10. You may have a snapshot where you expose sensitive data by accident and want to expire that single snapshot to clean up the datafiles created in that transaction. This would give you that flexibility. Expirations are a transaction, so a new *metadata.json* file is created with an updated list of valid snapshots.

There are six arguments that can be passed to the `expire_snapshots` procedure:

`table`
> Table to run the operation on

`older_than`
> Expires all snapshots on or before this timestamp

`retain_last`
> Minimum number of snapshots to retain

`snapshot_ids`
> Specific snapshot IDs to expire

`max_concurrent _deletes`
> Number of threads to use for deleting files

`stream_results`
> When true, sends deleted files to the Spark driver by Resilient Distributed Dataset (RDD) partition, which is useful for avoiding OOM issues when deleting large files

Another consideration when optimizing storage is orphan files. These are files and artifacts that accumulate in the table's data directory but are not tracked in the metadata tree because they were written by failed jobs. These files will not be cleaned up by expiring snapshots, so a special procedure should sporadically be run to deal with this. This procedure will look at every file in your table's default location and assess whether it relates to active snapshots. This can be an intensive process (which is why you should only do it sporadically). To delete orphan files, run a command such as the following:

```
CALL catalog.system.remove_orphan_files(table => 'MyTable')
```

You can pass the following arguments to the `removeOrphanFiles` procedure:

`table`
> Table to operate on

`older_than`
> Only deletes files created on or before this timestamp

`location`
> Where to look for orphan files; defaults to the table's default location

`dry_run`
> Boolean if true; won't delete files, but will return a list of what would be deleted

`max_concurrent_deletes`
> Lists the max number of threads for deleting files

While for most tables the data will be located in its default location, there are times you may add external files via the addFiles procedure (covered in Chapter 13) and later may want to clean artifacts in these directories. This is where the location argument comes in.

Write Distribution Mode

Write distribution mode requires an understanding of how massively parallel processing (MPP) systems handle writing files. These systems distribute the work across several nodes, each doing a job or task. The write distribution is how the records to be written are distributed across these tasks. If no specific write distribution mode is set, data will be distributed arbitrarily. The first X number of records will go to the first task, the next X number to the next task, and so on.

Each task is processed separately, so that task will create at least one file for each partition it has at least one record for. Therefore, if you have 10 records that belong in partition A distributed across 10 tasks, you will end up with 10 files in that partition with one record each, which isn't ideal.

It would be better if all the records for that partition were allocated to the same tasks so that they can be written to the same file. This is where the write distribution comes in, that is, how the data is distributed among tasks. There are three options:

none
> There is no special distribution. This is the fastest during write time and is ideal for presorted data.

hash
> The data is hash-distributed by partition key.

range
> The data is range-distributed by partition key or sort order.

In a hash distribution, the value of each record is put through a hash function and grouped together based on the result. Multiple values may end up in the same grouping based on the hash function. For example, if you have the values 1, 2, 3, 4, 5, and 6 in your data, you may get a hash distribution of data with 1 and 4 in task A, 2 and 5 in task B, and 3 and 6 in task C. You'll still write the smallest number of files needed for all your partitions, but less sequential writing will be involved.

In a range distribution, the data is sorted and distributed, so you'd likely have values 1 and 2 in task A, 3 and 4 in task B, and 5 and 6 in task C. This sorting will be done by the partition value or by the SortOrder if the table has one. In other words, if a SortOrder is specified, data will be grouped into tasks not just by partition value but also by the value of the SortOrder field. This is ideal for data that can benefit from clustering on certain fields. However, sorting the data for distribution sequentially has more overhead than throwing the data in a hash function and distributing it based on the output.

There is also a write distribution property to specify the behavior for deletes, updates, and merges:

```
ALTER TABLE catalog.MyTable SET TBLPROPERTIES (
    'write.distribution-mode'='hash',
    'write.delete.distribution-mode'='none',
    'write.update.distribution-mode'='range',
    'write.merge.distribution-mode'='hash',
);
```

In a situation where you are regularly updating many rows but rarely deleting rows, you may want to have different distribution modes, as a different distribution mode may be more advantageous depending on your query patterns.

Object Storage Considerations

Object storage is a unique take on storing data. Instead of keeping files in a neat folder structure such as a traditional filesystem, object storage tosses everything into what are called *buckets*. Each file becomes an object and gets a bunch of metadata tagged along with it. This metadata tells us all sorts of things about the file; enabling improved concurrency and resiliency when using object storage as the underlying files can be replicated for regional access or concurrency while all users just interact with it as a simple "object."

When you want to grab a file from object storage, you're not clicking through folders. Instead, you're using APIs. Just like you'd use a GET or PUT request to interact with a website, you're doing the same here to access your data. For example, you'd use a GET request to ask for a file, the system checks the metadata to find the file, and *voilà*, you've got your data.

This API-first approach helps the system juggle your data, like making copies in different places or dealing with loads of requests at the same time. Object storage, which most cloud vendors provide, is ideal for data lakes and data lakehouses, but it has one potential bottleneck.

Because of the architecture and how object stores handle parallelism (*https://oreil.ly/ jBLXG*), there are often limits on how many requests can go to files under the same "prefix." Therefore, if you wanted to access */prefix1/fileA.txt* and */prefix1/fileB.txt*, even though they are different files, accessing both counts toward the limit on *prefix1*. This becomes a problem in partitions with lots of files, as queries can result in many requests to these partitions and can then run into throttling, which slows down the query.

Running compaction to limit the number of files in a partition can help, but Apache Iceberg is uniquely suited for this scenario since it doesn't rely on how its files are physically laid out, meaning it can write files in the same partition across many prefixes.

You can enable this in your table properties like so:

```
ALTER TABLE catalog.MyTable SET TBLPROPERTIES (
    'write.object-storage.enabled'= true
);
```

This will distribute files in the same partition across many prefixes, including a hash to avoid potential throttling.

So, instead of this:

```
s3://bucket/database/table/field=value1/datafile1.parquet
s3://bucket/database/table/field=value1/datafile2.parquet
s3://bucket/database/table/field=value1/datafile3.parquet
```

you'll get this:

```
s3://bucket/4809098/database/table/field=value1/datafile1.parquet
s3://bucket/5840329/database/table/field=value1/datafile2.parquet
s3://bucket/2342344/database/table/field=value1/datafile3.parquet
```

With the hash in the filepath, each file in the same partition is now treated as if it were under a different prefix, thereby avoiding throttling.

Datafile Bloom Filters

A bloom filter is a way of knowing whether a value possibly exists in a dataset. Imagine a lineup of bits (those 0s and 1s in binary code), all set to a length you decide. Now, when you add data to your dataset, you run each value through a process called a *hash function*. This function spits out a spot on your bit lineup, and you flip that bit from a 0 to a 1. This flipped bit is like a flag that says, "Hey, a value that hashes to this spot might be in the dataset."

For example, let's say we feed 1,000 records through a bloom filter that has 10 bits. When it's done, our bloom filter might look like this:

```
[0,1,1,0,0,1,1,1,1,0]
```

Now let's say we want to find a certain value; we'll call it X. We put X through the same hash function, and it points us to spot number 3 on our bit lineup. According to our bloom filter, there's a 1 in that third spot. This means there's a chance our value X could be in the dataset because a value hashed to this spot before. So we go ahead and check the dataset to see if X is really there.

Now let's look for a different value; we'll call it Y. When we run Y through our hash function, it points us to the fourth spot on our bit lineup. But our bloom filter has a 0 there, which means no value hashed to this spot. So we can confidently say that Y is definitely not in our dataset, and we can save time by not digging through the data.

Bloom filters are handy because they can help us avoid unnecessary data scans. If we want to make them more precise, we can add more hash functions and bits. But remember, the more we add, the bigger our bloom filter gets, and the more space it will need. As with most things in life, it's a balancing act. Everything is a trade-off.

You can enable the writing of bloom filters for a particular column in your Parquet files (this can also be done for ORC files) via your table properties:

```
ALTER TABLE catalog.MyTable SET TBLPROPERTIES (
    'write.parquet.bloom-filter-enabled.column.col1'= true,
    'write.parquet.bloom-filter-max-bytes'= 1048576
);
```

Then engines querying your data may take advantage of these bloom filters to help make reading the datafiles even faster by skipping datafiles where bloom filters clearly indicate that the data you need doesn't exist.

Conclusion

This chapter explored various strategies for optimizing the performance of Iceberg tables. We looked at critical table performance optimization methods such as compaction, sorting, z-ordering, copy-on-write versus merge-on-read mechanisms, and hidden partitioning. Each of these components plays a pivotal role in enhancing query efficiency, reducing read and write times, and ensuring optimal utilization of resources. Understanding and implementing these strategies effectively can lead to significant improvements in the management and operation of Apache Iceberg tables.

In Chapter 5, we'll explore the concept of an Iceberg catalog, helping us make sure our Iceberg tables are portable and discoverable between our tools.

Iceberg Catalogs

In this chapter, we'll dive into Iceberg catalogs. You've seen how a catalog is a critical component of Iceberg that allows it to ensure consistency with multiple readers and writers and to discover what tables are available in the environment. In this chapter, we'll cover:

- The requirements of a catalog in general, and additional requirements recommended for the use of a catalog in production
- The different catalog implementations, including pros, cons, and how to configure Spark to use the catalog
- In what situations you may want to consider migrating catalogs
- How to migrate from one catalog to another

Requirements of an Iceberg Catalog

Iceberg provides a catalog interface (*https://oreil.ly/flAG3*) that requires the implementation of a set of functions, primarily ones to list existing tables, create tables, drop tables, check whether a table exists, and rename tables.

As it is an interface, it has multiple implementations, including Hive Metastore, AWS Glue, and a filesystem catalog (Hadoop). In addition to the requirement of implementing the functions defined in the interface, the primary high-level requirement for a catalog implementation to work as an Iceberg catalog is to map a table path (e.g., db1.table1) to the filepath of the metadata file that has the table's current state.

Since this is a generic requirement and there are a variety of catalog implementations with each system having inherent differences as to how they store data, different catalogs do this mapping differently. For example, with a filesystem as the catalog, there's a file called *version-hint.text* in the table's metadata folder that contains the version number of the current metadata file. With the Hive Metastore as the catalog, the table entry in the Hive Metastore has a table property called `location` that stores the location of the current metadata file.

While these are the bare minimum requirements to use a catalog implementation as an Iceberg catalog, there's a distinction between being able to functionally use a catalog and a catalog being recommended for production usage. That distinction is making sure there is no data loss when there are multiple concurrent jobs writing to the same table. For development and experimentation purposes, this requirement isn't necessary. However, in production, data loss can obviously have huge impacts on the business.

The primary requirement for an Iceberg catalog to be used in production is that it must support atomic operations for updating the current metadata pointer. This is required so that all readers and writers see the same state of the table at a given point in time and that when there are two concurrent writers, the second writer to commit doesn't overwrite the changes made by the first writer, resulting in data loss.

Catalog Comparison

In this section, we'll walk through the more popular Iceberg catalogs. For each catalog, we'll cover how the catalog maps a table path to the location of that table's current metadata file, pros and cons of the catalog, situations where you should consider using the catalog, and how to configure Apache Spark to use the catalog.

The main dimensions by which to compare and contrast the different catalogs are:

- Whether it's recommended for production
- Whether it requires an external system, and whether that external system is self-hosted or is a managed service (or can be)
- Whether it has wide engine and tool compatibility
- Whether it supports multitable and multistatement transactions
- Whether it is cloud agnostic

The Hadoop Catalog

The catalog that is the easiest to get started with Iceberg is the Hadoop catalog. This is because it doesn't require any external systems or processes. Despite its name, the Hadoop catalog works on any filesystem (or things that look like filesystems, such as cloud object stores), including the Hadoop Distributed File System (HDFS), Amazon Simple Storage Service (Amazon S3), Azure Data Lake Storage (ADLS), and Google Cloud Storage (GCS).

At its core, the Hadoop catalog maps the table path to its current metadata file by listing the contents of the table's metadata directory and choosing the most recently written metadata file based on the timestamp listed for each file in the filesystem. Generally, however, engines will write a file called *version-hint.txt* in the table's metadata folder containing a single number that the engine/tool then uses to retrieve the indicated metadata file by name—for example, v{n}.metadata.json.

Pros and cons of the Hadoop catalog

The main pro of the Hadoop catalog is that it doesn't require any external systems to run. All it requires is a filesystem, thereby lowering the barrier to getting started with Iceberg.

However, there is a big downside to the Hadoop catalog: it is not recommended for production usage. There are a few reasons for this.

One reason is that it requires the filesystem to provide a file/object rename operation that is atomic to prevent data loss when concurrent writes occur. Some filesystems and object stores support this, but not all. For example, ADLS and HDFS provide an atomic rename operation so that you won't have data loss if concurrent writes are made to the same table, but S3 does not. For S3, you can leverage a DynamoDB table to achieve the atomicity needed to prevent data loss during concurrent writes. However, at that point, you're using an external system anyway (and DynamoDB is supported as an Iceberg catalog on its own), so you might as well not use the Hadoop catalog.

A second reason is that when a system is configured to use the Hadoop catalog for a source, it can use only one warehouse directory, as it depends on the warehouse location for listing tables. For example, you can use a single bucket only if you're using cloud object storage such as S3 or ADLS. If you wanted to use more than one bucket for your set of tables in your environment, you would have to configure a separate source for each bucket.

A third reason is that when you're doing things that require listing the namespaces (aka databases) and/or tables, you may hit performance issues, especially when you have a large number of namespaces and tables. This is because the listing of namespaces and tables is performed by doing a list operation on the filesystem. For situations such as when you're running on S3 and you have a lot of namespaces and/or tables, this can take a while.

A final reason is that there is no ability to drop the table from the catalog or remove the reference to it in the catalog and keep the data. Dropping the table without removing the data allows you to undo the operation if needed (similar to time travel). For example, in Spark SQL, when you're using a catalog other than the Hadoop catalog, if you run DROP TABLE <tablename>, it only removes the reference from the catalog but doesn't delete the data. DROP TABLE <tablename> PURGE is how you can drop the table and delete the data if you are positive it wouldn't need to be undone at some point. This isn't possible if you use the Hadoop catalog, because even if the *version-hint.txt* file is deleted, the table still exists in the catalog definition since there are files in *warehouse_dir/namespace1/table1/metadata*. The current metadata file is still retrievable by doing a listing of the *metadata* directory and choosing the most recently created metadata file (going off the timestamp listed for the file in the filesystem).

Hadoop catalog use cases

Given these pros and cons, there are a couple of situations where you should consider using the Hadoop catalog. One very common situation is when you're new to Iceberg and want to get started quickly. Since you already have a distributed filesystem, you have all you need to use Iceberg with the Hadoop catalog; no other system or infrastructure is required. Plus, as we'll discuss later in this chapter, migrating catalogs is quick and easy, so you can get started with the Hadoop catalog and migrate to a production-ready catalog when you're ready to move into production. The other situation where you should consider using the Hadoop catalog is if you're experimenting or in a testing or development environment where either there won't be concurrent writers to the same table or, if there are, data loss won't be an issue.

Configuring Spark to use the Hadoop catalog

The following code snippet shows how to launch a Spark SQL shell where you can use my_catalog1 to write and read Iceberg tables using the Hadoop catalog:

```
spark-sql --packages
org.apache.iceberg:iceberg-spark-runtime-3.3_2.12:0.14.0\
    --conf
spark.sql.extensions=org.apache.iceberg.spark.extensions.Iceberg
SparkSessionExtensions \
    --conf
spark.sql.catalog.my_catalog1=org.apache.iceberg.spark.SparkCatalog \
    --conf spark.sql.catalog.my_catalog1.type=hadoop \
    --conf
spark.sql.catalog.my_catalog1.warehouse=<protocol>://<path>
```

The Hive Catalog

The Hive catalog is a popular implementation used for an Iceberg catalog. It maps a table's path to its current metadata file by using the location table property in the table's entry in the Hive Metastore. The value of this property is the absolute path in the filesystem where the table's current metadata file can be located.

Pros and cons of the Hive catalog

The primary pro of the Hive catalog is that it is compatible with a wide variety of engines and tools, since so many already support connecting to the Hive Metastore, albeit originally for tables arranged in the Hive table format. An additional advantage is that it is cloud agnostic.

There are two cons to the Hive catalog. The first is that it requires running an additional service yourself. Unlike some other catalogs, the Hive Metastore used for the Hive catalog needs to be set up and managed by the user. However, there are managed options available, such as Amazon EMR. The second con is that it doesn't provide support for multitable transactions. Multitable transactions are a key capability in databases, providing support for consistency and atomicity for one or more operations that involve more than one table. Their primary significance is their ability to maintain data consistency in an environment, which is key for maintaining data quality and trust in the data. Multitable transactions are discussed in more depth in Chapter 10.

Hive catalog use cases

The primary situation in which you might want to choose this catalog is if you already have a Hive Metastore running in your environment and plan to keep the instance around for a while. Keep in mind, though, that if you need multitable transactions, the Hive catalog doesn't support that.

Configuring Spark to use the Hive catalog

The following code snippet shows how to launch a Spark SQL shell where you can use my_catalog1 to write and read Iceberg tables using the Hive catalog:

```
spark-sql --packages
org.apache.iceberg:iceberg-spark-runtime-3.3_2.12:0.14.0\
    --conf
spark.sql.extensions=org.apache.iceberg.spark.extensions.Iceberg
SparkSessionExtensions \
    --conf
spark.sql.catalog.my_catalog1=org.apache.iceberg.spark.SparkCatalog \
    --conf spark.sql.catalog.my_catalog1.type=hive \
    --conf
spark.sql.catalog.my_catalog1.uri=thrift://<metastore-host>:<port>
```

The AWS Glue Catalog

The AWS Glue catalog is another implementation for Iceberg catalogs. It utilizes the AWS Glue Data catalog as a centralized metadata repository to track Iceberg table metadata. It maps a table's path to its current metadata file as a table property called metadata_location in the table's entry in Glue. The value for this property is the absolute path to the metadata file in the filesystem.

Pros and cons of the AWS Glue catalog

There are multiple advantages to using AWS Glue as your Iceberg catalog. One big one is that AWS Glue is a managed service, so it reduces operational overhead compared to managing your own metastore, as you would in Hive. Another advantage is that because it's a native AWS service, it has tight integration with other AWS services.

However, the AWS Glue catalog also has its downsides. Like the Hive catalog, it does not support multitable transactions. Furthermore, it's specific to the AWS ecosystem, meaning that operating in a multicloud environment and using AWS Glue as your Iceberg catalog can complicate your deployment.

AWS Glue catalog use cases

The AWS Glue catalog is a good choice if you're heavily invested in AWS services, don't need a multicloud solution, and/or need a managed solution for a catalog. It can also be useful for getting started with Iceberg quickly since you don't need to provision anything. But remember, if your data processing scenarios require multitable transactions, this catalog might not be suitable.

Configuring Spark to use the AWS Glue catalog

The following code snippet shows how you can launch a Spark SQL shell where you can use my_catalog1 to write and read Iceberg tables using the AWS Glue catalog:

```
spark-sql --packages "org.apache.iceberg:iceberg-spark-
runtime-x.x_x.xx:x.x.x,software.amazon.awssdk:bundle:x.xx.xxx,software.ama-
zon.awssdk:url-connection-client:x.xx.xxx" \
--conf spark.sql.catalog.my_catalog1=org.apache.iceberg.spark.SparkCatalog \
--conf spark.sql.catalog.my_catalog1.warehouse=s3://<path> \
--conf spark.sql.catalog.my_catalog1.catalog-impl=org.apache.ice-
berg.aws.glue.GlueCatalog \
--conf spark.sql.catalog.my_catalog1.io-impl=org.apache.iceberg.aws.s3.S3FileIO \
--conf spark.hadoop.fs.s3a.access.key=$AWS_ACCESS_KEY \
--conf spark.hadoop.fs.s3a.secret.key=$AWS_SECRET_ACCESS_KEY
```

The Nessie Catalog

Project Nessie is another option for an Iceberg catalog. With Nessie, a table's path is mapped to its current metadata file using a table property called metadataLocation stored within the table's entry in Nessie. This property's value is the absolute path of the current metadata file for the table.

Pros and cons of the Nessie catalog

One advantage of Project Nessie is that it introduces a Git-like experience to data lakes and enables the concept of "data as code," meaning data and its related metadata can be versioned and managed like source code. This is particularly valuable for data engineering and data science workflows where safe changes, reproducibility, and traceability are crucial. Another advantage of using Project Nessie as your Iceberg catalog is that it enables multitable and multistatement transactions like a data warehouse does. A third advantage is that it's cloud agnostic, so you can use the same catalog if you are multicloud today, will be multicloud tomorrow, or want to minimize cloud vendor lock-in.

There are two disadvantages of Project Nessie. One is that not all engines and tools support Nessie as a catalog. At the time of this writing, Spark, Flink, Dremio, Presto, Trino, and PyIceberg support Nessie as a catalog. The other disadvantage is that you have to run the infrastructure yourself, as you do in Hive Metastore. However, similar to how AWS Glue offers a hosted version (or at least a compatible one, so it looks like a Hive Metastore), Dremio offers a hosted version of Project Nessie.

Nessie catalog use cases

Nessie is a good choice for your Iceberg catalog if you need multitable/multistatement transactions, want to leverage the data-as-code paradigm, and/or have a goal to be cloud agnostic.

Configuring Spark to use the Project Nessie catalog

The following code snippet shows how you can launch a Spark SQL shell where you can use `my_catalog1` to write and read Iceberg tables using Project Nessie as your Iceberg catalog:

```
spark-sql --packages
"org.apache.iceberg:iceberg-spark-runtime-x.x_x.xx:x.x.x,org.projectnes-
sie:nessie-spark-extensions-x.x_x.xx:x.xx.x,software.amazon.awssdk:bun-
dle:x.xx.xxx,software.amazon.awssdk:url-connection-client:x.xx.xxx" \
--conf spark.sql.extensions="org.apache.iceberg.spark.extensions.Ice-
bergSparkSessionExtensions,org.projectnessie.spark.extensions.NessieSparkSes-
sionExtensions" \
--conf spark.sql.catalog.my_catalog1=org.apache.iceberg.spark.SparkCatalog \
--conf spark.sql.catalog.my_catalog1.catalog-impl=org.apache.iceberg.nessie.Nes-
sieCatalog \
--conf spark.sql.catalog.my_catalog1.uri=$NESSIE_URI \
--conf spark.sql.catalog.my_catalog1.ref=main \
--conf spark.sql.catalog.my_catalog1.authentication.type=BEARER \
--conf spark.sql.catalog.my_catalog1.authentication.token=$TOKEN \
--conf spark.sql.catalog.my_catalog1.warehouse=<protocol>://<path> \
--conf spark.sql.catalog.my_catalog1.io-impl=org.apache.iceberg.aws.s3.S3FileIO
```

The REST Catalog

The REST catalog, as the name suggests, leverages a RESTful service provider as an Iceberg catalog. This approach provides an interesting level of flexibility because the REST catalog is an interface rather than a specific implementation, unlike most other catalogs. The service implementing the REST catalog interface can choose to store the mapping of a table's path to its current metadata file in any way it chooses. It could even store it in one of the other catalogs mentioned in this section.

Pros and cons of the REST catalog

There are a few pros to the REST catalog. One is that it requires fewer packages and dependencies compared to other catalogs, simplifying deployment and management. This is because, at its core, it just uses standard HTTP communication. Another advantage is the flexibility it provides, since it can be provided by any service capable of handling RESTful requests and responses, and the service's data store can be many different things. A third advantage is that the REST catalog supports multitable transactions, offering flexibility for complex operations across multiple tables. Finally, it's cloud agnostic, so you can use the same catalog if you are multicloud today, will be multicloud tomorrow, or want to minimize cloud vendor lock-in.

There are three main disadvantages of the REST catalog. One is that you have to run a process to handle and respond to the REST calls from engines and tools. If you're running it in production, you'll also need to run or use an additional data storage service for storing state. A second disadvantage is that, at the time of this writing, there is no public implementation of the backend service to support REST catalog endpoints, meaning you'll have to write your own. An alternative for these two disadvantages is to use a REST catalog providing a hosted service such as Tabular. The third disadvantage is that not all engines and tools support the REST catalog. At the time of this writing, Spark, Trino, PyIceberg, and Snowflake support the REST catalog.

REST catalog use cases

The REST catalog would be a good choice if you're looking for a flexible, customizable solution that can integrate with a variety of backend data stores, if you need the ability to do multitable transactions, and/or if you have a goal to be cloud agnostic.

Configuring Spark to use the REST catalog

The following code snippet shows how you can launch a Spark SQL shell where you can use `my_catalog1` to write and read Iceberg tables using the REST catalog as your Iceberg catalog:

```
spark-sql --packages
org.apache.iceberg:iceberg-spark-runtime-3.3_2.12:0.14.0\
    --conf
spark.sql.extensions=org.apache.iceberg.spark.extensions.Iceberg
SparkSessionExtensions \
    --conf
spark.sql.catalog.my_catalog1=org.apache.iceberg.spark.SparkCatalog \
    --conf spark.sql.catalog.my_catalog1.type=rest \
```

```
--conf
spark.sql.catalog.my_catalog1.uri=http://<host>:<port>
```

The JDBC Catalog

The JDBC catalog leverages Java Database Connectivity (JDBC)–compliant data stores for Iceberg's catalog interface, making it a versatile choice if your data resides in a JDBC-supporting database such as MySQL or PostgreSQL. Note that the database to which JDBC connects must support atomic transactions.

The JDBC catalog maps a table's path to its current metadata file via a table property called metadata_location in the JDBC-compliant database, storing the location of the current metadata file for the table.

Pros and cons of the JDBC catalog

There are multiple advantages to using the JDBC catalog. One is that it can be easy to get started. If you have a JDBC-compliant data store, you already have the necessary infrastructure to start using the JDBC catalog. Common examples of such databases include MySQL and PostgreSQL. Even if you don't have one lying around, cloud providers make it easy to spin one up with, for instance, Amazon Relational Database Service (Amazon RDS) and Azure Database for MySQL/PostgreSQL. Another advantage is that these databases (especially the cloud-hosted ones) make it easy to have high availability built into the setup, ensuring that your data remains accessible and safe even if the primary database instance goes down. A third advantage is that it's cloud agnostic, so you can use the same catalog if you are multicloud today, will be multicloud tomorrow, or want to minimize cloud vendor lock-in.

There are two main disadvantages of the JDBC catalog. One is that it doesn't support multitable transactions. The second is that it requires all your engines and tools to either package a JDBC driver with its deployment or be able to pull one in dynamically, increasing the dependencies on your deployment.

JDBC catalog use cases

You might choose the JDBC catalog if you already have a JDBC-compliant database running or plan to use a database service offered by a cloud provider, such as Amazon RDS. It's also a good choice if your environment requires high availability and/or you want to be cloud agnostic.

Configuring Spark to use the JDBC catalog

The following code snippet shows how you can launch a Spark SQL shell where you can use my_catalog1 to write and read Iceberg tables using the JDBC catalog as your Iceberg catalog:

```
spark-sql --packages org.apache.iceberg:iceberg-spark-runtime-x.x_x.xx:x.x.x \
    --conf spark.sql.catalog.my_catalog1=org.apache.iceberg.spark.SparkCatalog \
    --conf spark.sql.catalog.my_catalog1.warehouse=<protocol>://<path> \
    --conf spark.sql.catalog.my_catalog1.catalog-impl=org.apache.ice-
berg.jdbc.JdbcCatalog \
    --conf spark.sql.catalog.my_catalog1.uri=jdbc:<protocol>://<host>:<port>/
<database> \
    --conf spark.sql.catalog.my_catalog1.jdbc.user=<username> \
    --conf spark.sql.catalog.my_catalog1.jdbc.password=<password>
```

Other Catalogs

Note that there are additional catalog implementations besides the ones covered here (e.g., in-memory, DynamoDB, Snowflake). However, here we chose to focus on the most common catalogs, since there can be a long tail of options because almost anything can act as an Iceberg catalog, as long as it provides the abilities mentioned in "Requirements of an Iceberg Catalog" on page 99.

Catalog Migration

One nice thing about the vast majority of an Iceberg table residing in data lake storage is that it makes migrating from one catalog instance to another or one catalog type to another a very lightweight operation—you're just changing where the mapping of the table path to the current metadata file is. However, while the operation itself is lightweight, as with all migrations a proper plan should be put in place to handle the surrounding complications, such as write jobs and the different tools and applications in your environment.

Being able to migrate catalogs easily mitigates vendor and catalog system lock-in risk and future-proofs your data. If a better or more cost-effective solution comes along, you can switch without much hassle.

There are a few situations where you might want to consider migrating catalogs. One is if you've been experimenting with and/or evaluating Iceberg with one catalog, such as Hadoop, to get started quickly, but you want to use a different catalog for production usage. A second situation is if you want to take advantage of additional capabilities that your current catalog doesn't have. A third situation is if you're changing the location of your environment. An example of this is if you're on premises and using the Hive Metastore from your old Hadoop deployment and you're migrating to AWS and want to use AWS Glue because it's a hosted offering. Note that this third situation requires additional consideration since you'll be migrating the data as well.

A nice thing about the migration being lightweight is that you can continue using your current catalog, register a set of tables in the new catalog, keep the entry in your current catalog, and do testing on the new catalog. Just note in this situation that the new catalog's entry will be stale, with any changes made to the table using the current catalog. You shouldn't make any changes to the table using the new catalog, as all existing usage of the current catalog won't see those changes.

There are two standard ways to migrate catalogs. We'll go through those next.

Using the Apache Iceberg Catalog Migration CLI

The Iceberg catalog migration tool (*https://oreil.ly/iCtJP*), which is a CLI, is an open source tool within Project Nessie. To maintain a clear emphasis that the Iceberg project focuses on the table format specification and engine integration, the Apache Iceberg community opted to maintain a distinct codebase for the tool, separate from the Iceberg repository. It enables bulk migration of Apache Iceberg tables from one catalog to another without the need to copy data. The tool supports all commonly used catalogs in Apache Iceberg, such as AWS Glue, Nessie, Dremio Arctic, Hadoop, Hive, REST, JDBC, and any custom catalogs.

The iceberg-catalog-migrator currently offers two main functions: migration and registration. Crucially, neither of these functions creates data copies. Also, both of them transfer the table's entire history, allowing for functionalities such as time travel in the new catalog after the migration or registration. Following is a summary of the `migrate` and `register` commands:

`migrate`

> The `migrate` command facilitates the bulk migration of Iceberg tables from the original (source) catalog to a new (target) catalog. Once the migration is successfully completed, the table entries will no longer exist in the source catalog; they are effectively moved to the target catalog.

`register`

> The `register` command lets you include (or register) Iceberg tables from the source catalog into the target catalog. Unlike the `migrate` operation, `register` does not involve removing tables from the source catalog. Therefore, following a successful registration, the tables will exist in both catalogs. This functionality is particularly useful for such tasks as conducting premigration validation testing or exploring new catalogs that offer unique features, all while ensuring that the original tables remain intact. When using the `register` command, you need to ensure that you do not write to the same table from multiple catalogs. Doing so can lead to missing updates, data loss, and potential table corruption. It's recommended to use the `migrate` command for this task, which automatically deletes the table from the source catalog after registration, avoiding these issues. Alternatively, avoid performing operations on tables from the source catalog after registration.

Note that it's not advisable to use the CLI tool during ongoing commits to tables in the source catalog. This is to prevent missing updates, data loss, and potential table corruption in the target catalog. During migration, the tool captures a specific state of the table (a metadata file) and uses that state for registering into the target catalog. If there are ongoing commits to the source catalog table, the new commits won't reflect on the target catalog, risking the integrity of your data. Adopting a batch-wise migration approach using a regex expression (e.g., all tables in namespace1 or all tables in namespace1 with names starting with the letter *a*) is generally recommended. This approach can be part of regular maintenance and downtime processes, allowing users to avoid writing data during this phase and pause any automated running jobs. Note that these jobs will need to be repointed to the new catalog before they start running again. An alternative can be to have a middle-layer shim that initially points to the existing catalog, configure your jobs to point at that shim, validate there are no issues, and then perform the migration. When the migration is complete, your jobs don't need to change; you just need to point the shim at the new catalog instead.

Here's an example usage of the CLI tool:

```
java -jar iceberg-catalog-migrator-cli-0.2.0.jar migrate \
--source-catalog-type GLUE \
--source-catalog-properties warehouse=s3a://bucket/gluecatalog/,io-
impl=org.apache.iceberg.aws.s3.S3FileIO \
--source-catalog-hadoop-conf
fs.s3a.secret.key=$AWS_SECRET_ACCESS_KEY,fs.s3a.access.key=$AWS_ACCESS_KEY_ID \
--target-catalog-type NESSIE \
--target-catalog-properties uri=http://localhost:19120/api/v1,ref=main,ware-
house=s3a://bucket/nessie/,io-impl=org.apache.iceberg.aws.s3.S3FileIO \
--identifiers db1.nominees
```

When executed, this command will migrate the table db1.nominees (specified by the --identifiers flag) from an AWS Glue catalog (specified by --source-catalog-type) for the AWS account corresponding to the AWS credentials (specified by the --source-catalog-hadoop-conf settings) to a Nessie catalog (specified by --target-catalog-type) running on localhost on port 19120 (specified by uri within --target-catalog-properties).

Using an Engine

The second standard way to migrate catalogs is to use an engine such as Apache Spark. When using Spark, there are a set of procedures that can be used from Spark SQL. You'll need to configure both the source catalog and the target catalog so that the Spark session can use these procedures.

For example, if you wanted to have a Hadoop catalog as your source catalog and an AWS Glue catalog as your target catalog, you could configure Spark SQL like this:

```
spark-sql --packages "org.apache.iceberg:iceberg-spark-
runtime-x.x_x.xx:x.x.x,software.amazon.awssdk:bundle:x.xx.xxx,software.ama-
zon.awssdk:url-connection-client:x.xx.xxx" \
    --conf
spark.sql.extensions=org.apache.iceberg.spark.extensions.Iceberg
SparkSessionExtensions \
    --conf
spark.sql.catalog.source_catalog1=org.apache.iceberg.spark.SparkCatalog \
    --conf spark.sql.catalog.source_catalog1.type=hadoop \
    --conf spark.sql.catalog.source_catalog1.warehouse=<protocol>://<path>
--conf spark.sql.catalog.target_catalog1=org.apache.iceberg.spark.SparkCatalog \
--conf spark.sql.catalog.target_catalog1.warehouse=s3://<path> \
--conf spark.sql.catalog.target_catalog1.catalog-impl=org.apache.ice-
berg.aws.glue.GlueCatalog \
--conf spark.sql.catalog.target_catalog1.io-impl=org.apache.ice-
berg.aws.s3.S3FileIO \
--conf spark.hadoop.fs.s3a.access.key=$AWS_ACCESS_KEY \
--conf spark.hadoop.fs.s3a.secret.key=$AWS_SECRET_ACCESS_KEY
```

When executed, this command will launch a Spark SQL shell configured to allow for migrating tables between a Hadoop catalog (specified by `--conf spark.sql.catalog.source_catalog1.type`) at the input location (specified by `--conf spark.sql.catalog.source_catalog1.warehouse`) and an AWS Glue catalog (specified by `--conf spark.sql.catalog.target_catalog1.catalog-impl=org.apache.iceberg.aws.glue.GlueCatalog`) for the AWS account corresponding to the AWS credentials (specified by `--conf spark.hadoop.fs.s3a.access.key` and `--conf spark.hadoop.fs.s3a.secret.key`).

Note that executing this command will just launch a Spark SQL shell that has the two catalogs configured (`source_catalog1` and `target_catalog1`), which allows commands to use these catalogs, rather than doing any immediate migration of tables. There are two main procedures to consider when migrating tables between catalogs. We'll go through these procedures next.

register_table()

The `register_table()` Spark SQL procedure creates a lightweight copy of the source table using the source table's datafiles. Any changes made to the target catalog's table will be done in the source catalog table's directories, but as long as the changes don't physically delete any of the datafiles (e.g., `expire_snapshot()`), the changes made to the tables registered in the target catalog won't be seen by the source catalog's table. That said, making changes to the target catalog's tables in this situation is not recommended.

This method can be useful for testing migration where no changes are required to the target catalog's table for validation. This method can also be useful if you want to migrate catalogs, but you want to keep the table's file location on data lake storage the same before and after migration.

Note that this method transfers the entire history of the table, so history operations such as time travel and viewing the history of the table via system tables are doable after using this procedure.

Table 5-1 details the arguments needed to run the `register_table()` procedure in Spark SQL.

Table 5-1. Arguments for the `register_table()` procedure

Argument name	Required?	Type	Description
table	Yes	String	Target table name to be registered
metadata_file	Yes	String	Metadata file that is to be registered as the current metadata file for the new target table

Table 5-2 details the output fields returned when the procedure is executed.

Table 5-2. Output for the `register_table()` procedure

Output name	Type	Description
current_snapshot_id	Long	Current snapshot ID of the newly registered Iceberg table
total_records_count	Long	Total record count of the newly registered Iceberg table
total_data_files_count	Long	Total datafile count of the newly registered Iceberg table

Following is an example usage of the `register_table` procedure, based on the Spark SQL shell configuration in the previous section:

```
CALL target_catalog.system.register_table(
'target_catalog.db1.table1', '/path/to/source_catalog_warehouse/db1/table1/
metadata/xxx.json'
)
```

snapshot()

Similar to `register_table()`, the `snapshot()` Spark SQL procedure creates a light-weight copy of the source table, using the source table's datafiles. However, unlike `register_table()`, any changes made to the target catalog's table will be done in the target table's table location, meaning any changes made to the target table won't interfere with the source table. That said, any changes made to the source table won't be visible to the users of the target table, and vice versa.

This method can be useful for testing migration where changes are required to be made to the target table for validation purposes, but you don't want anything using the source table to see these changes. Another consequence of the target catalog's table not owning the datafiles is that it is not allowed to run expire_snapshots() on the target table, since that would entail physically deleting datafiles owned by the source catalog's table. It can also be useful if you want a lightweight migration to the new catalog but want to change the table's file location, since, over time and with changes, more and more of the table's metadata and datafiles will be in the target catalog table's location. Further, if you want, you can leverage rewrite_data_files() at a later date postmigration to make the file migration happen more quickly (e.g., if migrating from on prem to the cloud or from one cloud to another).

Note that this method transfers the entire history of the table, so history operations such as time travel and viewing the history of the table via system tables are doable after using this procedure.

Table 5-3 details the arguments needed to run the snapshot() procedure in Spark SQL.

Table 5-3. Parameters for the snapshot() procedure

Argument name	Required?	Type	Description
source_table	Yes	String	Name of the table to snapshot
table	Yes	String	Name of the new Iceberg table to create
location		String	Table location for the new table (delegated to the catalog by default)
properties		map<string, string>	Properties to add to the newly created table

Table 5-4 details the output fields returned when the procedure is executed.

Table 5-4. Output for the snapshot() procedure

Output name	Type	Description
imported_files_count	Long	Number of files added to the new table

Following is an example usage of the snapshot() procedure, based on the Spark SQL shell configuration in the preceding section:

```
CALL target_catalog.system.snapshot(
'source_catalog.db1.table1',
'target_catalog.db1.table1'
)
```

Conclusion

In this chapter, we walked through a detailed exploration of Iceberg catalogs, taking a close look at their pivotal role in maintaining consistency among multiple readers and writers and their use in discovering available tables in a given environment.

We examined the fundamental requirements of a catalog, alongside additional necessities for deploying a catalog in a production setting. We also thoroughly compared various catalog implementations, detailing their pros and cons and explaining how to configure Spark for each of them. In addition, we discussed catalog migration, including the scenarios where one might want to consider migrating catalogs, and the two primary methods for how to go about doing so.

In Chapter 6, we'll go hands-on with Apache Iceberg in a variety of different tools.

Hands-on with Apache Iceberg

This part of the book will delve into the practical aspects of using Apache Iceberg with some widely used compute engines and standalone APIs, including Apache Spark, Dremio's SQL Engine, AWS Glue, Apache Flink, and PyIceberg. For a bonus chapter on the Iceberg Java/Python APIs, visit this supplemental repository (*https://oreil.ly/apache-ice_more-content*). The primary focus is to provide in-depth explanations and code examples to demonstrate how Apache Iceberg works with various compute engines so that you can apply and build on the theoretical concepts discussed in the previous chapters.

Visit the book's GitHub repository (*https://oreil.ly/supp-guide-apache-iceberg-ch6*) to learn how to create a data lakehouse environment on your computer with Docker and to get hands-on with tools such as Apache Spark, Apache Flink, and Dremio.

Apache Spark

Apache Spark stands out as a highly versatile distributed compute engine paired with Apache Iceberg due to its support for an extensive range of features. Leveraging Spark and Iceberg allows you to take advantage of the computational benefits of Iceberg's efficient data organization and management capabilities. In this chapter, we will explore the necessary steps to get started with Apache Iceberg and Spark as well as dive into some critical capabilities. By the end of this chapter, you will be able to configure Apache Iceberg; perform various Data Definition Language (DDL) operations (CREATE, ALTER), queries (SELECT), and Data Manipulation Language (DML) operations (INSERT, UPDATE, DELETE, MERGE); and manage Iceberg tables with different processing engines.

Configuration

We'll start by discussing how to configure Apache Iceberg tables and catalogs using Spark as the compute engine. The idea is to familiarize yourself with the basic configuration parameters needed to work with Iceberg and Spark seamlessly.

Configuring Apache Iceberg and Spark

To begin working with Apache Iceberg tables using Apache Spark, it's necessary to configure them to work together. There are a couple of ways to define these configurations. First you will see how to set these configs via feature flags for use in Spark Shell or Spark SQL, and then you will see how to do the same in a Python application.

Configuring via the CLI

As a first step, you'll need to specify the required packages to be installed and used with the Spark session. To do so, Spark provides the --packages option, which allows Spark to easily download the specified Maven-based packages (*https://oreil.ly/cVP-F*) and its dependencies to add them to the classpath of your application.

To use Iceberg with Spark, you use the --packages option and specify the iceberg-spark-runtime package. The generic format for specifying the package is groupId:artifactId:version. The iceberg-spark-runtime package includes the Iceberg classes that Spark needs to interact with Iceberg tables and metadata. By using the --packages option, you're ensuring that these necessary classes are included in the Spark classpath when your Spark shell or application runs.

Here is the command to start a Spark shell with Apache Iceberg:

```
spark-shell --packages org.apache.iceberg:iceberg-spark-runtime-3.3_2.12:1.3.0
```

This command tells Spark to download the iceberg-spark-runtime package from the org.apache.iceberg group where the Iceberg version is 1.3.0, the Spark version is 3.3, and the Scala version is 2.12. One critical thing to note here is that the package version and the Scala version must be compatible with your Apache Spark version. You can check the compatible versions in the official Iceberg documentation (*https://oreil.ly/JBlYq*). Otherwise, it may lead to compatibility issues.

Similarly, if you want to make these configurations in your Spark SQL session, you can include the package name, as shown in the following command:

```
spark-sql --packages org.apache.iceberg:iceberg-spark-runtime-3.3_2.12:1.3.0
```

An alternative to using the --package option in the CLI way of configuring is to add the required JAR files to Spark's *jars* folder in your installation. The JAR option can benefit local development and testing environments and eliminates the need to download the libraries from Maven repositories, whereas --package provides you flexibility in version management.

This JAR contains the Iceberg classes and extensions needed for Spark to interpret and manipulate Iceberg tables. Including the JAR file can be done via the command line when starting a Spark shell or Spark submit:

```
./bin/spark-shell --jars /path/to/iceberg-spark-runtime.jar
```

The two approaches allow you to configure Iceberg and Spark using the CLI. However, to make these configurations in your Python or Scala application, you must include the package in your code when creating a Spark session. Let's go through how to do that in a PySpark application.

Configuring via Python code (PySpark)

Before you start a PySpark session with Apache Iceberg, you will need to have the following installed:

- Java (v8 or v11)
- PySpark
- Apache Spark (the version depends on the Iceberg version)

To start a PySpark Session that includes all the Iceberg-related libraries, you will need to use the `SparkSession.builder` object in PySpark. This allows you to specify the required configuration options for your Spark session. Here is a snippet that shows how to achieve this:

```
from pyspark.sql import *
from pyspark import SparkConf

# Create a Spark Configuration
conf = SparkConf()

# Set Configurations
conf.set("spark.jars.packages", "org.apache.iceberg:iceberg-spark-
runtime-3.3_2.12:1.2.0")

# Create Spark Session
spark = SparkSession.builder.config(conf=conf).getOrCreate()

## Spark Session Object can then be used to run queries with
## the spark.sql("SELECT * FROM table") function
```

We first created a `SparkConf` object, which configures the properties for the Spark context in our application. We can specify various parameters here in key-value pairs. For this example, we set the `spark.jars.packages` config with our required package, `org.apache.iceberg:iceberg-spark-runtime-3.3_2.12:1.2.0`. Similar to the CLI method, this configuration will add external libraries directly by their Maven coordinates to the classpath. Finally, we created a `SparkSession` with the configuration object (`conf`) that we set up.

Configuring the Catalogs

The next important component in the configuration process is the Apache Iceberg catalog. Apache Iceberg supports a wide variety of catalogs for metadata management. We discussed the requirements for a catalog and its role in the Apache Iceberg table format in detail in Chapter 5. In a nutshell, a catalog is a logical namespace that holds metadata information about the Iceberg tables and provides a unified view of the data to various compute engines, bringing in reliability and consistency guarantees for the transactions. Therefore, a catalog is one of the first things you would configure to work with Iceberg tables.

Apache Spark provides an API to add table catalogs, which are utilized for loading, creating, and administering Iceberg tables. Configuring a catalog in Spark involves defining and naming it in the Spark session configuration, either programmatically in your PySpark code or in the Spark shell. This is done by setting the Spark property `spark.sql.catalog.<catalog-name>` with an implementation class for its value. The configuration signifies that a catalog of the given name should be created and managed using a defined implementation class. Here is an example of how to do this:

```
spark.sql.catalog.my_catalog =org.apache.iceberg.spark.SparkCatalog
```

Here we defined a catalog named `my_catalog` that will be implemented using Iceberg's implementation of the `SparkCatalog` class instead of Spark's default implementation. The implementation class is essentially the backbone of every catalog used by Spark, providing the logic and functionality that Spark will use to interact with your independent Apache Iceberg catalog (Nessie, AWS Glue) as a catalog in the Spark session. Before moving on to other configuration parameters, let's discuss the two built-in catalog implementation classes for Spark provided by Apache Iceberg.

Using org.apache.iceberg.spark.SparkCatalog

The first implementation class supports using either a Hive Metastore or a Hadoop (filesystem) catalog by default. This is the type of catalog we used in the previous example. When configured to use a Hive Metastore (by setting the catalog type to `hive`), `SparkCatalog` uses Hive's Metastore to store table metadata, allowing you to leverage Hive's metadata management features. Alternatively, if you set the catalog type to `hadoop`, `SparkCatalog` will use a directory-based catalog in Hadoop or any other filesystem to store table metadata. Here is an example of how to configure a `SparkCatalog` with Hive:

```
spark.sql.catalog.hive_catalog = org.apache.iceberg.spark.SparkCatalog

spark.sql.catalog.hive_catalog.type = hive

spark.sql.catalog.hive_catalog.uri = thrift://metastore-host:port
```

In this example, we configured a `SparkCatalog` called `hive_catalog`. The `type` parameter is set to `hive` to leverage the Hive Metastore in this particular case. Another parameter called `uri` is set to inform Spark to use the specified Hive Metastore URI for interacting with the Iceberg tables in the `hive_catalog`. Table 6-1 discusses details about the available catalog properties.

Table 6-1. Catalog properties

Property	Values	Description
spark.sql.cat alog.*catalog- name*.type	Hive, Hadoop, REST	Specifies the underlying Iceberg catalog implementation; remains unset if a custom catalog is used
spark.sql.cat alog.*catalog- name*.catalog-impl		Custom Iceberg catalog implementation class; must be defined if the type property is not set
spark.sql.cata log.*catalog-name*. io-impl		Custom FileIO implementation
spark.sql.cata log.*catalog-name*. default-namespace	default	Default namespace for the catalog
spark.sql.cata log.*catalog-name*.uri	thrift:// host:port	Hive Metastore URI, REST URI, or Nessie/Arctic server (custom catalog)
spark.sql.cat alog.*catalog- name*.warehouse	/path/to/ warehouse	Warehouse location for the catalog to store data

Using org.apache.iceberg.spark.SparkSessionCatalog

The SparkSessionCatalog is a more specialized implementation that wraps around Spark's built-in session catalog, adding support for Iceberg tables. This could benefit scenarios when you want to use Iceberg tables seamlessly alongside non-Iceberg tables in your Spark session. Here, all the non-Iceberg tables are managed by the built-in Spark catalog, while the tables specific to Iceberg are managed separately through the SparkSessionCatalog class. Here is an example of this configuration:

```
spark.sql.catalog.hive_spark_catalog = org.apache.iceberg.spark.SparkSessionCa-
talog

spark.sql.catalog.hive_spark_catalog.type = hive

spark.sql.catalog.hive_spark_catalog.uri = thrift://localhost:9083
```

In the preceding code, we configured a SparkSessionCatalog named hive_spark_ catalog to use a Hive Metastore (located at thrift:localhost:9083) for the metadata storage.

Using a custom catalog

There could be scenarios when you would like to go beyond Iceberg's built-in catalog implementations. For example, you might want to integrate with an existing platform in your organization, such as AWS Glue (*https://aws.amazon.com/glue*), or take advantage of the data-as-code paradigms with modern metastores such as Project Nessie (*https://projectnessie.org*). For such cases, Spark allows you to load a custom Iceberg catalog implementation. The custom catalog implementation needs to implement the `Catalog` interface in Iceberg and is specified using the `catalog-impl` property. The following example shows how to load a custom catalog:

```
spark.sql.catalog.custom_catalog = org.apache.iceberg.spark.SparkCatalog

spark.sql.catalog.custom_catalog.catalog-impl = com.my.custom.CatalogImpl

spark.sql.catalog.custom_catalog.my-additional-catalog-config = my-value
```

In this example, `custom_catalog` is a catalog that leverages Iceberg's `SparkCatalog`, but with a custom implementation defined by `com.my.custom.CatalogImpl`. The `my-additional-catalog-config` can be any additional configuration required by your `CatalogImpl`.

In the previous two sections we explored how to configure Apache Spark with Apache Iceberg and how to configure catalogs such as Hive Metastore and Hadoop to work with Iceberg tables. Now let's configure these components and get started with our hands-on exercises.

Starting Spark with All the Configurations (AWS Glue Example)

To follow along and execute the examples presented in this chapter, you can clone this repository (*https://oreil.ly/supp-guide-apache-iceberg*) and follow these instructions:

- In the *Chapter 6* folder of the repository, read the *developer_env.md* file for directions on how to set up your developer environment.
- Once it is set up, copy any notebook files you'll need for future exercises into the */notebooks* folder that will exist where your environment is established.

(If you'd rather use a local setup without the need for cloud infrastructure, refer to the book's GitHub repository (*https://oreil.ly/supp-guide-apache-iceberg-ch6*) for information on catalog setup and configurations.)

You will first need to set the AWS environment variables to interact with the Glue catalog:

```
%env AWS_REGION= region
%env AWS_ACCESS_KEY_ID= key
%env AWS_SECRET_ACCESS_KEY= secret
```

Make sure to replace these placeholders with the actual values:

```
import pyspark
from pyspark.sql import SparkSession
import os

conf = (
    pyspark.SparkConf()
        .setAppName('app_name')
        .set('spark.jars.packages', 'org.apache.iceberg:iceberg-
spark-runtime-3.3_2.12:1.2.0,software.amazon.awssdk:bundle:2.17.178,software.ama
zon.awssdk:url-connection-client:2.17.178')

        .set('spark.sql.extensions', 'org.apache.iceberg.spark.extensions.Ice
bergSparkSessionExtensions')
        .set('spark.sql.catalog.glue', 'org.apache.iceberg.spark.SparkCatalog')

        .set('spark.sql.catalog.glue.catalog-impl', 'org.apache.ice
berg.aws.glue.GlueCatalog')

        .set('spark.sql.catalog.glue.warehouse', 's3://my-bucket/warehouse/')

        .set('spark.sql.catalog.glue.io-impl', 'org.apache.iceberg.aws.s3.S3Fil
eIO')
)

spark = SparkSession.builder.config(conf=conf).getOrCreate()
```

Next, you will pass the necessary packages for Iceberg and Spark along with an AWS SDK package that will help you interact with the AWS services (S3, Glue) we plan to use. Define a catalog called glue that leverages Iceberg's SparkCatalog as its foundation, but with a custom implementation defined by org.apache.iceberg.aws.glue.GlueCatalog. Then set the catalog warehouse location to s3://my-bucket/warehouse/. This is where the compute engine will write the data and metadata files.

Finally, the org.apache.iceberg.aws.s3.S3FileIO value set in the custom FileIO implementation property indicates the implementation provided by Iceberg for reading and writing data to AWS S3. Upon executing this code, you will have your Spark app up and running with all the configurations:

```
--------------------------------------------------------------------
|                     |         |         modules         ||  artifacts  |
|       conf          | number| search|dwnlded|evicted|| number|dwnlded|
--------------------------------------------------------------------
|      default        |   35  |   0   |   0   |   1   ||   34  |   0   |
--------------------------------------------------------------------
:: retrieving :: org.apache.spark#spark-submit-parent-18734b47-4777-4ae3-
b1e0-1caa56050c4a
    confs: [default]
    0 artifacts copied, 34 already retrieved (0kB/234ms)

23/08/22 23:48:58 WARN NativeCodeLoader: Unable to load native-hadoop library
for your platform... using builtin-java classes where applicable

Setting default log level to "WARN".
To adjust logging level use sc.setLogLevel(newLevel). For SparkR, use
setLogLevel(newLevel).

23/08/22 23:49:07 WARN Utils: Service 'SparkUI' could not bind on port 4040.
Attempting port 4041.
Spark Running
```

Data Definition Language Operations

This section will familiarize you with the various DDL operations available within Apache Iceberg using Spark. In Iceberg, DDL operations are intuitive and well aligned with standard SQL. Apache Spark allows you to perform these operations using the SQL API or DataFrame API (DataFrameWriterV2) and provides similar results irrespective of the API used. Please note that the DataFrame API does not support all the DDL operations. We will present examples of how to run these operations with both the SQL API and the DataFrame API (wherever applicable).

CREATE TABLE

The first step is to create an Iceberg table using the CREATE TABLE command. Following are examples of how to do so using the Spark SQL API and the DataFrame API.

Spark SQL:

```
spark.sql("""
    CREATE TABLE glue.test.employee (
        id INT,
        role STRING,
        department STRING,
        salary FLOAT,
        region STRING)
    USING iceberg
""")
```

Here, glue refers to the catalog instance, test refers to the database/namespace name (which must already exist in your Glue catalog), and employee is the new table. The table will be created with five columns. The USING iceberg clause in the SQL API indicates that you're leveraging Iceberg as your table format.

DataFrame API:

```
from pyspark.sql.types import StructType, StructField, StringType, IntegerType

# Define the schema
schema = StructType([
    StructField("id", IntegerType(), True),
    StructField("role", StringType(), True),
    StructField("department", StringType(), True),
])

# Create an empty DataFrame with the schema
df = spark.createDataFrame([], schema)

# Write the DataFrame to the catalog as a new table
df.writeTo("glue.test.employee").create()
```

Create a table with partitions

Partitioning is a way to segregate your data into smaller, manageable units, enabling you to optimize data operations by leaving out irrelevant data. When a table is partitioned, data is physically divided and stored across different directories based on the partition column values. For example, if you partition a product data table by region, the data for each region will be stored separately, and when you query data specific to a particular region, only the relevant data is read and returned. We discussed partitioning in detail in Chapter 4. Here is how to create a partitioned table in Iceberg using Spark.

Spark SQL:

```
spark.sql("""
    CREATE TABLE glue.test.emp_partitioned (
        id INT,
        role STRING,
        department STRING)
    USING iceberg
    PARTITIONED BY (department)
""")
```

Here, the PARTITIONED BY (department) clause instructs Iceberg to partition the data based on the department column. This would result in data being stored in separate partitions based on the distinct values present in the department column.

DataFrame API:

```
from pyspark.sql.types import StructType, StructField, StringType, IntegerType
from pyspark.sql.functions import col

# Define the schema
schema = StructType([
    StructField("id", IntegerType(), True),
    StructField("role", StringType(), True),
    StructField("department", StringType(), True)
])

# Create an empty DataFrame with the schema
df = spark.createDataFrame([], schema)

# Write the DataFrame to the catalog as a new table
df.writeTo("glue.test.emp_partitioned").partitionedBy(col("department")).create()
```

Apache Iceberg also supports hidden partitioning, which means you don't have to add or manage explicit partition columns, unlike in table formats such as Hive. Iceberg takes a column and internally transforms it into a partition value while keeping track of the relationship. This happens behind the scenes, so users won't have to deal with it when querying data. You can read more about hidden partitioning in Chapter 4.

The PARTITIONED BY clause supports certain transform expressions to generate hidden partitions. Here is an example using Spark SQL:

```
spark.sql("""
    CREATE TABLE glue.test.emp_partitioned_month (
        id INT,
        role STRING,
        department STRING,
        join_date DATE
    )
    USING iceberg
    PARTITIONED BY (months(join_date))
""")
```

This statement will create an Iceberg table called emp_partitioned_month that is partitioned by month of join_date. In this case, Iceberg does the transformation of join_date to months(ts) internally and tracks the relationship between these two, avoiding the need to create an additional partition column. This way, users don't have to worry about the physical layout of the table. Other supported transformations include the following:

- year(ts): Partition by year.
- months(ts): Partition by month.
- days(ts) or date(ts): dateint partitioning.
- hours(ts) or date_hour(ts): dateint and hour partitioning.

- bucket(N, col): Partition by hash value mod N (Number) buckets.

- truncate(L, col): Partition by value truncated to L (Length).

Use the CREATE TABLE...AS SELECT statement

The CREATE TABLE...AS SELECT (CTAS) statement allows you to create and populate a new table with records simultaneously. This can be particularly useful for scenarios where you want to create a new table based on the results of complex queries or transformations applied to existing tables. One important thing to note when running CTAS in the context of Apache Iceberg is that it works as an atomic operation only when using the SparkCatalog class. If you use the SparkSessionCatalog class, CTAS is supported but is not atomic, which may cause inconsistencies when concurrent writes are occurring. Here is how to execute a CTAS statement in Apache Iceberg using Spark.

Spark SQL:

```
spark.sql("""
    CREATE TABLE glue.test.employee_ctas
    USING iceberg
    AS SELECT * FROM glue.test.sample
""")
```

In this example, a new table, employee_ctas, is created within the glue.test catalog and is populated with the data from an existing table called sample.

DataFrame API:

```
# Read an existing table into a DataFrame
df_ctas = spark.read.table("glue.test.sample")

# Use the DataFrame's writeTo method with the create operation to do a CTAS
df_ctas.writeTo("glue.test.employee_ctas").create()
```

Note that the original table's partition specification and other properties are not automatically inherited when using CTAS. You can manually set these properties by using the PARTITIONED BY clause and the TBLPROPERTIES command in your CTAS statement. Here is an example.

Spark SQL:

```
spark.sql("""
    CREATE TABLE glue.test.emp_ctas_partition
    USING iceberg
    PARTITIONED BY (category)
    TBLPROPERTIES (write.format.default='avro')
    AS SELECT *
    FROM glue.test.sample
""")
```

DataFrame API:

```
from pyspark.sql.functions import col

df_new = spark.read.table("glue.test.sample")
df_new.writeTo("glue.test.emp_ctas_partition") \
    .partitionedBy(col("category")) \
    .create()
```

ALTER TABLE

As your business requirements change, the existing table structure may need to evolve or change. These changes could span from simply renaming a table's column and adding or dropping columns to more complex modifications such as altering table properties and changing schema or column types. Apache Iceberg provides support for a variety of ALTER TABLE operations. Note that these operations are only possible using Spark SQL, not the DataFrame API.

Let's look at a few of these operations.

Rename a table

There might be situations where you would want to adjust the naming scheme of an Iceberg table for better organization of your data assets or when the table's current name no longer accurately depicts its data contents. In such cases, you can use the ALTER TABLE...RENAME TO command to easily rename a table:

```
spark.sql("""
    ALTER TABLE glue.test.employee RENAME TO glue.test.emp_renamed
""")
```

In this example, we've renamed the table from employee to emp_renamed within the catalog glue.test (this does not change the storage path, just the namespace in the catalog).

Set table properties

You can set table-specific properties in Iceberg to customize and manage the behavior of individual tables, such as changing the write distribution strategy for performance improvements and enabling specific features. This can be achieved using the SET TBLPROPERTIES command:

```
spark.sql("""
    ALTER TABLE glue.test.employee SET TBLPROPERTIES ('write.wap.enabled'='true')
""")
```

This command sets the write.wap.enabled property of the employee table to true, which enables write-audit-publish writes (a pattern of staging writes for auditing before publishing).

Add a column

To add more fields to your existing Iceberg table, you can use the `ALTER TABLE...ADD COLUMN` command:

```
spark.sql("""
    ALTER TABLE glue.test.employee ADD COLUMN manager STRING
""")
```

Here, we added another column called `manager`, which is of type `string`, to our existing table `employee` using the `ADD COLUMN` clause.

You can add multiple columns at the same time using separated commas:

```
spark.sql("""
    ALTER TABLE glue.test.employee ADD COLUMN details STRING, manager_id INT
""")
```

To add columns to a specific position, you can leverage the `FIRST` and `AFTER` clauses:

```
spark.sql("""
ALTER TABLE glue.test.employee ADD COLUMN new_column bigint AFTER department
""")
```

This query will add a new column called `new_column` to a specific position, in this case, after the `department` column.

Similarly, the following query will add a new column, `first_column`, to the very first position of the table:

```
spark.sql("""
ALTER TABLE glue.test.employee ADD COLUMN first_column bigint FIRST
""")
```

Rename a column

Renaming a column is another operation that you might require to adhere to a new naming convention or to accommodate changing data needs. Here is an example of how this command can be applied:

```
spark.sql("""
    ALTER TABLE glue.test.employee RENAME COLUMN role TO title
""")
```

In this query, we altered the `employee` table within the `glue.test` catalog by renaming `role` to `title` to better reflect the relevant column name.

Modify a column

To modify the attributes of a column, such as its type or nullability, or to set comments and reordering fields, Iceberg provides the `ALTER TABLE...ALTER COLUMN` command:

```
spark.sql("""
    ALTER TABLE glue.test.employee ALTER COLUMN id TYPE BIGINT
""")
```

This command changes the id column's data type to BIGINT from INT in the employee table.

Iceberg allows you to flexibly modify column types while ensuring that the updates are safe. Safe updates are essential so that there is no data loss or misinterpretation. Some of the recommended safe updates include the following:

- Changing an integer (int) to a bigint
- Changing a float to a double
- Transforming decimal(P, S) to decimal(P2, S) given that scale S remains unchanged

Iceberg also allows you to reorder columns using the FIRST and AFTER clauses:

```
spark.sql("ALTER TABLE glue.test.employee ALTER COLUMN salary FIRST")
```

The preceding query changes the order of the salary column and brings it to the very beginning of the table.

Drop a column

To remove unnecessary columns from an Iceberg table, you can use the ALTER TABLE...DROP COLUMN command:

```
spark.sql("""
    ALTER TABLE glue.test.employee DROP COLUMN department
""")
```

The preceding SQL statement removes the column department from the employee table.

Alter a Table with Iceberg's Spark SQL Extensions

Apache Iceberg has an extension module in Spark that allows you to run additional operations that are not part of standard SQL. (You can find a quick reference of the operations that work with SQL extensions in Table 6-2.) For example, you can execute various Spark procedures to clean up your metadata in Iceberg using the CALL clause or change the existing table's schema with a variety of ALTER statements. To leverage these SQL commands, you will need to add the Iceberg Spark extensions property to your Spark CLI or code. Here is an example of how to set this property in PySpark code:

```
import pyspark
from pyspark.sql import SparkSession
import os

conf = (
    pyspark.SparkConf()
        .setAppName('app_name')

    # This property allows us to add any extensions that we want to use
        .set('spark.sql.extensions', 'org.apache.iceberg.spark.extensions.Ice
bergSparkSessionExtensions')
    spark = SparkSession.builder.config(conf=conf).getOrCreate()
```

Let's take a look at some of these SQL extensions and how they can help with the ALTER statements.

Add/drop/replace a partition

Iceberg allows you to modify the partitioning schema and specify additional partition fields (enabling partitioning the table on future writes based on an existing table field), as well as remove or replace existing partitioning fields using the Spark SQL extension. In the following query, a new partition field, region, is added to the employee table. Therefore, the data in this table will now be divided based on the values in the region column, thereby making reads faster for specific regions:

```
spark.sql("""
    ALTER TABLE glue.test.employee ADD PARTITION FIELD region
""")
```

The following query will remove the partitioning on the department field in the employee table. There is, however, no impact on the existing column or schema of the table due to removal of a partition column:

```
spark.sql("""
    ALTER TABLE glue.test.employee DROP PARTITION FIELD department
""")
```

To replace a partitioning field with a new one, you can use the ALTER TABLE...REPLACE PARTITION FIELD command:

```
spark.sql("""
    ALTER TABLE glue.test.employee REPLACE PARTITION FIELD region WITH department
""")
```

The preceding example replaces the existing region partition field with a new partition field, department, in the employee table.

Adding, dropping, or replacing a partition field is a metadata-only operation, which means no existing datafiles will be changed. The current data will remain in the old partition (if applicable), and new datafiles will be written as per the new partitioning strategy. However, files rewritten based on table maintenance procedures will be rewritten based on the current partitioning scheme.

Set the write order

In Iceberg, tables can be configured with a sort order that instructs the compute engine to sort the data written to the table automatically. To set a sort order for a table, Iceberg provides the `ALTER TABLE...WRITE ORDERED BY` command.

Here is an example of ordering the `employee` table by the `id` field in ascending order:

```
spark.sql("""
    ALTER TABLE glue.test.employee WRITE ORDERED BY id ASC
""")
```

Set the write distribution

Iceberg gives you control over how the data is distributed among writers. The command `ALTER TABLE...WRITE DISTRIBUTED BY PARTITION` is instrumental in managing data distribution during writes. It ensures that each data partition is handled by a single writer. This strategy can be beneficial for avoiding uneven data distribution during the write process. The default implementation of this feature uses *hash* distribution.

Here is how to apply this setting to the table:

```
spark.sql("""
    ALTER TABLE glue.test.employee WRITE DISTRIBUTED BY PARTITION
""")
```

Upon executing this query, every partition in the `employee` table will be handled by an individual writer.

Set/drop identifier fields

To assign certain fields as identifiers (a field that can make it possible for an engine to realize two rows refer to the same entity) or to drop existing ones, Iceberg allows using the `ALTER TABLE...SET/DROP IDENTIFIER FIELDS` command:

```
spark.sql("""
    ALTER TABLE glue.test.employee SET IDENTIFIER FIELDS id
""")
```

In the preceding example, the `id` field is set as the identifier for the `employee` table, uniquely identifying each record.

The following query shows how to drop an identifier field from the table:

```
spark.sql("""
    ALTER TABLE glue.test.employee DROP IDENTIFIER FIELDS id
""")
```

Table 6-2 provides a brief overview of the ALTER operations covered in this section, outlining situations where SQL extensions could be necessary and where they are not required.

Table 6-2. Operations supported with and without SQL extension

Operation	Without SQL extension	With SQL extension
Rename table	☑	☐
Set table properties	☑	☐
Add/rename/modify/drop column	☑	☐
Add/drop/replace partition	☐	☑
Set write order	☐	☑
Set write distribution	☐	☑
Set/drop identifier field	☐	☑

DROP TABLE

The final DDL command in Iceberg is the DROP statement. DROP allows you to remove an existing table from the catalog. It is important to note that prior to Iceberg v0.14, executing a DROP TABLE command would remove the table from the catalog along with its metadata and data contents. However, from v0.14 onward, this behavior has been modified to only remove the table from the catalog and to keep the table's contents.

The following query will remove the employee table from glue.test, but the table's contents will remain intact:

```
spark.sql("DROP TABLE glue.test.employee")
```

If you intend to delete the table and its contents, you can use the DROP TABLE...PURGE command:

```
spark.sql("DROP TABLE glue.test.employee PURGE")
```

Reading Data

In this section, we will focus on how to read data from Apache Iceberg tables using Spark. First you will see how to query and explore data using Spark SQL, and then we'll discuss how to use DataFrameWriterV2 to do the same.

The Select All Query

The SELECT * command pulls all the records from an existing Iceberg table.

Spark SQL:

```
spark.sql("SELECT * FROM glue.test.employee").show()
```

The preceding query selects all the records from the employee table present in the glue catalog under the namespace test.

DataFrame API:

```
df_emp = spark.table("glue.test.employee")
```

Here, the spark.table() method is used to load the Iceberg table employee into a DataFrame.

The Filter Rows Query

To filter out your data based on specific conditions, you can use conditional queries. Here is an example.

Spark SQL:

```
spark.sql("SELECT * FROM glue.test.employee WHERE department = 'Market
ing'").show()
```

DataFrame API:

```
df_emp = spark.table("glue.test.employee")

# Filter the data
filtered_df = df_emp.filter(df_emp['department'] == 'Marketing')

filtered_df.show()
```

Aggregation Queries

Aggregation queries allow you to perform calculations over groups of data points. By leveraging aggregate functions such as SUM, AVG, MAX, MIN, and COUNT, you can efficiently extract valuable insights and statistics from your dataset. Following are a few examples.

Count the records

To count the number of rows in an Iceberg table, you can use the COUNT() method in the Spark SQL and DataFrame APIs. The following queries will give the count of all records in the glue.test.employee table.

Spark SQL:

```
spark.sql("SELECT COUNT(*) FROM glue.test.employee").show()
```

DataFrame API:

```
df_emp = spark.table("glue.test.employee")
print(df_emp.count())
```

Find the average

The AVG() method calculates the average of all the records in an Iceberg table. The following queries will return the average of all the salaries (salary) from the glue.test.employee table.

Spark SQL:

```
spark.sql("SELECT AVG(salary) FROM glue.test.employee").show()
```

DataFrame API:

```
df_emp = spark.table("glue.test.employee")
df_emp.agg({'salary': 'avg'}).show()
```

Sum the values

SUM() calculates the total sum of the rows in a table. The following queries will return the sum of all the salaries (salary) from the glue.test.employee table.

Spark SQL:

```
spark.sql("SELECT SUM(salary) FROM glue.test.employee").show()
```

DataFrame API:

```
df_emp = spark.table("glue.test.employee")
df_emp.agg({'salary': 'sum'}).show()
```

Find the maximum

These queries will group the employees by their category and then find the maximum salary within each category.

```
spark.sql("SELECT category, MAX(salary) FROM glue.test.employee GROUP BY cate
gory").show()
```

DataFrame API:

```
df_emp = spark.table("glue.test.employee")
df_emp.groupBy("category").max("salary").show()
```

Using Window Functions

Window functions are highly beneficial for performing calculations across a set of rows that are related to the current row. Unlike aggregate functions, window functions don't group rows into a single output. They are typically used for tasks such as ranking items and calculating rolling averages. Here is an example of how you can use window functions in Spark with Apache Iceberg tables.

Spark SQL:

```
spark.sql("""
SELECT * , RANK() OVER (PARTITION BY department ORDER BY salary DESC) as rank
FROM glue.test.employee
""").show()
```

In the preceding query, RANK() OVER (PARTITION BY department ORDER BY salary DESC) creates a window partitioned by the department column and orders by salary in descending order. For each partition, RANK() gives a unique rank starting from 1.

Here is what the output looks like:

id	department	salary	region	rank
2	Marketing	10000	NA	1
6	Marketing	5000	EMEA	2
5	Product	25000	NA	1
4	Product	17000	EMEA	2
3	Sales	8000	APAC	1

DataFrame API:

```
from pyspark.sql import Window
from pyspark.sql.functions import row_number

df_emp = spark.table("glue.test.employee")

windowSpec = Window.partitionBy(df_emp['department']).orderBy(df_emp['sal
ary'].desc())

df_emp = df_emp.withColumn("row_number", row_number().over(windowSpec))
df_emp.toPandas()
```

In the preceding query, Window.partitionBy(df['department']).orderBy(df['salary'].desc()) creates a window specification that groups data by department and orders it by salary in descending order. Then, row_number().over(windowSpec) applies the row_number() function over the defined window to generate a new row_number column. The withColumn function adds this new column to the DataFrame.

Here is the output:

id	department	salary	region	row_number
2	Marketing	10000	NA	1
6	Marketing	5000	EMEA	2
5	Product	25000	NA	1
4	Product	17000	EMEA	2
3	Sales	8000	APAC	1

Writing Data

Apache Iceberg brings atomicity and transactional guarantees when writing data to data lakes, thereby making these operations safe. In this section, we will explore the INSERT INTO, MERGE INTO, INSERT OVERWRITE, DELETE, and UPDATE write operations so that you can gain hands-on experience with these critical data management functions. We will use both Spark SQL and the DataFrameWriterV2 APIs wherever applicable to understand these examples. Note that the DataFrameWriterV2 API does not support all of these operations.

INSERT INTO

INSERT INTO allows you to insert new records into an existing Iceberg table.

Spark SQL:

```
spark.sql("INSERT INTO glue.test.employee VALUES (1, 'Software Engineer', 'Engi
neering', 25000, 'NA'), (2, 'Director', 'Sales', 22000, 'EMEA')")
```

DataFrame API:

```
from pyspark.sql import Row

# Create a DataFrame with the values
data = [Row(id=1, role='Software Engineer', department='Engineering', sal
ary=25000, region='NA'),
        Row(id=2, role='Director', department='Sales', salary=22000,
region='EMEA')]

df = spark.createDataFrame(data)

df.writeTo("glue.test.employee").append()
```

Both of these APIs insert two records into the `employee` table.

MERGE INTO

`MERGE INTO` is used to update an existing row based on whether a specific condition is met. If it is not met, you just insert the new record into the table.

Spark SQL:

```
spark.sql("""
MERGE INTO glue.test.employee AS target
USING (SELECT * FROM employee_updates) AS source
ON target.id = source.id
WHEN MATCHED AND source.role = 'Manager' AND source.salary > 100000 THEN
    UPDATE SET target.salary = source.salary
WHEN NOT MATCHED THEN
    INSERT *
""")
```

The preceding query first compares each row in the `employee_updates` table with rows in the `employee` table based on the condition `target.id = source.id`. If a match is found and if the role in the staging table is `Manager` with a salary greater than `100000`, the salary is updated with the data from the source table. If there is no match, the new record is simply inserted.

INSERT OVERWRITE

To replace the data in an Iceberg table or partition with the result of a query, `INSERT OVERWRITE` is used. Apache Spark provides two overwrite modes for this operation: static and dynamic (by default, the mode is static). Let's discuss these two modes in detail.

Static overwrite

In static overwrite mode, Spark converts the `PARTITION` clause into a filter (predicate) for determining which partitions to overwrite. If you run the query without the `PARTITION` clause, it will replace all partitions. The following query overwrites only the EMEA partition of the `employee` table with data from the `employee_source` table. Note that this mode cannot replace hidden partitions because the `PARTITION` clause can only reference table columns.

Spark SQL:

```
spark.sql("""
INSERT OVERWRITE glue.test.employees
PARTITION (region = 'EMEA')
SELECT *
FROM employee_source
```

```
WHERE region = 'EMEA'
""")
```

DataFrame API:

```
from pyspark.sql.functions import col

# Read from the source table
source_df = spark.read.table("glue.test.employee")

# Filter rows where region is 'EMEA'
filtered_df = source_df.filter(col("region") == 'EMEA')

# Overwrite in Iceberg table
filtered_df.writeTo("glue.test.employee").overwrite(col("region") == 'EMEA')
```

Dynamic overwrite

To configure dynamic overwrite mode, set the Spark config property, `spark.sql.sources.partitionOverwriteMode=dynamic`. In this mode, any partitions that correspond to rows returned by the SELECT query are replaced:

```
spark.conf.set("spark.sql.sources.partitionOverwriteMode", "dynamic")
```

In the following query, any partition in the `employee` table that matches the data produced by the SELECT query will be replaced. Since we filter the `employee_source` table with only the EMEA region data, only the corresponding EMEA partition will be overwritten in the `employee` table.

Spark SQL:

```
spark.sql("""
INSERT OVERWRITE glue.test.employee
SELECT * FROM employee_source
WHERE region = 'EMEA'
""")
```

DataFrame API:

```
from pyspark.sql.functions import col

# Configure dynamic partition overwrite mode
spark.conf.set("spark.sql.sources.partitionOverwriteMode", "dynamic")

# Read from the source table
source_df = spark.read.table("glue.test.employee")

# Filter rows where region is 'EMEA'
filtered_df = source_df.filter(col("region") == 'EMEA')

# Overwrite in Iceberg table
filtered_df.writeTo("glue.test.employee").overwritePartitions()
```

The dynamic overwrite mode is generally recommended when writing to Iceberg tables because it provides granular control over which partitions get overwritten based on the query's outcome.

DELETE FROM

`DELETE FROM` allows you to remove records from an Iceberg table based on a filter. The following query removes all rows from the `employee` table where the `id` value is less than 3.

Spark SQL:

```
spark.sql("DELETE FROM glue.test.employee WHERE id < 3")
```

Apache Iceberg supports two types of deletions depending on the filter condition specified. If the filter condition matches entire partitions of a table, a metadata-only delete is performed. This is a highly efficient operation as no datafiles are touched. On the other hand, if the delete condition matches specific rows within a table, Iceberg will rewrite the affected datafiles.

UPDATE

You can modify existing rows in a table using the `UPDATE` command based on conditions specified in the query.

Spark SQL:

```
spark.sql("""
UPDATE glue.test.employee
SET region = 'APAC', salary = 6000
WHERE id = 6
""")
```

In this example, we updated the `region` and `salary` fields of the employee with `id=6` in the `employee` table.

Here is another example:

```
spark.sql("""
UPDATE glue.test.employee AS e
SET region = 'NA'
WHERE EXISTS (SELECT id FROM emp_history WHERE emp_NA.id = e.id)
""")
```

In this case, we updated the `region` field for all employees whose `id` exists in the emp_NA table. This showcases how you can use subqueries in your UPDATE commands to base your updates on conditions across multiple tables.

Iceberg Table Maintenance Procedures

Managing the datafiles and metadata files in your data lake is of paramount importance as your data grows over time. In Iceberg, metadata files are core to so many critical operations, such as time travel and query optimization. However, with the increase in the number of datafiles, the number of metadata files also increases. Additionally, streaming-based ingestion jobs can lead to a lot of small files being generated as data is written in smaller chunks as and when they arrive. It is therefore important to have a strategy as part of your organization's regular maintenance process to remove these unnecessary metadata files or to compact smaller files into larger ones for better read performance.

Apache Spark provides procedures for easy maintenance of Iceberg tables. In this section, we will look at a few of these procedures. For a detailed read, please refer to Chapter 4.

Expire Snapshots

Any modification to the data in Iceberg—be it an insert, update, delete, or upsert—generates a new snapshot. These snapshots are retained by Iceberg for supporting capabilities such as time travel. However, over a period of time you might end up with a lot of snapshots and not all of them might be necessary. The `expire_snapshots` procedure in Spark helps remove these older, unnecessary snapshots along with their datafiles.

This procedure removes manifest lists, manifests, datafiles, and delete files that are uniquely associated with expired snapshots, ensuring that files still in use by active snapshots are retained.

Here is the generic function and an example of how to run this procedure:

```
# Generic procedure
CALL catalog_name.system.expire_snapshots(table, older_than, retain_last)

spark.sql("CALL glue.system.expire_snapshots('test.employees',
date_sub(current_date(), 90), 50)")
```

This procedure deletes snapshots from the `employee` table that are older than 90 days from the current date, while preserving the most recent 50 snapshots.

Rewrite Datafiles

The number of datafiles in a table has a direct impact on the performance of the queries since there is a huge cost associated with opening, reading, and closing each of the datafiles that are covered by the query. Also, a larger number of small files may cause unnecessary metadata overhead. The `rewrite_data_files` procedure in Spark allows you to compact these small files into larger ones for addressing these issues.

This procedure can also be used to organize the layout of your datafiles by leveraging techniques such as sorting and z-ordering so that they are optimized for the queries. This topic was also covered in Chapter 4.

Here is the generic procedure and a simple example of running it:

```
# Generic procedure
CALL catalog_name.system.rewrite_data_files(table, strategy, sort_order, options)

spark.sql("CALL glue.system.rewrite_data_files('test.employee')")
```

The preceding procedure rewrites the datafiles by combining the small files in the employee table using the default binpack algorithm and splits larger ones into smaller files as per the default write size of the table.

Rewrite Manifests

Manifest files in Iceberg tables play a crucial role in optimizing scan planning as they keep statistical information about the datafiles. The rewrite_manifests procedure allows you to rewrite these manifests in parallel, thereby improving the speed and efficiency of data scans. The following example procedure rewrites the manifests of the employee table:

```
# Generic procedure
CALL catalog_name.system.rewrite_manifests(table)

spark.sql("CALL test.system.rewrite_manifests('test.employee')")
```

Remove Orphan Files

Over time, certain datafiles in an Iceberg table might lose their reference in any metadata files and become "orphaned." These files take up unnecessary storage space and might lead to inconsistencies. The remove_orphan_files procedure takes care of removing these orphaned files.

Here is an example of how to call this procedure:

```
# Generic procedure
CALL catalog_name.system.remove_orphan_files(table, older_than, dry_run)

CALL glue.system.remove_orphan_files(table => 'test.employee', dry_run => true)
```

This procedure lets you do a dry run to preview the orphaned files associated with the employee table to be deleted as part of this operation.

Conclusion

This chapter explored methods for interacting with Iceberg tables from Apache Spark. We looked at the different aspects of these interactions, such as doing the initial configuration, creating and modifying structures with DDL, performing analysis, writing data, and performing table maintenance operations.

Chapter 7 will emphasize the engine-agnostic nature of Apache Iceberg, covering how to perform these same operations from a different engine, Dremio's SQL Engine.

Dremio's SQL Query Engine

Dremio's SQL Query Engine, which is part of the Dremio Lakehouse Platform, is widely used to support various analytical workloads such as ad hoc SQL or low-latency business intelligence (BI) queries directly on the data stored in a data lake. Dremio allows you to query data across multiple data sources, thereby enabling federation of queries and providing a unified view of the data without the need to move or copy it. All of this is done with the support of a vectorized query engine that allows Dremio to achieve fast query results even on extremely large datasets. This, when combined with the capabilities of the Apache Iceberg table format, provides a potent combination to manage and query datasets with improved performance and ease of the UI.

This chapter will provide an overview of how to get hands-on with Dremio and Iceberg.

Configuration

Dremio's Lakehouse Platform has both software- and cloud-based options. In this chapter, the examples will use Dremio Cloud. As discussed in Chapter 6, the first step to get started with Iceberg tables is to define the catalog configuration. To configure an Iceberg catalog in the Dremio Lakehouse Platform, all you need to do is add a new source by going to the Sources section of the Dremio interface and selecting Add Data Source, as shown in Figure 7-1.

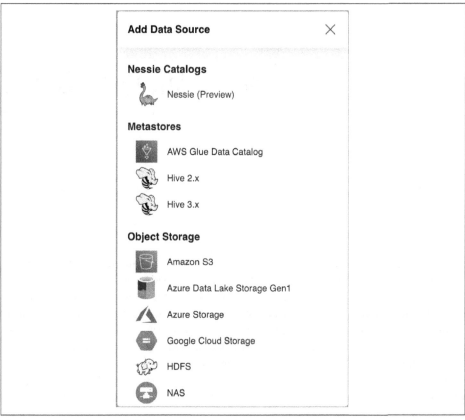

Figure 7-1. Sources available to connect to in Dremio

Here, you can add a new source and choose between AWS Glue, Amazon Simple Storage Service (Amazon S3), or relational databases. Once you make your choice, Dremio will use the proper Iceberg catalog for that data source. Table 7-1 maps the Dremio source to the Iceberg catalog type.

Table 7-1. Apache Iceberg catalog to Dremio source mapping

Dremio source type	Iceberg catalog
AWS Glue	AWS Glue catalog
Amazon Simple Storage Service, Azure Data Lake Storage, Hadoop Distributed File System, Google Cloud Storage	Hadoop catalog
Arctic/Nessie	Nessie catalog

After the configuration is successful, Dremio will automatically connect to the respective Iceberg catalog, and you can start creating your Iceberg table (you may have to specify a warehouse location for certain catalogs for creating tables; refer to the Dremio documentation for your use case).

Data Definition Language Operations

In this section, we will explore how to do DDL operations in Dremio's SQL Query Engine to work with Iceberg tables.

CREATE TABLE

You can create an Iceberg table using Dremio's CREATE TABLE statement. We will discuss a few variations of this command so that you can become familiar with the available options.

Let's start with basic table creation:

```
CREATE TABLE employee (ID int, role varchar, department varchar, salary float,
region varchar)
```

The preceding statement will create a table called employee with five columns and will store it in the source specified. In this case, it is an Amazon S3 source.

CREATE TABLE...AS SELECT

Like other compute engines, such as Spark, Dremio provides the CREATE TABLE...AS SELECT statement to create an Iceberg table from an existing table or datafile:

```
CREATE TABLE employee AS SELECT * FROM mySource."myFolder"."empData.csv"
```

Here, assuming the datafile exists in the Dremio source mySource, Dremio will run the query and create a table called employee to match the schema and records of the query result set.

CREATE TABLE with partitioning and sorting

You can optimize your tables for specific types of queries using specific clauses such as PARTITION BY and LOCALSORT BY. Whereas the PARTITION BY clause partitions the table by specific columns, the LOCALSORT BY clause sorts each Parquet file fragment by the specified column for faster data retrieval.

The following example creates a table called emp_partitioned, which is partitioned by department and is locally sorted by id. This will optimize queries that often filter by department and sort- or range-filter by id:

```
CREATE TABLE emp_partitioned (id int, role varchar, department varchar)
  PARTITION BY (department)
  LOCALSORT BY (id)
```

With Iceberg tables, you can also use more advanced partitioning strategies by employing partition transform functions such as year(), month(), day(), hour(), bucket(), and truncate(). These transformations allow you to partition the data based on time components, hashed values, or truncated values, providing more flexibility and optimization possibilities.

Here is how you can create a table and partition it by a month transform:

```
CREATE TABLE emp_partitioned_by_month
(id int, role varchar, department varchar, join_date date)
  PARTITION BY (month(join_date))
```

CREATE TABLE with row access and column masking

Dremio also allows you to create tables with row access and column masking policies, providing an additional layer of security. The row access policy determines which rows a user can see or modify, while the column masking policy masks specific column data based on a user-defined function (UDF).

Here are some examples that assume you have the UDFs restrict_region and mask_salary:

```
-- Create the restrict_region UDF
CREATE FUNCTION restrict_region(region VARCHAR)
RETURNS BOOLEAN
RETURN SELECT CASE
    WHEN query_user()='jdoe@dremio.com' OR is_member('HR') THEN true
    WHEN region = 'North' THEN true
    ELSE false
END;

-- Create the regional_employee_data table with the row access policy
CREATE TABLE regional_employee_data (
    id INT,
    role VARCHAR,
    department VARCHAR,
    salary FLOAT,
    region VARCHAR,
    ROW ACCESS POLICY restrict_region(region)
);
```

The preceding statement creates a table, regional_employee_data, while restricting access to specific regions.

```
-- Create the mask_salary UDF
CREATE FUNCTION mask_salary(salary VARCHAR)
RETURNS VARCHAR
RETURN SELECT CASE
    WHEN query_user()='jdoe@dremio.com' OR is_member('HR') THEN salary
    ELSE 'XXX-XX'
END;
```

```
-- Create the employee_salaries table with the column masking policy
CREATE TABLE employee_salaries (
    id INT,
    salary VARCHAR MASKING POLICY mask_salary (salary),
    department VARCHAR
);
```

The preceding query creates a table, `employee_salaries`, while masking the salary column for security reasons.

ALTER TABLE

The `ALTER TABLE` statement allows you to modify the structure of an existing table. This can include adding or dropping columns, changing data types, renaming columns, setting or unsetting masking policies, and more.

Let's dive into some examples.

ADD COLUMNS

Let's say you need to add a column called `date_of_birth` to keep track of each employee's birth date. You can use the `ADD COLUMNS` command, like this:

```
ALTER TABLE employee
ADD COLUMNS (date_of_birth DATE);
```

MODIFY COLUMN

If you want to set or unset column masking policies for a particular column, you can do so using the `MODIFY COLUMN` command:

```
-- Setting a Masking Policy on an Existing Table
ALTER TABLE employee
MODIFY COLUMN ssn_col
SET MASKING POLICY protect_ssn;

-- Unsetting a Masking Policy
ALTER TABLE employee
MODIFY COLUMN ssn_col
UNSET MASKING POLICY;+
```

ALTER COLUMN

To rename a specific column present in an Iceberg table using Dremio, you can leverage the `ALTER COLUMN` command:

```
ALTER TABLE employee
ALTER COLUMN role title VARCHAR;
```

This statement changes the `role` column to `title` in the `employee` table.

DROP COLUMN

If for some reason you no longer need the `department` column in your table, you can use the `DROP COLUMN` command to remove it:

```
ALTER TABLE employee
DROP COLUMN department;
```

DROP TABLE

The `DROP TABLE` statement allows you to remove a table from your data source. However, it is important to note that the effect of this command varies based on the data source type. For example, if your data source is an Amazon S3 bucket, the `DROP TABLE` command permanently deletes all the data and metadata files, and hence they cannot be restored. If your data source is AWS Glue, the command deletes only the table from the catalog; the datafiles will still exist in the warehouse location.

Let's assume that you want to drop the `employee` table. The SQL statement would look like this:

```
DROP TABLE employee;
```

This will permanently delete the table with all the associated data and metadata files since the data source here is Amazon S3.

Reading Data

Dremio, with its support for standard SQL, provides a simple and intuitive way to query data. This section will guide you through the different ways to read data from an Iceberg table.

Using the SELECT Query

The most basic way to retrieve data is to use a `SELECT` query, which can query the entire table or specific columns. For instance, to retrieve all data from the employee table, you can use the following query:

```
SELECT * FROM employee;
```

Filtering Rows

Often, we want to retrieve only a subset of the records that meet certain criteria. This is achieved with the `WHERE` clause:

```
SELECT * FROM employee
WHERE department = 'Engineering';
```

The preceding query will filter out rows that don't meet the criterion `department = 'Engineering'`.

Using Aggregated Queries

Aggregated queries allow you to compute aggregated values, such as the sum, average, maximum, and minimum, from an Iceberg table using Dremio. Here are a few examples.

Count records

The `COUNT()` function in Dremio gives you the number of records in a table:

```
SELECT role, COUNT(*) as employee_count
FROM employee
GROUP BY role;
```

This query counts the number of employees for each unique `role`.

Find the average

To find the average salary in each region, you can use the following query, which uses the `AVG()` function:

```
SELECT region, AVG(salary) FROM employee GROUP BY region;
```

Here, the `GROUP BY` clause groups the data by `region`, and the `AVG()` function computes the average of each group.

Sum the value

The `SUM()` function calculates the total for a given column. The following example calculates the total salary for each `department`:

```
SELECT department, SUM(salary) as total_salary
FROM employee
GROUP BY department;
```

Find the maximum

The `MAX()` function in Dremio gives you the maximum value of each column. For example, to find the highest salary in each `job` category, you can use the following query:

```
SELECT department, MAX(salary) as highest_salary
FROM employee
GROUP BY department;
```

Using Window Functions

Window functions perform calculations across a set of table rows related to the current row. They provide an easy way to perform complex computations.

For example, let's say you want to rank employees within each `region` based on their `salary`. You could use the `RANK()` function in Dremio:

```
SELECT salary, region,
RANK() OVER (PARTITION BY region ORDER BY salary DESC) AS salary_rank
FROM company_data.employee;
```

Here, the `RANK()` function is applied to each partition of the data, and ranks are ordered by `salary` within each `region`. A new column called `salary_rank` is added to show the rank of each employee's salary within their region.

Here is the output:

salary	region	salary_rank
28000	EMEA	1
16000	EMEA	2
30000	NA	1
18000	NA	2

Writing Data

Dremio provides multiple data manipulation options, ranging from inserting new data to updating or deleting existing rows from an Iceberg table. We will explore a few of these operations in this section.

INSERT INTO

The `INSERT INTO` operation allows you to add new records into an Iceberg table. For instance, let's say that you want to add two new employees to the employee table:

```
INSERT INTO employee VALUES
    (7, 'Solution Architect', 'Sales', 15000, 'EMEA'),
    (8, 'Product Manager', 'Product', 28000, 'NA');
```

Here, two new rows for each employee with IDs 7 and 8 will be added to the `employee` table.

COPY INTO

Another easy way to insert new data to an Iceberg table is to use the COPY INTO statement. This statement allows you to load data from CSV, JSON, or Parquet files stored in different sources and convert them into Iceberg tables. Here is an example of using the COPY INTO statement:

```
COPY INTO employee
FROM '@mySource/myFolder/'
FILE_FORMAT 'csv';
```

The preceding statement copies all the CSV files present in the folder *myFolder* and inserts them into the employee table. The @mySource can be any storage source connected to Dremio (HDFS, S3, ADLS, etc.).

Here is how to copy just one specific file:

```
COPY INTO employee
FROM '@mySource/myFolder/employee_data.csv';
```

The result of the COPY INTO operation would show the number of rows inserted from the source datafiles to your Iceberg table.

MERGE INTO

When you want to insert new data or update existing data conditionally, you can use the MERGE function in Dremio. This function matches records from two tables (source and target) based on a given condition and performs INSERT or UPDATE operations accordingly.

For example, suppose you have another table named new_employee with updated salary data for existing employees and some new employees. Now you want to merge this table with the employee table. Here is how you can do it:

```
MERGE INTO employee AS e USING new_employee AS ne ON (e.id = ne.id)
  WHEN MATCHED THEN UPDATE SET salary = ne.salary
  WHEN NOT MATCHED THEN INSERT (id, role, department, salary, region) VALUES
(ne.id, ne.role, ne.department, ne.salary, ne.region);
```

DELETE

The DELETE operation allows you to eliminate rows based on specific conditions. For example, if you need to remove all employees from the NA region in the employee table, you would use this query:

```
DELETE FROM employee WHERE region = 'NA';
```

UPDATE

UPDATE lets you modify existing rows in an Iceberg table. For instance, let's say you want to increase the salary of all employees of the Marketing team by $2,000. You could do this with an UPDATE operation:

```
UPDATE employee
SET salary = salary + 2000
WHERE department = 'Marketing';
```

This query updates the salary field in the employee table, adding $2,000 to the current salary for every employee whose job department is Marketing.

Note that Dremio doesn't support join conditions in WHERE clauses when using UPDATE. If you need to use a join condition, you should use a MERGE statement.

Iceberg Table Maintenance

Building upon the discussions from "Iceberg Table Maintenance Procedures" on page 141, it becomes apparent that the maintenance of Apache Iceberg tables plays a pivotal role in managing table size, enhancing query performance, and keeping the relevant versions of data. This involves systematic administration and regular purging of extraneous data and metadata files associated with your Iceberg tables. Dremio, as the compute engine, provides a couple of intuitive SQL commands to deal with a range of table maintenance operations. Let's take a look at a few of these.

Expire Snapshots

Expiring unnecessary snapshots is critical because, over time, they can take up an increasing amount of storage space. Additionally, the accumulation of snapshots increases the metadata size of the table, which can impact the performance of queries. Dremio provides the VACUUM method to expire snapshots from a specific Iceberg table. Here is an example:

```
VACUUM TABLE 'employee'
    EXPIRE SNAPSHOTS older_than TIMESTAMP '2023-07-10 00:00:00.000' retain_last
30;
```

In this case, all snapshots older than 2023-07-10 00:00:00.000 from the employee_data table will be removed, while keeping the 30 most recent snapshots.

Rewrite Datafiles

Dremio provides the capability to optimize query performance by rewriting datafiles. This process of compaction logically combines smaller files into an optimal file size or splits larger files to reduce metadata overhead and runtime file-open costs. Dremio by default uses the binpack strategy to compact datafiles. Let's say you want to rewrite datafiles of the `employee` table to an optimal size of 128 MB. The SQL query would look like this:

```
OPTIMIZE TABLE 'employee'
    REWRITE DATA (TARGET_FILE_SIZE_MB=128);
```

Dremio also allows you to rewrite datafiles for specific partitions. For instance, let's say the `employee` table is partitioned by `year`. Now, if you want to rewrite datafiles only for the partition corresponding to the year `2023`, Dremio allows you to achieve such granular control using a query such as the following:

```
OPTIMIZE TABLE 'employee'
    FOR PARTITIONS year=2023;
```

Rewrite Manifests

Manifest files are used by Iceberg to keep track of data, functioning as an index on the table's datafiles. These manifests are extremely useful for efficient query planning and processing, thereby helping to prune the irrelevant datafiles. However, as with other metadata files, manifests can grow in size, specifically with ingestion of streaming data or frequent DML operations. To mitigate this, Dremio provides a feature to rewrite manifest files based on specific size criteria. The default target size for manifest files is 8 MB.

For example, if you want to rewrite manifest files of the `employee` table, the SQL command will be as follows:

```
OPTIMIZE TABLE 'employee'
    REWRITE MANIFESTS;
```

Conclusion

This chapter explored methods for interacting with Iceberg tables from Dremio. We looked at the different aspects of these interactions, such as initial configuration, creating and modifying structures with DDL, performing analysis, writing data, and performing table maintenance operations.

Chapter 8 will continue to emphasize the engine-agnostic nature of Apache Iceberg, covering how to perform operations from AWS Glue.

AWS Glue

AWS Glue is a fully managed data integration service that provides a streamlined way to prepare and integrate data for various analytical workloads, such as business intelligence (BI) and machine learning (ML). It also offers a user-friendly visual interface that simplifies the process of job creation, execution, and management. By leveraging AWS Glue, users can use the scalable, serverless data catalog to manage their workflows. AWS Glue 3.0 and later versions support the Apache Iceberg table format. This means you can use Glue with Iceberg for a range of operations, such as creating Iceberg tables on object stores such as Amazon Simple Storage Service (Amazon S3), performing read and write operations, or just leveraging the Glue catalog for storing all your Iceberg tables.

In this chapter, you will learn how to configure AWS Glue with Apache Iceberg tables and perform various operations such as CREATE, READ, and INSERT.

As of this writing, AWS Glue 4.0 supports Iceberg v1.0.0, whereas AWS Glue 3.0 supports Iceberg v0.13.1.

Configuration

The AWS Glue integration tool works based on "jobs" that represent a single unit of work, moving data from a source (anywhere) to a destination (an Apache Iceberg table, for our purposes). We will review the configurations needed when creating a job using Apache Iceberg as a source or destination.

Creating a Glue Database

The first step is to create a database in the AWS Glue Data catalog. The Glue Data catalog acts as a centralized repository that stores all the metadata information of your tables. A Glue catalog database acts as a namespace under which many tables can be grouped and governed in the catalog.

To create the database, navigate to the AWS Glue console, and in the left navigation pane, click Databases under Data Catalog. Then click "Add database" and enter a unique name for your database. For this demonstration, let's call it "test." Click Create Database to finalize the creation.

Configuring the Glue ETL Job

To create a new ETL job, we will leverage the Visual ETL interface of Glue. Navigate to the Visual ETL section of AWS Glue in the left navigation pane and select Visual with a Blank Canvas. You will be redirected to the visual editor, where you can begin creating your job.

Configure the data source

Before you start configuring the job, it is important to note that you will create the Iceberg table using an existing dataset stored in an S3 bucket. You will leverage the CREATE TABLE...AS SELECT (CTAS) command to create the table. So, as a first step, you will need to add an S3 source to your visual canvas. To do so, click the Add Node button and select "Amazon S3 (source)" from the list.

Now, in Data Source Properties, add the location of the S3 bucket that stores the dataset, and set the Data Format as CSV. You can find images of the UI for reference on the book's GitHub repository (*https://oreil.ly/supp-guide-apache-iceberg*).

After adding the data source node, go to the "Job details" tab. This is where you will fill in all the necessary information for the Glue job to connect with Apache Iceberg. Let's explore these configurations.

Basic properties

In the Basic Properties section, you'll need to configure several key settings for your Glue job as part of the Apache Iceberg integration. First, provide a name for your job; for example, you can name it "Iceberg_ETL." Next, select an appropriate IAM role that has the necessary permissions for Glue operations. Choose "Glue 4.0" as the Glue version since it supports Apache Iceberg 1.0.0. Set the script language to "Python 3" to specify the programming language for your ETL script. Lastly, specify the requested number of workers as "2" to utilize standard workers for your task.

Advanced properties

Under Advanced Properties, you will see the Job Parameters section, where you will specify the parameters for the job; the parameters are key-value pairs that allow you to customize the job when it runs. The two key parameters for Apache Iceberg usage are `--datalake-formats` and `--conf`.

Set the `--datalake-formats` value to `iceberg` to enable the Iceberg table format for this job. The `--conf` field includes a set of key-value pairs to configure the Iceberg catalog in the Apache Spark session that runs when the job begins (this should be familiar to you as the configurations you used in Chapter 5). Here, you specify the extensions for Iceberg, catalog implementation, and other details.

Here is how the `--conf` parameter value would look (note that the initial `--conf` isn't needed as that is passed as the key of the parameter; also, be mindful of unseen line breaks that may result in configurations being skipped over):

```
--conf spark.sql.extensions=org.apache.iceberg.spark.extensions.IcebergSparkSes-
sionExtensions
--conf spark.sql.catalog.glue_catalog=org.apache.iceberg.spark.SparkCatalog
--conf spark.sql.catalog.glue_catalog.warehouse=s3://<your-warehouse-dir>/
--conf spark.sql.catalog.glue_catalog.catalog-impl=org.apache.ice-
berg.aws.glue.GlueCatalog
--conf spark.sql.catalog.glue_catalog.io-impl=org.apache.iceberg.aws.s3.S3FileIO
```

Finally, ensure that you replace *<your-warehouse-dir>* with the S3 path where you want your tables to be written to.

After defining the required configurations, you can save the job and then head to the Script tab. You should see the job's PySpark script, as presented here:

```
import sys
from awsglue.transforms import *
from awsglue.utils import getResolvedOptions
from pyspark.context import SparkContext
from awsglue.context import GlueContext
from awsglue.job import Job

args = getResolvedOptions(sys.argv, ["JOB_NAME"])
sc = SparkContext()
glueContext = GlueContext(sc)
spark = glueContext.spark_session
job = Job(glueContext)
job.init(args["JOB_NAME"], args)

# Script generated for node Amazon S3
AmazonS3_node1689692483975 = glueContext.create_dynamic_frame.from_options(
    format_options={"quoteChar": '"', "withHeader": True, "separator": ","},
    connection_type="s3",
    format="csv",
    connection_options={
```

```
        "paths": ["s3://dm-iceberg/datasets/salesdata.csv"],
        "recurse": True,
    },
    transformation_ctx="AmazonS3_node1689692483975",
)

job.commit()
```

Note that the imported data here is in a Glue `DynamicFrame`, which is a custom DataFrame construct for AWS Glue. As an additional step, you will convert this `DynamicFrame` to a Spark DataFrame using the method `toDF()`. This conversion is necessary because DataFrames have some methods you'll need in order to convert them into an SQL view. Finally, turn the DataFrame into a temporary SQL view using the `createOrReplaceTempView()` method, as shown in the following snippet:

```
import sys
from awsglue.transforms import *
from awsglue.utils import getResolvedOptions
from pyspark.context import SparkContext
from awsglue.context import GlueContext
from awsglue.job import Job

args = getResolvedOptions(sys.argv, ["JOB_NAME"])
sc = SparkContext()
glueContext = GlueContext(sc)
spark = glueContext.spark_session
job = Job(glueContext)
job.init(args["JOB_NAME"], args)

# Script generated for node Amazon S3, add toDF()
# To Convert DynamicFrame into a DataFrame
df = glueContext.create_dynamic_frame.from_options(
    format_options={"quoteChar": '"', "withHeader": True, "separator": ","},
    connection_type="s3",
    format="csv",
    connection_options={
        "paths": ["s3://dm-iceberg/datasets/salesdata.csv"]
    },
    transformation_ctx="AmazonS3_node1689692483975",
).toDF()

# Turn Dataframe into an SQL Temporary View
df.createOrReplaceTempView("temp_df")
```

Now that all the required configurations have been set, you should be ready to start interacting with Iceberg via Glue. Let's review a few of these operations so that you have a practical understanding of them.

Create a Table Using the Glue Data Catalog

To create an Iceberg table using the Glue catalog, you can leverage the CTAS statement. Note that in the previous step, you created a temporary view, `temp_df`, based on your dataset. So all you need to do is use this view to create the Iceberg table. Go to the Script tab in the Glue job and add the following code:

```
df.createOrReplaceTempView("temp_df")

query = f"""
CREATE TABLE glue_catalog.test.employee
USING iceberg
AS SELECT * FROM temp_df
"""
spark.sql(query)
```

The preceding code created an Iceberg table called `employee` and stored it in the `glue_catalog` within the database `test`.

Read the Table

The `GlueContext` object, which allows you to interact with the Glue catalog, includes a `create_data_frame.from_catalog()` method to return a table in the Glue catalog as a DataFrame. Run the following code in the Script tab of your Glue job:

```
from awsglue.context import GlueContext
from pyspark.context import SparkContext

sc = SparkContext()
glueContext = GlueContext(sc)

additional_options = {}

# Use the create_data_frame.from_catalog() method to read an Iceberg table
df = glueContext.create_data_frame.from_catalog(
    database="test",
    table_name="employee",
    additional_options=additional_options
)
```

Insert the Data

While you can use Spark SQL to do any operation with the Apache Iceberg tables in your Glue catalog, if you want to use the Spark DataFrame API to write to a table, you should use the `GlueContext.write_data_frame.from_catalog()` method. This method writes a DataFrame to the target table in the target database in your Glue catalog. A prerequisite for this is to set the `--enable-glue-datacatalog` job parameter, which allows AWS Glue to use the Glue Data catalog as an Apache Spark Hive Metastore.

The following code inserts data from a df DataFrame into the Iceberg employee table using the Glue Data catalog:

```
from awsglue.context import GlueContext
from pyspark.context import SparkContext

sc = SparkContext()
glueContext = GlueContext(sc)

additional_options = {}

# Use the write_data_frame.from_catalog() method of GlueContext to insert data
into an Iceberg table
glueContext.write_data_frame.from_catalog(
    frame=df,
    database="test",
    table_name="employee",
    additional_options=additional_options
)
```

Conclusion

In this chapter, we explained how you can use AWS Glue to reduce much of the friction in using Spark to do ETL (deploying/configuring clusters, scheduling jobs, submitting jobs, etc.). With its visual editor and integration with table formats such as Apache Iceberg, AWS Glue becomes an effective tool for data integration with Apache Iceberg.

In Chapter 9, we will explore how to use Apache Iceberg with Apache Flink.

Apache Flink

Apache Flink is an efficient stream processing framework that can process batch and real-time data with high throughput and low latency. It has robust features, such as event-time processing, exactly-once semantics, and diverse windowing mechanisms. The combination of Apache Flink and Apache Iceberg brings several advantages. Capabilities in Iceberg, such as snapshot isolation for reads and writes, the ability to handle multiple concurrent operations, ACID-compliant queries, and incremental reads, allow Flink to do operations that were typically difficult with older table formats. Together they provide an efficient and scalable platform for processing large-scale data, specifically for streaming use cases.

In this chapter, we will delve into hands-on usage of Apache Flink with Apache Iceberg. We will primarily look at configuring and setting up the Flink SQL Client with an Iceberg catalog for most of the examples, such as running DDL commands, executing read and write queries, and showing how to do some of these operations using the Flink DataStream and Table APIs in Java. All of these can run on your local machine with the steps provided.

Configuration

Let's start by going over the basic configuration and setup of a Flink cluster, whether you are using standard Flink with jobs written in Java or whether you are using PyFlink, which compiles jobs from Python to Java.

Prerequisites

You can either download and unpack the latest binary from the official Apache Flink website (*https://flink.apache.org/downloads*) or use a specific supported version of Flink with Iceberg. For this demonstration, we'll use Flink 1.16.1. Here are the commands that will set appropriate environment variables, download the binary, and unpack it (it is assumed that you already have Java installed):

```
FLINK_VERSION=1.16.1

SCALA_VERSION=2.12

APACHE_FLINK_URL=https://archive.apache.org/dist/flink/

wget ${APACHE_FLINK_URL}/flink-${FLINK_VERSION}/flink-${FLINK_VERSION}-bin-
scala_${SCALA_VERSION}.tgz

tar xzvf flink-${FLINK_VERSION}-bin-scala_${SCALA_VERSION}.tgz
```

Next, download the compatible Iceberg runtime JAR file and place it in the *FLINK_HOME/lib* directory. This runtime library enables Iceberg integration with Flink. If you want to download the latest JAR, you can get it from the `iceberg-flink-runtime` JAR page on the Maven repository website (*https://oreil.ly/X0W_B*). We will use `iceberg-flink-runtime-1.16` here. Table 9-1 highlights the supported Flink version with Iceberg and the corresponding runtime JAR. These are the two latest versions of Flink maintained as of writing this chapter.

Table 9-1. Flink version and Iceberg support

Version	Initial Iceberg support	Latest Iceberg support	Latest runtime JAR
1.16	1.1.0	1.3.0	`iceberg-flink-runtime-1.16`
1.17	1.3.0	1.3.0	`iceberg-flink-runtime-1.17`

The Hadoop Common libraries are necessary for Flink to interact with filesystems such as the Amazon Simple Storage Service (Amazon S3) and Hadoop Distributed File System (HDFS). Here, you will run the Flink cluster within a Hadoop environment and use a Hadoop catalog for your Iceberg tables. Therefore, you must download a compatible Hadoop version comprising these common libraries. However, if you are running Flink outside Hadoop, you can download the JAR file (v2.8.3 (*https://oreil.ly/hEabL*) is a stable version):

```
APACHE_HADOOP_URL=https://archive.apache.org/dist/hadoop/

HADOOP_VERSION=2.8.5

wget ${APACHE_HADOOP_URL}/common/hadoop-${HADOOP_VERSION}/hadoop-${HADOOP_VER-
SION}.tar.gz

tar xzvf hadoop-${HADOOP_VERSION}.tar.gz
```

Next, set `HADOOP_HOME` to point to the downloaded version of Hadoop and add Hadoop's classpath to your environment variables, like this (this will be used by the Flink cluster when it starts up):

```
HADOOP_HOME=`pwd`/hadoop-${HADOOP_VERSION}
export HADOOP_CLASSPATH=`$HADOOP_HOME/bin/hadoop classpath`
```

You may also need the following classes:

Hadoop AWS classes
> This is required only if you plan to read or write data specifically from Amazon S3. You can download it from the Maven repository (*https://oreil.ly/BKwiq*).

AWS bundled classes
> These classes facilitate interaction with numerous AWS services, including S3, IAM, AWS Lambda, and more. Although the Hadoop AWS library offers basic S3 operations, the AWS bundle allows you to do more complex tasks, such as uploading and downloading items. You can find a stable version on the Maven repository (*https://oreil.ly/xkVum*).

Before we start the Flink cluster, there are two important concepts to understand regarding Flink's architecture:

JobManager
> The JobManager is an orchestrator. It is responsible for coordinating and managing different activities within a Flink application. This includes scheduling tasks, coordinating checkpoints, and handling the execution of code (directed graphs called *JobGraphs*).

TaskManager
> The TaskManager is responsible for executing the tasks assigned by the JobManager. It has a set of slots (the smallest unit of resource scheduling) that allows it to execute multiple tasks in separate threads.

These two components and related parameters can be modified to adhere to your requirements in the configuration file, *flink-conf.yaml*, present in the *FLINK_HOME/lib* directory.

Start the Flink Cluster and Flink SQL Client

Now start the Flink cluster with the following command:

```
./bin/start-cluster.sh
```

This will start the Flink cluster locally on your machine, and you should see something like this:

```
Starting cluster.
Starting standalonesession daemon on host Dipankars-MBP.
Starting taskexecutor daemon on host Dipankars-MBP.
```

Once the Flink cluster is up and running, you can launch the Flink SQL Client using this command:

```
./bin/sql-client.sh embedded
```

As it begins, you will see an ASCII text version of the Flink logo with your prompt changing to "Flink SQL>" to indicate you are now in Flink SQL.

Data Definition Language Operations

Flink SQL provides a range of DDL operations for Apache Iceberg tables. In this section, we will go through some of the common DDL operations that you can run.

CREATE CATALOG

The first thing to configure to start working with Apache Iceberg tables is the catalog. Iceberg by default ships with Hadoop JARs for the Hadoop catalog, but there are also lots of other catalog options available with Apache Flink, such as Hive, REST, and custom catalogs like AWS Glue and Project Nessie.

To create an Iceberg catalog using Flink SQL, you can use the following query:

```
CREATE CATALOG <catalog_name> WITH (
    'type'='iceberg',
    'catalog-type'=<values>
    <config_key>=<config_value>
);
```

There are essential properties to consider when configuring catalogs for Apache Iceberg tables in Flink SQL. The `type` property must always be set to `iceberg` to indicate the catalog type. When working with built-in catalogs such as Hive, Hadoop, and REST, you should specify the `catalog-type` accordingly. However, if you're dealing with custom catalogs such as AWS Glue and Project Nessie, it's important to leave the `catalog-type` unset. Additionally, suppose you're using a custom catalog and have left `catalog-type` unset. In that case, you must specify the `catalog-impl` property, which should contain the fully qualified class name of your custom catalog implementation. These properties play a crucial role in configuring and defining the behavior of your Iceberg catalog within the Flink SQL environment.

The Hadoop catalog

Iceberg supports directory-based catalogs such as the Hadoop catalog in HDFS. Here is an example that shows how to configure a Hadoop catalog using Flink SQL:

```
CREATE CATALOG local_catalog WITH (
  'type'='iceberg',
  'catalog-type'='hadoop',
  'warehouse'='hdfs://nn:8020/warehouse/path'
);
```

This statement will create an Iceberg catalog named `local_catalog`. The `type = 'iceberg'` is a required parameter to let Flink know to create an Iceberg catalog. The `'catalog-type'='hadoop'` parameter tells Flink that this Iceberg catalog is a Hadoop catalog, meaning that it will use any directory-based catalog to manage and store the metadata and datafiles. The `'warehouse'='hdfs://nn:8020/warehouse/path'` parameter specifies the HDFS directory that the Hadoop catalog will use to store metadata files and datafiles. Whenever you create a new table in this catalog, these files will be stored in this HDFS directory. If you want to use a local folder here instead of the HDFS directory, you can do so by using something like `'warehouse'='file:///absolute/path/to/warehouse'`. Another common option is to use cloud object storage here, which can be specified by setting `'warehouse'= 's3://my-bucket/hadoopcatalog/'`. Please be sure to set the `'io-impl'= 'org.apache.iceberg.aws.s3.S3FileIO'` property and download the required AWS dependencies to interact with AWS S3 (as discussed in Chapter 5).

You can validate whether your catalog was created successfully by using the following command:

```
show catalogs;
```

You should see output similar to the following:

```
[Flink SQL> show catalogs;
catalog name
default_catalog
local_catalog
2 rows in set
```

After creating the catalog, you can set it as the current catalog using the following command:

```
USE CATALOG local_catalog;
```

The Hive catalog

Since Iceberg by default doesn't come with Hive JARs, you must make sure that the required dependencies are available in your Flink environment and are loaded when starting the Flink SQL Client. You can download the latest JAR from the Maven repository (*https://oreil.ly/fR1k_*). Once you have the *flink-sql-connector-hive-2.3.9_2.12-1.16.1.jar* file, it needs to be made available to the Flink SQL Client. To do so, you can place the JARs in the */lib* directory of your Flink folder. Once the JARs are in the correct location, you can start the Flink SQL Client.

Once the dependencies are set and the Flink SQL Client is started, you can create an Iceberg Hive catalog using the following query:

```
CREATE CATALOG hive_catalog WITH (
  'type'='iceberg',
  'catalog-type'='hive',
  'uri'='thrift://localhost:9083',
  'clients'='5',
  'warehouse'='hdfs://nn:8020/warehouse/path'
);
```

There are key properties to consider in the context of Hive-specific parameters for configuring Apache Iceberg tables. The 'uri' property pertains to the Hive Metastore's thrift URI, essential for establishing a connection to the Hive Metastore. The 'clients' property, though optional, allows you to specify the pool size for Hive Metastore clients, with a default value of 2. Finally, the 'warehouse' property is crucial as it denotes the storage location, specifying where the metadata and datafiles associated with your Hive-based Iceberg catalog will be stored. These parameters are instrumental in tailoring the behavior of your Iceberg catalog when integrated with Hive within the Apache Flink SQL environment.

After creating the catalog, you can set it as the current catalog using the following command:

```
USE CATALOG hive_catalog;
```

Custom catalogs

Flink also provides support for creating a custom Iceberg catalog implementation by specifying the catalog-impl property. Here is an example:

```
CREATE CATALOG custom_catalog WITH (
  'type'='iceberg',
  'catalog-impl'='com.my.custom.CatalogImpl',
  'my-additional-catalog-config'='my-value'
);
```

The catalog-impl property expects the class name of your custom catalog implementation. For example, if you are using Nessie as a custom catalog, the class name would be org.apache.iceberg.nessie.NessieCatalog.

CREATE DATABASE

Flink SQL comes with a default database. If you want to create a new database, here is how you can do so:

```
CREATE DATABASE iceberg_db;
```

The preceding code will create a new database named `iceberg_db`. This database will be stored within the currently active catalog. To switch your operations into this new database, you need to use the USE statement:

```
USE iceberg_db;
```

CREATE TABLE

The next step is to create an Iceberg table using Flink SQL. Here is an example of creating a table:

```
CREATE TABLE employee (
    id BIGINT,
    role STRING,
    department STRING,
    salary FLOAT,
    region STRING
) WITH (
    'connector'='iceberg'
);
```

The preceding query creates an Iceberg table, `emp`, with five columns. The `'connector'='iceberg'` property tells Flink that you are using the Iceberg connector to create this table.

CREATE TABLE...PARTITIONED BY

To create a partitioned Iceberg table using Flink SQL, you can use a query such as this:

```
CREATE TABLE emp_partitioned_table (
    id BIGINT,
    role STRING,
) PARTITIONED BY (role) WITH (
    'connector'='iceberg'
);
```

The preceding query creates a table called `emp_partitioned_table` that is partitioned by the `role` column.

It is important to note that while Iceberg supports hidden partitioning, Flink has no support for partitioning on columns by function. Therefore, there is no support for hidden partitions when using the Flink DDL.

CREATE TABLE...LIKE

There might be scenarios where you need to create a new table that mirrors the structure and properties of an existing table. Flink SQL provides a very handy command, `CREATE TABLE...LIKE`, for this purpose. This command creates a new table with the same schema, partitioning, and table properties as an existing table.

Say you have a table named emp with two columns, id and role, and you want to create a new table with the same schema and properties. You can use a query such as this:

```
CREATE TABLE emp_like LIKE employee;
```

This will create a new table, emp_like, that will have the exact same schema, partitioning strategy, and properties as the emp table. This is a quick and easy way to duplicate the structure of a table.

ALTER TABLE

Flink SQL provides statements to change the structure of an existing Iceberg table using the ALTER TABLE statement. Here are a few examples.

To rename an Iceberg table, you can use the following query:

```
ALTER TABLE employee RENAME TO emp_new;
```

Let's say you want to change the default write format of a table named emp to avro. Here's how you can do so:

```
ALTER TABLE employee SET ('write.format.default'='avro');
```

DROP TABLE

To remove a table from the catalog, you can use the DROP TABLE statement:

```
DROP TABLE employee;
```

Reading Data

Flink SQL provides both batch and streaming capabilities for reading data from your Iceberg tables. It allows for flexible execution modes, customizable query parameters, and the ability to inspect various metadata properties associated with the tables. In this section, we will delve into the different read operations in Iceberg using Flink SQL.

Flink SQL Batch Read

To read batch data using Flink SQL, you should first set the execution runtime mode to batch. Here is how you can read all data from a table named employee in batch mode:

```
SET execution.runtime-mode = batch;
SELECT * FROM employee;
```

This query runs as a batch job and retrieves the entire dataset at once.

Flink SQL Streaming Read

If you need to process incremental data, you can utilize the Flink SQL streaming mode by setting the execution runtime mode to `streaming`. Here is an example:

```
SET execution.runtime-mode = streaming;

SELECT * FROM employee /*+ OPTIONS('streaming'='true', 'monitor-
interval'='1s')*/ ;
```

Here, the `SELECT` statement starts reading all the records from the `employee` table's current snapshot and then continues to read incremental data. The `/*+ OPTIONS('streaming'='true', 'monitor-interval'='1s')*/` is an SQL hint. In Flink, SQL hints are optional instructions placed within an SQL statement that provide additional information to the SQL planner to change the execution plan. In this case, we specify that the query should be executed in `streaming` mode and that the monitor interval should be set to `1s`, which means Flink will check the Iceberg table every second for any new data or changes.

Metadata Table

To gain insights into your table's historical data, snapshot details, and overall health, such as understanding the number of small files or orphan files the table contains, Iceberg provides metadata tables. These metadata tables can be accessed by appending a $ followed by the metadata table name in Flink SQL. Let's take a look at a few of these metadata tables.

History

The history metadata table allows you to view the evolution of your table over time. You can access this table using the following statement:

```
SELECT * FROM `catalog`.`database`.`table`$history;
```

The result is a history of the table, which can help you understand whether any of the transactions were rolled back, among other things.

Metadata logs

Metadata logs keep track of all the metadata files, including information such as the `latest_snapshot_id` and `latest_schema_id`, as well as the `timestamp`. Here is how to query a metadata log table:

```
SELECT * FROM `catalog`.`database`.`table`$metadata_log_entries;
```

Snapshots

To get information about the snapshots in the Iceberg table, you can query the snapshots metadata table. Here is an example:

```
SELECT * FROM `catalog`.`database`.`table`$snapshots;
```

This table gives you information such as the number of added or deleted records after any write operation and the Flink job ID.

There are also other available metadata tables, such as manifests and partitions. These and others are covered in depth in Chapter 10.

Writing Data

Flink SQL provides a variety of write operations, such as INSERT INTO, INSERT OVERWRITE, and UPSERT, for Apache Iceberg tables. These operations can be utilized in both batch and streaming modes with certain limitations. Let's look at these operations.

INSERT INTO

The INSERT INTO command is used to append new data to an Iceberg table. Here are a few examples:

```
INSERT INTO employee VALUES (1, 'Software Engineer', 'Engineering', 25000, 'NA');

INSERT INTO employee SELECT id, role from emp_new;
```

The first query inserts a single row into the employee table in the selected Iceberg catalog. The second query inserts id and role field values by selecting the id and the role from a different table, emp_new.

INSERT INTO is supported in both the batch and streaming modes of Flink SQL.

INSERT OVERWRITE

To replace data in a table with the result of a query, INSERT OVERWRITE is used in Flink SQL. Since overwrites are atomic operations in Apache Iceberg, they provide data consistency when executing such queries.

Here is an example of using INSERT OVERWRITE in a batch job:

```
INSERT OVERWRITE employee VALUES (1, 'Software Tester', 'Engineering', 23000,
'NA');
```

The preceding query replaces all the existing data in the emp table with the row specified.

Iceberg also allows you to overwrite specific partitions by selecting values. Let's say your `employee` table is partitioned by `department` and you want to make some updates specifically for the employees in the `Engineering` department. You can do so in Flink SQL using the following query:

```
INSERT OVERWRITE employee PARTITION(department='Engineering') SELECT * FROM upda
ted_emp_data WHERE department='Engineering';
```

This query will take the records from the `updated_emp_data` table for employees in the `Engineering` department and overwrite the corresponding partition in the `employee` table.

Note that `INSERT OVERWRITE` is only supported in batch mode, not streaming mode.

UPSERT

Apache Iceberg supports `UPSERT`, a combination of `INSERT` and `UPDATE`. If the record exists, it will be updated, and if it doesn't, it will just be inserted as a new record. This is similar to the `MERGE INTO` operation discussed for engines such as Spark and Dremio. Note that you need a primary identifier in the table to execute this operation. There are two ways to do an `UPSERT`.

First, you can enable `UPSERT` mode as a table-level property, as shown in the following example:

```
CREATE TABLE employee (
    `id`  INT UNIQUE,
    `role` STRING NOT NULL,
    `department` STRING NOT NULL,
    `salary` FLOAT,
    `region` STRING NOT NULL,
  PRIMARY KEY(`id`) NOT ENFORCED
) WITH ('format-version'='2', 'write.upsert.enabled'='true');
```

Here, `UPSERT` mode is set when you create the table and will be applied to both batch and stream modes unless the property is overwritten by the second approach.

You can then do an `INSERT INTO`, and based on the primary identifier of the table, Iceberg will decide whether it has to do an update or an insert, as shown in the following example:

```
INSERT INTO employee VALUES (1, 'Director', 'Product', 33000, 'APAC');
```

Alternatively, you can enable `UPSERT` mode using `upsert-enabled` in write options.

In this approach, `UPSERT` mode is enabled for specific `INSERT` operations, which offers more flexibility. Here is an example:

```
INSERT INTO employee /*+ OPTIONS('upsert-enabled'='true') */ VALUES (3, 'Mana
ger', 'Engineering', 26000, 'NA');
```

Flink DataFrame and Table API with Apache Iceberg Tables

In the previous section, we went through a couple of exercises to explore how to do operations such as executing DDL statements and reading and writing data using Flink SQL. In this section, we will discuss how to leverage the DataFrame and Table APIs using Java, and we'll do some basic operations with Apache Iceberg tables.

Prerequisites

Like before, you will first need to download Apache Flink and all the required JAR files for your configuration. Here is a list of the JAR files we will be using with the Maven download links (note that these are the stable versions as of writing the chapter). Keep in mind that if you are using the alexmerced/flink-iceberg Docker image as per this exercise, all these JARs are already inside the image:

- *Iceberg-flink-runtime-1.16-1.3.0.jar* (*https://oreil.ly/HKUhy*) (Iceberg-Flink runtime)
- *Hadoop-common-2.8.3.jar* (*https://oreil.ly/MJyfc*) (Hadoop common classes)
- *Flink-shaded-hadoop-2-uber-2.8.3-10.0.jar* (*https://oreil.ly/s5TnM*) (Hadoop AWS classes)
- *Bundle-2.20.18.jar* (*https://oreil.ly/KerlT*) (AWS bundled classes)

You will also want to make sure you have Java 8+ and Maven installed. If you'd like to create a local Flink environment for the following exercise, please refer to the book's GitHub repository (*https://oreil.ly/supp-guide-apache-iceberg-ch9*).

Configuring the Flink Job

The first step is to create an empty Maven project. To do so, use the following command:

```
mvn archetype:generate
```

There will be several prompts around the project that you can skip by hitting Enter. You will input the artifactID as **flink_job** and the groupID as **com.my_flink_job**. The artifactID will be the name of your project.

Your project directory will look something like Figure 9-1 after the build is successful.

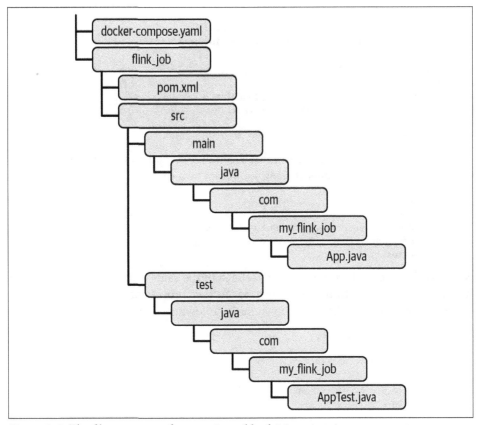

Figure 9-1. The file structure after creating a blank Maven project

Note the following regarding the files listed in Figure 9-1:

- The *pom.xml* file is where you will define your project's dependencies and plug-ins.
- The *App.java* file will contain your application logic.
- The *AppTest.java* file will be used for unit testing.

Since you will be importing a couple of libraries in your application, you will need to specify them in the *pom.xml* file so that Maven can automatically download and include them during the project's build process. Here is a snippet:

```
<dependencies>
  <dependency>
      <groupId>org.apache.flink</groupId>
      <artifactId>flink-java</artifactId>
      <version>1.16.1</version>
  </dependency>
```

```
<dependency>
    <groupId>org.apache.iceberg</groupId>
    <artifactId>iceberg-flink-runtime-1.16</artifactId>
    <version>1.3.0</version>
</dependency>
<dependency>
    <groupId>org.apache.iceberg</groupId>
    <artifactId>iceberg-core</artifactId>
    <version>1.3.0</version>
</dependency>
```

Additionally, you will need to ensure that the Maven compiler properties are set to 1.8 Java 8 or to the proper number if using a different Java version:

```
<properties>
<project.build.sourceEncoding>UTF-8</project.build.sourceEncoding>
<maven.compiler.source>1.8</maven.compiler.source>
<maven.compiler.target>1.8</maven.compiler.target>
</properties>
```

Next, you'll create a class called EmployeeData in the same folder as *App.java*, which will serve as a schema to map your data for further processing. This class includes a few getter and setter methods, as shown in the following code:

```
package com.my_flink_job;

public class EmployeeData {
    private Long id;
    private String department;
    private Long salary;

    public EmployeeData() {
    }

    public EmployeeData(Long id, String department, Long salary) {
        this.id = id;
        this.department = department;
        this.salary = salary;
    }

    public Long getId() {
        return id;
    }

    public void setId(Long id) {
        this.id = id;
    }

    public String getDepartment() {
        return department;
    }

    public void setDepartment(String department) {
```

```
        this.department = department;
    }

    public Long getSalary() {
        return salary;
    }

    public void setSalary(Long salary) {
        this.salary = salary;
    }
}
```

Finally, you'll write the logic for the *App.java* file, which will utilize Flink's Data-Stream and Table APIs to create an Iceberg catalog and a table and insert a few records. Here is an abbreviated version of the code (to see the full code for *App.java*, visit the book's GitHub repository (*https://oreil.ly/supp-guide-apache-iceberg*)):

```
public class App
{
    public static void main(String[] args) throws Exception {

        // setup environment
        // ...

        // create the Nessie catalog
        tableEnv.executeSql(
                "CREATE CATALOG iceberg WITH ("
                    + "'type'='iceberg',"
                    + "'catalog-impl'='org.apache.iceberg.nessie.
                    NessieCatalog',"
                    + "'io-impl'='org.apache.iceberg.aws.s3.S3FileIO',"
                    + "'uri'='http://catalog:19120/api/v1',"
                    + "'authentication.type'='none',"
                    + "'ref'='main',"
                    + "'client.assume-role.region'='us-east-1',"
                    + "'warehouse' = 's3://warehouse',"
                    + "'s3.endpoint'='http://{id-address}:9000'"
                    + ")");

        // Set the current catalog to the new catalog
        tableEnv.useCatalog("iceberg");

        // Create a database in the current catalog
        tableEnv.executeSql("CREATE DATABASE IF NOT EXISTS db");

        // create the table
        tableEnv.executeSql(
                "CREATE TABLE IF NOT EXISTS db.employees ("
                    + "id BIGINT COMMENT 'unique id',"
                    + "department STRING,"
                    + "salary BIGINT"
                    + ")");
```

```
        // Setup Sample Data
        // ...

        // write the DataStream to the table
        tableEnv.executeSql(
                "INSERT INTO db.employees SELECT * FROM my_datastream");
    }
}
```

The preceding code creates a `StreamExecutionEnvironment`, env, that sets up the Flink job and the computation environment. Then a `StreamTableEnvironment`, `tableEnv`, is created that allows you to work with both Flink's DataStream and Table APIs and enables you to convert between the two (as shown in the code). Here, the table environment is used to execute SQL statements such as creating an Iceberg catalog, database, and table.

One last thing to do before you build the package and run the job is to provide the IP address in the `CREATE CATALOG` section. To get the IP address, start the cluster. This is necessary if you are running `docker-compose setup` as mentioned at the beginning of the exercise. If you have a Nessie server deployed with a static IP address or under a domain name, you can just use that as your URI. In this case, we are determining the IP address of the Nessie container in the Docker network.

Starting the Cluster and Building the Package

To spin up your environment, just open your shell/terminal environment and run the `docker-compose up` command.

Once all your configurations are set up correctly, you can connect to the storage container's shell with `docker exec -it storage /bin/bash` and then use `ifconfig` to find the IP address.

From the output, copy the `inet` value of `eth0`. You will use this value to update your catalog configuration. Here's how your updated code would look:

```
"'s3.endpoint'='http://172.27.0.4:9000'"
```

Finally, build the Maven package by traversing to the directory where the *pom.xml* file exists and running the `mvn package` command. The expected output of this build is the *flink_job-1.0-SNAPSHOT.jar* file generated under the */target* directory. This is the file that you will need to use to submit a Flink job to do all sorts of Iceberg operations defined in your code.

Running the Job

Apache Flink provides a web interface that you can see in your browser from `local host:8081`. This UI allows you to manage all things related to a Flink job, including submitting jobs, checking job status, and analyzing logs. To submit and run your job from the UI, click Submit New Job and then click Add New to upload the JAR file. Under Entry Class, enter `com.my_flink_job.App` (the name of your package) and hit Submit.

You can also check the job status from the web UI.

The records should be inserted in your Apache Iceberg table and be queryable with a query engine of your choice.

Conclusion

Using the information covered in this chapter, you should be able to begin taking advantage of Apache Iceberg in your Flink jobs to read and write streaming and batch data. You have learned how to write a basic Apache Iceberg Flink job, the different types of read and write transactions available, and how to configure the jobs for streaming or batch jobs.

PART III
Apache Iceberg in Practice

Using Apache Iceberg as part of your data platform goes beyond the ability to read and write data. You also want to be able to observe your tables' health via its metadata, version your data to isolate ingestion and handle disaster recovery, migrate your existing data to Iceberg, and use Iceberg in several typical use cases. This part of the book aims to guide you through tools and practices you should take advantage of as an Iceberg practitioner.

Apache Iceberg in Production

Data engineers are responsible for collecting, storing, and processing data in a way that is efficient, reliable, and secure. When putting data into production, they need to follow a set of best practices to ensure that the data is accurate, consistent, and accessible. In this chapter, we will discuss many of the tools that can be used to help monitor and maintain Apache Iceberg tables in production. We will start with a discussion of Apache Iceberg metadata tables, which you can use to better understand your Iceberg tables. Then we will cover ways to ensure data quality, including branching to isolate ingestion at the table or catalog level; catalog versioning to carry out multitable transactions; and rolling back the state of a table or catalog when things go wrong.

All the practices discussed in this chapter can be applied in reactive or proactive ways. A *reactive* approach means reacting to situations that already exist, such as rewriting a partition that has already become too large or rolling back a table that has already ingested bad data.

Proactive techniques attempt to prevent problems like these in the first place and include monitoring partition sizes before they affect query performance using metadata tables, and using branching to isolate ingestion so that no bad data makes it into production before quality checks have occurred.

You will want to apply both approaches so that you can prevent problems from occurring and address problems that sneak through. The techniques in this chapter should help you in both cases.

Apache Iceberg Metadata Tables

One of the most powerful features of Apache Iceberg is that from its robust metadata, several metadata tables can be generated that can be used to help monitor the health of the table and diagnose where bottlenecks may exist.

In the past, to see table data with formats such as Hive, you'd have to depend on a particular engine implementing one-off commands, such as SHOW PARTITIONS. Since Apache Iceberg exposes this data as traditional SQL supporting tables, you get the full power of SQL when working with these tables, allowing for sorts, aggregations, joins, and anything else possible with SQL, even time travel.

```
SELECT * FROM catalog.table.history AS OF VERSION 10590355530770364194
```

These tables are generated from the metadata across Apache Iceberg metadata files at query time. Let's first go over the metadata tables that exist and their schemas and then discuss novel ways they can be used to monitor your Apache Iceberg tables. Keep in mind that the metadata tables built into Apache Iceberg are accessible using slightly different syntax depending on the query engine you are using. We will use the Spark, Dremio, and Trino syntax for each applicable metadata table.

As we go through the metadata tables, you'll be able to see an overview of the schema in this text. In the book's GitHub repository (*https://oreil.ly/supp-guide-apache-iceberg*) we have also provided sample table data.

The history Metadata Table

The history metadata table records the table's evolution. Each of the four fields in this table provides unique insights into the table's history.

The first field, made_current_at, represents the exact timestamp when the corresponding snapshot was made the current snapshot. This gives you a precise temporal marker for when changes to the table were committed.

Next, the snapshot_id field serves as a unique identifier for each snapshot. This identifier enables you to track and reference specific snapshots within the table's history.

Following this, the parent_id field provides the unique ID of the parent snapshot of the current snapshot. This effectively maps out the lineage of each snapshot, thus facilitating the tracking of the table's evolution over time.

Finally, the is_current_ancestor field indicates whether a snapshot is an ancestor of the table's current snapshot. This boolean value (true or false) helps identify snapshots that are part of the table's present state lineage and those that have been invalidated from table rollbacks.

Table 10-1 lays out the schema of the `history` metadata table.

Table 10-1. Schema of the `history` metadata table

Field name	Data type	Example value
made_current_at	Timestamp	2023-02-08 03:29:51.215
snapshot_id	Int	5179289226185056830
parent_id	Int or null	5781947345336215154
is_current_ancestor	Boolean	true

You can use the `history` metadata table for data recovery and version control as well as to identify table rollbacks.

With a snapshot ID, you can restore your data and minimize potential data loss. In case of any issues or errors, users can retrieve earlier versions of the data by referring to the snapshot history. You can just query the table to get the snapshot prior to the disaster you want to recover from. Then you can use the snapshot ID to roll back the table using one of the methods discussed later in this chapter.

In the following code snippet, we run a query to get the `snapshot_id` from all snapshots prior to July 11, which we can use to roll back the table to a snapshot before any incident that occurred on that date. Rollbacks will be discussed later in this book.

```
SELECT snapshot_id
FROM catalog.table.metadata_log_entries
WHERE made_current_at < '2023-07-11 00:00:00'
ORDER BY made_current_at ASC
```

The data from this table can be used to identify a rollback of the table. This can be useful to identify when recovery actions have been taken when trying to build context for the table's history. There are two signals to look for in the `history` table to identify a table rollback:

- Two or more snapshots have the same `parent_id`.
- Only one of those snapshots has `is_current_ancestor` set to `true` (`true` would mean it's part of the current table history).

For example, based on the table information provided earlier, it can be inferred that there was a rollback in the table's history at the given snapshot IDs (296410040247533565 and 2999875608062437345). This conclusion is drawn from the fact that snapshot 296410040247533565 is not a current ancestor and shares a parent with snapshot 2999875608062437345.

The following code snippet shows how to query all entries from the history meta-data table:

```
-- Spark SQL
SELECT * FROM my_catalog.table.history;

-- Dremio
SELECT * FROM TABLE(table_history('catalog.table'))

-- Trino
SELECT * FROM "table$history"
```

The metadata_log_entries Metadata Table

The metadata_log_entries metadata table keeps track of the evolution of the table by logging the metadata files generated during table updates. Each field within this table holds significant information about the state of the table at a given point in time.

The timestamp field records the exact date and time when the metadata was updated. This timestamp serves as a temporal marker for the state of the table at that specific moment.

Next, the file field indicates the location of the datafile that corresponds to that particular metadata log entry. This location acts as a reference point to access the actual data associated with the metadata entry.

The latest_snapshot_id field provides the identifier of the most recent snapshot at the time of the metadata update. It is a useful reference point for understanding the state of the data when the metadata was updated.

Following that, the latest_schema_id field contains the ID of the schema being used when the metadata log entry was created. This gives context about the structure of the data at the time of the metadata update.

Finally, the latest_sequence_number field signifies the order of the metadata updates. It's an incrementing count that helps track the sequence of metadata changes over time.

Table 10-2 lays out the schema of the metadata-log-entries table.

Table 10-2. Schema of the metadata-log-entries metadata table

Field name	Data type	Example value
timestamp	Timestamp	2023-07-28 10:43:57.487
file	String	.../v1.metadata.json
latest_snapshot_id	Int	180260833656645300
latest_schema_id	Int	0
latest_sequence_number	Int	1

You can use the `metadata_log_-entries` metadata table to find the latest snapshot with a previous schema. For example, maybe you made a change to the schema and now you want to go back to the previous schema. You'll want to find the latest snapshot using that schema, which can be determined with a query that will rank the snapshots for each `schema_id` and then return only the top-ranked snapshot for each:

```
WITH Ranked_Entries AS (
    SELECT
        latest_snapshot_id,
        latest_schema_id,
        timestamp,
        ROW_NUMBER() OVER(PARTITION BY latest_schema_id ORDER BY timestamp
DESC) as row_num
    FROM
        catalog.table.metadata_log_entries
    WHERE
        latest_schema_id IS NOT NULL
)
SELECT
    latest_snapshot_id,
    latest_schema_id,
    timestamp AS latest_timestamp
FROM
    Ranked_Entries
WHERE
    row_num = 1
ORDER BY
    latest_schema_id DESC;
```

The following code snippet will query all entries from this table:

```
-- Spark SQL
SELECT * FROM my_catalog.table.metadata_log_entries;
```

The snapshots Metadata Table

The `snapshots` metadata table is essential for tracking dataset versions and histories. It maintains metadata about every snapshot for a given table, representing a consistent view of the dataset at a specific time. The details about each snapshot serve as a historical record of changes and portray the state of the dataset at the snapshot's creation. The table includes several fields, each with a unique role.

First, the `committed_at` field signifies the precise timestamp when the snapshot was created, giving an indication of when the snapshot and its associated data state were committed.

The `snapshot_id` field is a unique identifier for each snapshot. This field is crucial for distinguishing between the different snapshots and for specific operations such as snapshot retrieval or deletion.

The `operation` field lists a string of the types of operations that occurred, such as APPEND and OVERWRITE.

The `parent_id` field links to the snapshot ID of the snapshot's parent, providing context about the lineage of snapshots and allowing for the reconstruction of a historical sequence of snapshots.

Further, the `manifest_list` field offers detailed insights into the files comprising the snapshot. It's like a directory or inventory that keeps a record of all the datafiles associated with a given snapshot.

Lastly, the `summary` field holds metrics about the snapshot, such as the number of added or deleted files, number of records, and other statistical data that provides a quick glance into the snapshot's content.

Table 10-3 summarizes the schema for the `snapshots` metadata table.

Table 10-3. Schema of the snapshots metadata table

Field name	Data type	Example value
committed_at	Timestamp	2023-02-08 03:29:51.215
snapshot_id	Int	57897183625154
parent_id	Int or null	NULL
operation	String	append
manifest_list	String	.../table/metadata/snap-57897183999154-1.avro
summary	Map/struct	{ added-records -> 400404, total-records -> 3000000, added-data-files -> 300, total-data-files -> 500, spark.app.id -> application_1520379268916_155055 }

There are many possible ways to use the `snapshots` metadata table. One use case is to understand the pattern of data additions to the table. This could be useful in capacity planning or understanding data growth over time. Here is an SQL query that shows the total records added at each snapshot:

```
SELECT
    committed_at,
    snapshot_id,
    summary['added-records'] AS added_records
FROM
    catalog.table.snapshots;
```

Another use case for the `snapshots` metadata table is to monitor the types and frequency of operations performed on the table over time. This could be useful for understanding the workload and usage patterns of the table. Here is an SQL query that shows the count of each operation type over time:

```
SELECT
    operation,
    COUNT(*) AS operation_count,
    DATE(committed_at) AS date
FROM
    catalog.table.snapshots
GROUP BY
    operation,
    DATE(committed_at)
ORDER BY
    date;
```

The `snapshots` metadata table in Apache Iceberg serves as a valuable resource for managing dataset versions, supporting time-travel queries, and performing incremental processing, optimization, and replication. It enables users to effectively track changes, access historical states, and efficiently manage datasets.

The following SQL will allow you to query the `snapshots` table to see all of its data:

```
-- Spark SQL
SELECT * FROM my_catalog.table.snapshots;
-- Dremio
SELECT * FROM TABLE(table_snapshot('catalog.table')
-- Trino
SELECT * FROM "table$snapshots"
```

The files Metadata Table

The `files` metadata table showcases the current datafiles within a table and furnishes detailed information about each of them, from their location and format to their content and partitioning specifics.

The first field, `content`, represents the type of content in the file, with a 0 signifying a datafile, 1 a position delete file, and 2 an equality delete file.

Next, `file_path` gives the exact location of each file. This helps facilitate access to each datafile when needed.

The `file_format` field indicates the format of the datafile; for instance, whether it's a Parquet, Avro, or ORC file.

The `spec_id` field corresponds to the partition spec ID that the file adheres to, providing a reference to how the data is partitioned.

The `partition` field provides a representation of the datafile's specific partition, indicating how the data within the file is divided for optimized access and query performance.

The `record_count` field reports the number of records contained within each file, giving a measure of the file's data volume.

The `file_size_in_bytes` field provides the total size of the file in bytes, while `column_sizes` furnishes the sizes of the individual columns.

The `value_counts`, `null_value_counts`, and `nan_value_counts` fields provide the count of non-null, null, and NaN (Not a Number) values, respectively, in each column.

The `lower_bounds` and `upper_bounds` fields hold the minimum and maximum values in each column, providing essential insights into the data range within each file.

The `key_metadata` field contains implementation-specific metadata, if any exists.

The `split_offsets` field provides the offsets at which the file is split into smaller segments for parallel processing.

The `equality_ids` and `sort_order_id` fields correspond to the IDs relating to equality delete files, if any exist, and the IDs of the table's sort order, if it has one.

Table 10-4 summarizes the schema of the `files` metadata table.

Table 10-4. Schema of the `files` metadata table

Field name	Data type	Example value
content	Int	0
file_path	String	.../table/data/00000-3-8d6d60e8-d427-4809-bcf0-f5d45a4aad96.parquet
file_format	String	PARQUET
spec_id	Int	0
partition	Struct	{1999-01-01, 01}
record_count	Int	1
file_size_in_bytes	Int	597
columns_sizes	Map	[1 -> 90, 2 -> 62]
value_counts	Map	[1 -> 1, 2 -> 1]
null_value_counts	Map	[1 -> 0, 2 -> 0]
nan_value_counts	Map	[]
lower_bounds	Map	[1 -> , 2 -> c]
upper_bounds	Map	[1 -> , 2 -> c]
key_metadata	Binary	null
split_offsets	List	[4]
equality_ids	List	null
sort_order_id	Int	null

There are many possible use cases for the `files` metadata table, including determining whether a partition should be rewritten, identifying partitions that need data repair, finding the total size of a snapshot, and getting a list of files from a previous snapshot.

If a partition has many small files, it may be a good candidate for compaction to improve performance, as discussed in Chapter 4. The following query can help you break down each partition's number of files and average file size to help identify partitions to rewrite:

```
SELECT
    partition,
    COUNT(*) AS num_files,
    AVG(file_size_in_bytes) AS avg_file_size
FROM
    catalog.table.files
GROUP BY
    partition
ORDER BY
    num_files DESC,
    avg_file_size ASC
```

Some fields probably shouldn't have null values in your data. Using the `files` metadata table you can identify partitions or files that may have missing values in a much more lightweight operation than scanning the actual data. The following query returns the partition and filename of any files with null data in their third column:

```
SELECT
    partition, file_path
FROM
    catalog.table.files
WHERE
    null_value_counts['3'] > 0
GROUP BY
    partition
```

You can also use the `files` metadata table to sum all the file sizes to get a total size of the snapshot:

```
SELECT sum(file_size_in_bytes) from catalog.table.files;
```

Using time travel you can get the list of files from a previous snapshot:

```
SELECT file_path, file_size_in_bytes
FROM catalog.table.files
VERSION AS OF <snapshot_id>;
```

The `files` metadata table in Apache Iceberg offers detailed information about individual datafiles, enabling granular data processing, schema management, lineage tracking, and data quality assurance. It serves as a valuable resource for various use cases, empowering users with enhanced data understanding and control. The following SQL allows you to pull up the data in the `files` table:

```
-- Spark SQL
SELECT * FROM my_catalog.table.files;
-- Dremio
SELECT * FROM TABLE(table_files('catalog.table')
-- Trino
SELECT * FROM "table$files"
```

The manifests Metadata Table

The `manifests` metadata table details each of the table's current manifest files. This table offers an array of useful information that assists in understanding the table's structure and changes over time.

The `path` field provides the filepath where the manifest is stored, enabling quick access to the file. The `length` field, on the other hand, shows the size of the manifest file.

The `partition_spec_id` field indicates the specification ID of the partition that the manifest file is associated with, which is valuable for tracking changes in partitioned tables. The `added_snapshot_id` field provides the ID of the snapshot that added this manifest file, offering a link between snapshots and manifests.

Three count fields—`added_data_files_count`, `existing_data_files_count`, and `deleted_data_files_count`—respectively relay the number of new files added in this manifest, the number of existing datafiles that were added in previous snapshots, and the number of files deleted in this manifest. This trio of fields is instrumental in understanding the evolution of the data.

Lastly, the `partition_summaries` field is an array of `field_summary` structs that summarize partition-level statistics. It contains the following information: `contains_null`, `contains_nan`, `lower_bound`, and `upper_bound`. These fields indicate whether the partition contains null or NaN values, and they provide the lower and upper bounds of data within the partition. It's important to note that `contains_nan` could return `null` when the information isn't available from the file's metadata, which usually occurs when reading from a V1 table. Table 10-5 summarizes the schema for the `manifests` metadata table.

Table 10-5. Schema of the `manifests` metadata table

Field name	Data type	Example value
path	String	.../table/metadata/45b5290b-ee61-4788-b324-b1e2735c0e10-m0.avro
length	Int	4479
partition_spec_id	Int	0
added_snapshot_id	Int	6668963634911763636
added_data_files_count	Int	8
existing_data_files_count	Int	0
deleted_data_files_count	Int	0
partition_summaries	List	[[false,null,2019-05-13,2019-05-15]]

With the `manifests` metadata table, users can perform various operations, including finding manifests that need rewriting, summing the total number of files added per snapshot, finding snapshots where files were deleted, and determining whether the table is sorted well.

With the following query, you can find which manifests are below the average size of manifest files, which can help you discover which manifests can be compacted with `rewrite_manifests`:

```
WITH avg_length AS (
    SELECT AVG(length) as average_manifest_length
    FROM catalog.table.manifests
)

SELECT
    path,
    length
FROM
    catalog.table.manifests
WHERE
    length < (SELECT average_manifest_length FROM avg_length);
```

You may be curious about the pace of file growth in your table. With this query, you can see how many files were added for each snapshot:

```
SELECT
    added_snapshot_id,
    SUM(added_data_files_count) AS total_added_data_files
FROM
    catalog.table.manifests
GROUP BY
    added_snapshot_id;
```

Perhaps you want to monitor your deletion patterns for the purposes of complying with requests to clean personal identifiable information (PII). Knowing which snapshots have deletes can help you monitor which snapshots may need expiration to hard-delete the data:

```
SELECT
    added_snapshot_id
FROM
    catalog.table.manifests
WHERE
    deleted_data_files_count > 0;
```

The following code snippet examines the manifest's upper and lower bounds to see whether they are sorted well or should be rewritten for better clustering:

```
SELECT path, partition_summaries
FROM db.table.manifests;
```

The manifests metadata table can also play a role in managing, analyzing, and optimizing datasets stored in Apache Iceberg:

```
-- Spark SQL
SELECT * FROM my_catalog.table.manifests;
-- Dremio
SELECT * FROM TABLE(table_manifests('catalog.table'))
-- Spark SQL
SELECT * FROM "table$manifests"
```

The partitions Metadata Table

The partitions metadata table in Apache Iceberg provides a snapshot of how the data in a table is divided into distinct, nonoverlapping regions, known as *partitions*. Each row represents a specific partition within the table.

The first field, partition, represents the actual partition values, usually based on certain columns of your data. This allows your data to be organized in a meaningful way and enables efficient query processing as data can be retrieved based on specific partition values.

Next is the record_count field, which indicates the total number of records within a given partition. This metric can be helpful in understanding data distribution across the partitions and can guide optimization strategies such as repartitioning and rebalancing.

The file_count field gives the total number of datafiles present in the partition. It's crucial in managing and optimizing storage, as having too many small files can impact query performance.

Finally, the spec_id field corresponds to the ID of the partition specification used to generate this partition. Partition specifications define how the data is split into partitions, and having the ID readily available aids in understanding the partitioning strategy used.

It's worth noting that for unpartitioned tables, the `partitions` metadata table will have a single record that will contain only the `record_count` and `file_count` fields, as no partitioning is applied to such tables. Also included are delete file record counts and file counts in the `position_delete_record_count`, `position_delete_file_count`, `equality_delete_record_count`, and `equality_delete_file_count` fields, respectively.

While the `partitions` metadata table provides a snapshot of the current state of partitions, it's important to note that delete files are not applied. As a result, in certain scenarios, partitions may be listed even though all their data rows have been marked for deletion by delete files. Table 10-6 summarizes the schema of the `partitions` metadata table.

Table 10-6. Schema of the `partitions` metadata table

Field name	Data type	Example value
partition	List	{20211001, 11}
spec_id	Int	0
record_count	Int	1
file_count	Int	1
position_delete_record_count	Int	0
position_delete_file_count	Int	0
equality_delete_record_count	Int	0
equality_delete_record_count	Int	0

There are many use cases for the `partitions` metadata table, including finding how many files are in a partition, summing the total size in bytes of a partition, and finding the number of partitions per partition scheme. For instance, you may want to see how many files are in a partition, because if a particular partition has a large number of files, it may be a candidate for compaction. The following code accomplishes this:

```
SELECT partition, file_count FROM catalog.table.partitions
```

Along with looking at the number of files, you may want to look at the size of the partition. If one partition is particularly large, you may want to alter your partitioning scheme to better balance out distribution, as shown here:

```
SELECT partition, SUM(file_size_in_bytes) AS partition_size FROM cata
log.table.files GROUP BY partition
```

With partition evolution, you may have different partitioning schemes over time. If you're curious how different partitioning schemes affected the number of partitions for the data written with it, the following query should be helpful:

```
SELECT
    spec_id,
    COUNT(*) as partition_count
FROM
    catalog.table.partitions
GROUP BY
    spec_id;

-- Spark SQL
SELECT * FROM my_catalog.table.partitions;
-- Trino
SELECT * FROM "test_table$partitions"
```

The all_data_files Metadata Table

The all_data_files metadata table in Apache Iceberg provides comprehensive details about every datafile across all valid snapshots in the table.

The first field, content, signifies the type of the file. A value of 0 indicates a datafile, 1 a position delete file, and 2 an equality delete file.

The file_path field is a string that represents the complete path to the datafile. This usually includes the storage system location (e.g., *s3://my-bucket/folder/subfolder/myfile.xyz*), the table name, and the unique file identifier.

The file_format field indicates the format of the datafile. In our example, it's Parquet, but it could be another file format such as AVRO or ORC.

The spec_id field corresponds to the ID of the partition specification used to generate this partition.

The partition field represents the partition to which this datafile belongs. It's usually based on the partitioning scheme defined for the table.

The record_count field gives the total number of records within the file, while file_size_in_bytes represents the size of the datafile in bytes. Both metrics are essential for understanding the volume of data and can be used in query optimization strategies.

The column_sizes field provides a map between the column ID and the size of that column in bytes.

The value_counts field gives a map that represents the total count of values for each column in the datafile. Similarly, null_value_counts and nan_value_counts provide a count of null and NaN values for each column, respectively.

The lower_bounds and upper_bounds fields are maps that store the minimum and maximum values for each column in the datafile. These fields are instrumental in pruning data during query execution.

The key_metadata field contains implementation-specific metadata.

The split_offsets field provides information about split points within the file. It's an array of long values and is especially useful in distributed processing scenarios, where datafiles can be split into smaller chunks for parallel processing.

The equality_ids field relates to equality deletes and helps in identifying rows deleted by equality deletes.

The sort_order_id field contains the ID of the sort order used to write the datafile.

The readable_metrics field is a derived field that provides a human-readable representation of the file's metadata including column size, value counts, null counts, and lower and upper bounds.

Remember, the all_data_files metadata table may produce more than one row per datafile because a file could be part of multiple table snapshots. This table helps in understanding the state and organization of your data at a granular level. Table 10-7 summarizes the schema of the all_data_files metadata table.

Table 10-7. Schema of the all_data_files metadata table

Field name	Data type	Example value
content	Int	0
file_path	String	.../dt=20210103/00000-0-26222098-032f-472b-8ea5...
file_format	String	PARQUET
spec_id	Int	0
partition	List	{20210102}
record_count	Int	14
file_size_in_bytes	Int	2444
column_sizes	Map	{1 -> 94, 2 -> 17}
value_counts	Map	{1 -> 14, 2 -> 14}
null_value_counts	Map	{1 -> 0, 2 -> 0}
nan_value_counts	Map	{1 -> 0, 2 -> 0}
lower_bounds	Map	{1 -> 1, 2 -> 20210102}
upper_bounds	Map	{1 -> 2, 2 -> 20210102}
key_metadata	Binary	NULL
split_offsets	List	[4]
equality_ids	List	NULL
sort_order_id	Int	0
readable_metrics	List	{{48, 2, 0, null, Benjamin, Brandon}}

There are many use cases for the `all_data_files` metadata table, including finding the largest table across all snapshots, finding the total file size across all snapshots, and assessing partitions across snapshots.

The following query first makes sure you have only distinct files since the same file can have multiple records. It then returns the five largest files from that list of distinct files:

```
WITH distinct_files AS (
    SELECT DISTINCT file_path, file_size_in_bytes
    FROM catalog.table.all_data_files
)
SELECT file_path, file_size_in_bytes
FROM distinct_files
ORDER BY file_size_in_bytes DESC
LIMIT 5;
```

If you want to see a total picture of the number of files, the size of those files, and the number of records you have across all snapshots, you can run this query:

```
WITH unique_files AS (
    SELECT DISTINCT file_path, record_count, file_size_in_bytes
    FROM catalog.table.all_data_files
)
SELECT COUNT(*) as num_unique_files,
       SUM(record_count) as total_records,
       SUM(file_size_in_bytes) as total_file_size
FROM unique_files;
```

With the following query you can see the number of files, number of records, and total file size of each partition across all snapshots. You can use this information to help understand your data storage status by partition:

```
WITH unique_files AS (
    SELECT DISTINCT file_path, partition, record_count, file_size_in_bytes
    FROM catalog.table.all_data_files
)
SELECT partition,
       COUNT(*) as num_unique_files,
       SUM(record_count) as total_records,
       SUM(file_size_in_bytes) as total_file_size
FROM unique_files
GROUP BY partition;

-- Spark SQL for All Data Files
SELECT * FROM my_catalog.table.all_data_files;
```

The all_manifests Metadata Table

The `all_manifests` metadata table in Apache Iceberg provides detailed insights into every manifest file across all valid snapshots in the table.

The first field, content, signifies the type of the file, similar to the all_data_files table. A value of 0 indicates the manifest tracks datafiles; a value of 1 indicates that it tracks delete files.

The path field is a string representing the complete path to the manifest file. Like the all_data_files table, this includes the storage system location (e.g., s3://...), the table name, and a unique file identifier.

The length field represents the size of the manifest file in bytes. This can provide insights into the volume of metadata stored in the manifest.

The partition_spec_id field corresponds to the ID of the partition specification used to write this manifest file. This indicates how the datafiles listed in the manifest are partitioned.

The added_snapshot_id field represents the ID of the snapshot when the manifest was created.

The added_data_files_count, existing_data_files_count, and deleted_data_files_count fields provide a summary of the changes in datafiles that this manifest file represents. The added_delete_files_count, existing_delete_files_count, and deleted_delete_files_count fields provide a similar summary for delete files.

The partition_summaries field is an array of structures, where each structure provides a summary for a specific partition in the manifest file. Each structure indicates whether the partition contains null or NaN values, as well as the lower and upper bounds of the partition.

The reference_snapshot_id field represents the ID of the snapshot that this record is associated with. You'll see a manifest listed once for each snapshot it was valid for.

Remember, the all_manifests metadata table may produce more than one row per manifest file because a manifest file may be part of multiple table snapshots. This table helps in understanding the state and organization of your data at a more holistic level than the all_data_files table. Table 10-8 summarizes the schema of the all_manifests metadata table.

Table 10-8. Schema of the all_manifests metadata table

Field name	Data type	Example value
content	Int	0
path	String	.../metadata/a85f78c5-3222-4b37-b7e4-faf944425d48-m0.avro
length	Int	6376
partition_spec_id	Int	0
added_snapshot_id	Int	6272782676904868561

Field name	Data type	Example value
added_data_files_count	Int	2
existing_data_files_count	Int	0
deleted_data_files_count	Int	0
added_delete_files_count	Int	2
existing_delete_files_count	Int	0
deleted_delete_files_count	Int	0
partition_summaries	List	[{false, false, 20210101, 20210101}]
reference_snapshot_id	Int	6272782676904868561

There are many use cases for the all_manifests metadata table, including finding all manifests for a particular snapshot, monitoring the growth of manifests from snapshot to snapshot, and getting the total size of all valid manifests.

While the manifests table will tell you all the manifests for the current snapshot, you can generate this data for any snapshot using the all_manifests table with a query such as this one:

```
SELECT *
FROM catalog.table.all_manifests
WHERE reference_snapshot_id = 1059035530770364194;
```

The following query returns the total manifest size and datafile counts for each snapshot to see the growth of files and manifest size from snapshot to snapshot:

```
SELECT reference_snapshot_id, SUM(length) as manifests_length,
SUM(added_data_files_count + existing_data_files_count)AS total_data_files
FROM catalog.table.example.all_manifests
GROUP BY reference_snapshot_id;
```

With this query you can get the storage being used by all valid manifests:

```
SELECT
    SUM(length) AS total_length
FROM (
    SELECT DISTINCT path, length
    FROM catalog.table.all_manifests

-- Spark SQL for All Manifests
SELECT * FROM my_catalog.table.all_manifests;
```

The refs Metadata Table

The refs metadata table in Apache Iceberg provides a list of all the named references within an Iceberg table. Named references can be thought of as pointers to specific snapshots of the table data, providing an ability to bookmark or version the table state.

The first field, `name`, represents the unique identifier for a named reference. Named references are categorized into two types, which brings us to the second field, `type`. The type can be one of two values: `BRANCH`, a mutable reference that can be moved to a new snapshot; or `TAG`, an immutable reference that, once created, always points to the same snapshot.

The `max_reference_age_in_ms` field indicates the maximum duration in milliseconds that a snapshot can be referenced. This age is measured from the time the snapshot was added to the table. If the age of a snapshot exceeds this duration, it will no longer be valid and will be a candidate for cleanup during maintenance operations.

The `min_snapshots_to_keep` field provides a lower limit on the number of snapshots to keep in the table history. The Iceberg table will always maintain at least this many snapshots, even if they are older than the `max_snapshot_age_ms` setting.

Lastly, the `max_snapshot_age_in_ms` field indicates the maximum age in milliseconds for any snapshot in the table. Snapshots that exceed this age could be removed by the maintenance operations, unless they are protected by the `min_snapshots_to_keep` setting.

Remember, the `refs` metadata table helps you understand and manage your table's snapshot history and retention policy, making it a crucial part of maintaining data versioning and ensuring that your table's size is under control. Table 10-9 summarizes the schema of the `refs` metadata table.

Table 10-9. Schema of the refs metadata table

Field name	Data type	Example value
name	String	main
type	String	BRANCH
snapshot_id	Int	4686954189838128572
max_reference_age_in_ms	Int	10
min_snapshots_to_keep	Int	20
max_snapshot_age_in_ms	Int	30

There are many uses for the `refs` metadata table, including finding references at risk of losing snapshots and finding the latest snapshot of a particular reference.

In addition, you may be wondering whether a particular branch's rules may result in the invalidation of a snapshot on its next update. This query should help filter just references that have max snapshot rules:

```
SELECT name, min_snapshots_to_keep, max_snapshot_age_in_ms
FROM catalog.table.refs
WHERE min_snapshots_to_keep IS NOT NULL AND max_snapshot_age_in_ms IS NOT NULL;
```

The following query will give you just the snapshot ID for each ref:

```
SELECT name, snapshot_id
FROM catalog.table.refs;

-- Spark SQL
SELECT * FROM my_catalog.table.refs;
```

The entries Metadata Table

The `entries` metadata table in Apache Iceberg offers insightful details about each operation that has been performed on the table's data and deletes files across all snapshots. Each row in this table captures operations that affected many files at a certain point in the table's history, making it an essential resource for understanding the evolution of your dataset.

The first field, `status`, is an integer that indicates whether a file was added or deleted in the snapshot. A value of 0 represents an existing file, while 1 indicates an added file and 2 a deleted file. This field allows you to track the lifecycle of each file, providing a glimpse into the changes and modifications the dataset has undergone over time.

Next, `snapshot_id` is the unique identifier of the snapshot in which the operation took place. This ID allows you to connect each file operation to a particular snapshot, which can be beneficial in tracking changes made in specific versions of the table.

The `sequence_number` field indicates the order of operations. This is a global counter across all snapshots of the table, and it increments for each change made, whether the change is an addition, a modification, or a deletion. By understanding the sequence number, you can reconstruct the exact series of operations that led to the current state of the table.

Finally, `data_file` is a struct that encapsulates extensive details about the file involved in the operation. The struct includes fields such as the following:

`file_path`
The complete path to the file in the storage system

`file_format`
The format of the file, such as Parquet or AVRO

`partition`
Information about the partition the file belongs to

`record_count`
The total number of records in the file

`file_size_in_bytes`
The size of the file in bytes

column_sizes
> A map of the size in bytes of each column

value_counts
> A map with a count of total values in each column

null_value_counts
> A map with a count of null values in each column

nan_value_counts
> A map with a count of NaN values in each column

lower_bounds *and* upper_bounds
> Maps containing the minimum and maximum values of each column

key_metadata
> Implementation-specific metadata

split_offsets
> Information about split points within the file

By querying the entries table, you can keep track of each operation applied to your table, offering a comprehensive audit trail of your data evolution. Table 10-10 summarizes the schema of the entries metadata table.

Table 10-10. Schema of the entries metadata table

Field name	Data type	Example value
status	Int	1
snapshot_id	Int	1059035530770364194
sequence_number	Int	0
data_file	List	{0, s3://….parquet, PARQUET, 0, {A}, 6, 609, {1 -> 83}, {1 -> 6}, {1 -> 0}, {}, {1 -> Adriana}, {1 -> Antonio}, null, null, null, 0}

There are many use cases for the entries metadata table, including identifying files added in a particular snapshot, tracking changes to a file over time, and tracking table size changes over time.

For example, the following query will find all entries that match a snapshot representing an added file:

```
SELECT data_file
FROM catalog.table.entries
WHERE snapshot_id = <your_snapshot_id> AND status = 1;
```

This query will return all records for a particular file, whether it was existing, added, or deleted:

```
SELECT snapshot_id, sequence_number, status, data_file
FROM catalog.table.entries
WHERE data_file.file_path = '<your_file_path>'
ORDER BY sequence_number ASC;
```

With the following query, you'll get the size of added files for each snapshot to see the growth in storage needs across snapshots:

```
SELECT snapshot_id, SUM(data_file.file_size_in_bytes) as total_size_in_bytes
FROM catalog.table.entries
WHERE status = 1
GROUP BY snapshot_id
ORDER BY snapshot_id ASC;

-- Spark SQL
SELECT * FROM my_catalog.table.entries;
```

Using the Metadata Tables in Conjunction

By joining these metadata tables together, you can extract even more valuable insights and tailor your data operations more effectively. Let's consider a few examples of how these metadata tables can be joined for different use cases.

Get data on all the files added in a snapshot

You can assess the data added in a snapshot to verify the right number of records have been added, see the growth in file storage in a particular snapshot, and more. To bring up all the file metadata for a particular snapshot, use the following query:

```
SELECT f.*, e.snapshot_id
FROM catalog.table.entries AS e
JOIN catalog.table.files AS f
ON e.data_file.file_path = f.file_path
WHERE e.status = 1 AND e.snapshot_id = <your_snapshot_id>;
```

Get a detailed overview of the lifecycle of a particular datafile

You may be curious when a file was added, deleted, and existed as well as about the state of table operations at each point. Using the following query, you can build a detailed log of a particular datafile's history, allowing you to also see how many files were added and deleted at each point in the file's lifecycle. Also, using the filepath you can identify each operation where the file was involved and use the `entries` and `manifests` tables to gather more information and context around those operations:

```
SELECT e.snapshot_id, e.sequence_number, e.status, m.added_snapshot_id,
m.deleted_data_files_count, m.added_data_files_count
FROM catalog.table.entries AS e
```

```
JOIN catalog.table.manifests AS m
ON e.snapshot_id = m.added_snapshot_id
WHERE e.data_file.file_path = '<your_file_path>'
ORDER BY e.sequence_number ASC;
```

Track the evolution of the table by partition across snapshots

You may want to see how partitions evolve across snapshots, such as how many files
are added. Here is an example query of how you can build that data view. You can use
this as the base for such assessments as the number of files added and the size of files
added by partition:

```
SELECT e.snapshot_id, f.partition, COUNT(*) AS files_added
FROM catalog.table.entries AS e
JOIN catalog.entries.files AS f
ON e.data_file.file_path = f.file_path
WHERE e.status = 1
GROUP BY e.snapshot_id, f.partition;
```

Monitor files associated with a particular branch

If you're using table branching, you may want to monitor those branches to keep
track of storage and optimization needs. With this query you can bring up the files
for the current snapshot of a particular branch:

```
SELECT r.name as branch_name, f.*
FROM catalog.table.refs AS r
JOIN catalog.table.entries AS e
ON r.snapshot_id = e.snapshot_id
JOIN catalog.table.files AS f
ON e.data_file.file_path = f.file_path
WHERE r.type = 'BRANCH' AND r.name = '<your_branch_name>';
```

Find file differences between two branches of a table

If you want to see what files two branches don't share, you can use this query. This
unions the results of two queries to get the unique files in both branches:

```
-- files in branch1 but not in branch2
SELECT 'branch1' as branch, f.*
FROM catalog.table.refs AS r1
JOIN catalog.table.entries AS e1
ON r1.snapshot_id = e1.snapshot_id
JOIN catalog.table.files AS f
ON e1.data_file.file_path = f.file_path
WHERE r1.type = 'BRANCH' AND r1.name = 'branch1'
AND f.file_path NOT IN (
    SELECT f2.file_path
    FROM catalog.table.refs AS r2
    JOIN catalog.table.entries AS e2
    ON r2.snapshot_id = e2.snapshot_id
    JOIN catalog.table.files AS f2
```

```
        ON e2.data_file.file_path = f2.file_path
        WHERE r2.type = 'BRANCH' AND r2.name = 'branch2'
    )

    UNION ALL

    -- files in branch2 but not in branch1
    SELECT 'branch2' as branch, f.*
    FROM catalog.table.refs AS r1
    JOIN catalog.table.entries AS e1
    ON r1.snapshot_id = e1.snapshot_id
    JOIN catalog.table.files AS f
    ON e1.data_file.file_path = f.file_path
    WHERE r1.type = 'BRANCH' AND r1.name = 'branch2'
    AND f.file_path NOT IN (
        SELECT f2.file_path
        FROM catalog.table.refs AS r2
        JOIN catalog.table.entries AS e2
        ON r2.snapshot_id = e2.snapshot_id
        JOIN catalog.table.files AS f2
        ON e2.data_file.file_path = f2.file_path
        WHERE r2.type = 'BRANCH' AND r2.name = 'branch1'
    )
```

Find the growth in storage by the latest snapshot of each branch

Branches are great for isolation and experimentation, but many branches where experimental data has been ingested over time can have storage costs you may want to monitor. This query will allow you to see how much data was added on the current snapshot of each branch:

```
SELECT r.name as branch_name, e.snapshot_id, SUM(f.file_size_in_bytes) as
total_size_in_bytes
FROM catalog.table.refs AS r
JOIN catalog.table.entries AS e
ON r.snapshot_id = e.snapshot_id
JOIN catalog.table.files AS f
ON e.data_file.file_path = f.file_path
WHERE r.type = 'BRANCH'
GROUP BY r.name, e.snapshot_id
ORDER BY r.name, e.snapshot_id;
```

Using the Apache Iceberg metadata tables, you can better monitor the state of your tables to avoid performance bottlenecks and other issues, which helps with taking advantage of Apache Iceberg in a production environment.

Isolation of Changes with Branches

The practice of isolating changes to your data in a Git-like branch can be significantly valuable in modern data workflows, which is why more practitioners should begin adopting it. This approach allows for the separation of different lines of work, enabling developers to make changes independently without interfering with other developers' work or destabilizing the main codebase. It's akin to having multiple parallel universes, where changes in one universe do not affect the others. You can experiment, make mistakes, and learn without the fear of impacting the broader system.

In the context of Apache Iceberg tables, there are two ways to implement this concept: at the table level, which is native to Apache Iceberg regardless of catalog; and at the catalog level, which is possible when using the Project Nessie catalog.

The first method, isolating changes at the table level, involves creating branches for specific tables. Each branch contains a full history of changes made to that table. This approach allows for concurrent schema evolution, rollbacks, and other advanced use cases. It is a powerful tool for handling table-specific changes, but it lacks the ability to provide a holistic view of changes across the entire data catalog.

Isolating changes at the catalog level allows you to manage a complete data lake as a single entity, capturing changes across multiple tables within a branch. Using Nessie, you can take a snapshot of the entire catalog at a particular point in time. This practice facilitates a more comprehensive version control strategy, enabling you to test data transformations, track data lineage, and maintain data integrity across multiple tables.

There are advantages and drawbacks to both methods. Table-level isolation provides granular control and flexibility for individual tables but might become complex to manage in a large-scale data environment. Catalog-level isolation provides a comprehensive, unified view of changes but might be overkill for small-scale or single-table scenarios.

The value of isolating changes to your data on a Git-like branch is multifaceted. It provides developers with the freedom to experiment and make changes without fear of widespread impact, allows for version control and rollback of changes, and promotes greater data integrity and lineage tracking. Whether you choose to implement this at the table level or at the catalog level, using Project Nessie will depend on your specific use case (ingesting data, testing in production, experimental environments) and the complexity of your data environment.

Table Branching and Tagging

Built into the Apache Iceberg specification is the ability for the metadata to track snapshots under different paths, known as *branching*, or to give particular snapshots a name, known as *tagging*. This enables isolation, reproducibility, and experimentation in your data operations with an individual table.

Table branching

Table branching in Apache Iceberg allows you to create independent lineages of snapshots, each with its own lifecycle. A branch is essentially a named reference pointing to a divergent chain of snapshots. Each branch points to the head of the branch, which is the most recent snapshot in the branch's snapshot history. Each branch also has settings for maximum snapshot age and minimum number of snapshots that should exist in the branch.

Consider a data management scenario where you have a pipeline of data to be ingested into an existing table. Before merging the data into the main table, you want to isolate it for validation and quality checks. To achieve this isolation, you can leverage Apache Iceberg's branching mechanism.

In this scenario, the incoming data can be directed to a separate branch (say, "ingestion-validation-branch") without interfering with the main table. You can achieve this with Iceberg's Java API using the toBranch operation while writing to the table (the Java API consists of Java libraries that are part of the Apache Iceberg project that enable common operations on Iceberg tables). This method isolates the incoming data, allowing for validation and checks before it's merged with the main table data.

Here is a Java code snippet demonstrating this process:

```
// Using Iceberg Java API
// String to be used as branch name
String branch = "ingestion-validation-branch";

// Create a branch
table.manageSnapshots()
    // Create a branch from a particular snapshot
    .createBranch(branch, 3)
    // Specify how many snapshots to keep
    .setMinSnapshotsToKeep(branch, 2)
    // Specify max age of those snapshots
    .setMaxSnapshotAgeMs(branch, 3600000)
    // Set max age of branch
    .setMaxRefAgeMs(branch, 604800000)
    .commit();

// Write incoming data to the new branch
table.newAppend()
```

```
    // Append incoming file to the branch
    .appendFile(INCOMING_FILE)
    // Specify the branch to do this operation on
    .toBranch(branch)
    .commit();

// Read from the branch for validation
TableScan branchRead = table
    .newScan()
    .useRef(branch);
```

The creation of "ingestion-validation-branch" allows for the testing and validation of new incoming data, making it an invaluable tool in data engineering workflows. Once the data on the new branch is validated and passes all the quality checks,
the main branch can be updated to the head of "ingestion-validation-branch"
using the fastForward operation:

```
// Updating the main branch to incorporate validated changes from the new branch
table
    .manageSnapshots()
    // Set that the main branch's latest commit should match the new branch
    .fastForward("main", "ingestion-validation-branch")
    .commit();
```

In this way, branching in Apache Iceberg provides an effective mechanism to isolate,
validate, and merge incoming data, thus maintaining data quality and integrity in the
main table.

To achieve the same isolation and validation workflow using SQL, you can use the
ALTER TABLE statement provided by Apache Iceberg. The first step is to create a new
branch, "ingestion-validation-branch", on your table. Let's say you're working
with a table named sales_data in a catalog called my_catalog and a database named
my_db. The branch is configured to retain snapshots for seven days and to always
keep at least two snapshots. Here is the code to do this:

```
-- Create the new branch
ALTER TABLE my_catalog.my_db.sales_data
    CREATE BRANCH ingestion-validation-branch
    RETAIN 7 DAYS
    WITH RETENTION 2 SNAPSHOTS;
```

Next, set the newly created branch as the active writing branch using the SET command:

```
-- Set the new branch to the write branch
SET spark.wap.branch = 'ingestion-validation-branch';
```

Now you can write your incoming data to "ingestion-validation-branch". This
isolates the new data and allows you to conduct validation and quality checks before
it is merged into the main data. The term *WAP* (Write Audit Publish) is a pattern

where you write the data, audit the data for quality issues, and then publish it when complete. For this example, let's assume you are inserting some data into the sales_data table:

```
-- Write incoming data to the new branch
INSERT INTO my_catalog.my_db.sales_data (column1, column2, column3)
VALUES (value1, value2, value3), (value4, value5, value6);
```

Once you're done with any validations, you will need to use Java to run the fastFor ward procedure.

Table tagging

While branching provides a way to create separate lineages of data, Iceberg also provides a mechanism for tagging. Tagging in Iceberg allows for named references to snapshots, facilitating reproducibility.

In the context of supply chain management, consider a scenario where you need to reproduce the state of the table at the end of a quarter for auditing purposes. Tagging enables you to retain important historical snapshots, thereby allowing state reproduction. A tag can be created for a snapshot using the createTag operation, and you can specify how long the tag should be retained:

```
// create a tag
String tag = "end-of-quarter-Q3FY23";
table.manageSnapshots()
    // create a tag out of snapshot 8
    .createTag(tag, 8)
    // set the max age of the tag
    .setMaxRefAgeMs(tag, 1000 * 60 *60 * 2486400000)
    .commit();
```

In this example, a tag named "end-of-quarter-Q3FY23" is created at snapshot 8, and it is retained for one day. Reading from a tag is as straightforward as passing it to the useRef API when setting up a table scan, as shown here:

```
// Read from a tag
String tag = "end-of-quarter-Q3FY23";
Table tagRead = table
    .newScan()
    .useRef(tag);
```

This can also be done from SQL like so:

```
-- Spark SQL
-- Create a tag with a life of 14 days
ALTER TABLE catalog.db.closed_invoices
  CREATE TAG 'end-of-quarter-Q3FY23'
  AS OF VERSION 8
  RETAIN 14 DAYS;
```

Branching and tagging together form a powerful combination for managing large datasets. They allow for isolated testing, easier auditing, and the ability to reproduce the state of your data at any given point in time. Whether you're handling General Data Protection Regulation (GDPR) requirements or navigating the complexities of supply chain management, these features of Apache Iceberg offer the flexibility and control needed for efficient data operations. However, when dealing with many tables, using an abstraction at the catalog level may be a better option.

Catalog Branching and Tagging

Project Nessie, often referred to as Git for data lakes, introduces powerful features such as catalog branching and tagging to enhance your management of Apache Iceberg tables. Essentially, Nessie facilitates a more organized approach to managing vast amounts of data, all while preserving the integrity and consistency of your data.

What distinguishes Nessie is its ability to maintain an always-consistent view of your data across all tables in your catalog. By isolating and independently processing changes, Nessie ensures that users never encounter incomplete changes. Once all changes are finalized, they can be consistently and atomically applied, enhancing the overall data management experience.

With Nessie, keeping track of individual datafiles becomes effortless. It knows which datafiles are in use and which ones can safely be deleted. It allows multiple environments, such as production, staging, and development, to coexist within the same data lake without compromising the integrity of production data.

Crucially, Nessie is designed to optimize data management by avoiding unnecessary duplication. Instead of copying data, Nessie employs a reference system to the existing immutable datafiles. This characteristic, similar to Git, enables Nessie to record all modifications in the data lake as commits without needing to duplicate the actual data.

One of the significant advantages of Nessie is its catalog-level versioning, which offers conveniences over individual table versioning. When working with many tables, managing each table's versioning individually can become complicated and cumbersome. In contrast, catalog-level versioning with Nessie allows you to handle many tables simultaneously and more efficiently, greatly simplifying your data management processes.

Let's further explore how catalog-level branching and tagging using Nessie and Apache Iceberg can enhance your data management strategies.

Catalog branching

Branching, an advantageous feature of Project Nessie when used alongside Apache Iceberg, provides a secure environment for testing new data before it's incorporated into the catalog. By creating a new branch, you can safely ingest and validate batches of data across multiple tables, reducing the risk of erroneous entries across your catalog of tables.

Imagine you are working with a series of large datasets related to an ongoing project, and you receive weekly batches of data. Instead of directly adding this data to your catalog, you can first ingest it into a separate branch, perhaps named "weekly_ingest_branch". This approach would allow you to validate the data before merging it with the main production branch of your catalog.

Here's an example of this workflow using Spark SQL:

```
-- Create a new branch for weekly data ingestion
CREATE BRANCH IF NOT EXISTS weekly_ingest_branch IN catalog;

-- Switch to the new branch
USE REFERENCE weekly_ingest_branch IN catalog;

-- Ingest new data into each table from the branch
INSERT INTO table_name (...);
```

After you've validated the data in your tables, you can merge it into the main branch:

```
MERGE BRANCH weekly_ingest_branch INTO main IN catalog;
```

Catalog tagging

Tagging in the Project Nessie catalog, paired with Apache Iceberg, allows you to mark specific versions of your data, providing an easy way to track and reproduce states of the data at different points in time. This can be particularly useful when conducting quarterly analytics, where you need to reproduce data exactly as it was at the end of each quarter.

For instance, suppose you're conducting financial analysis every quarter. By creating tags such as Q1_end_snapshot and Q2_end_snapshot, you can easily retrieve the state of your data at the end of each quarter. The following Spark SQL command can be used to create these quarterly tags:

```
-- Create a tag for the end of the first quarter
CREATE TAG IF NOT EXISTS Q1_end_snapshot IN catalog;
```

To retrieve the data as it was at the end of Q1, you can switch to the following tag and query the data:

```
-- Switch to the end of Q1 snapshot
USE REFERENCE Q1_end_snapshot IN catalog;

-- Query data as it was at the end of Q1
SELECT * FROM table_name;
```

Using catalog branching and tagging with Apache Iceberg and Project Nessie provides the following benefits:

- Facilitates the safe and isolated testing and validation of new data batches
- Enables easy reproduction of data at regular intervals, such as at the end of each quarter, improving the reliability of analytics
- Assists in maintaining an audit trail of data changes over time
- Aids in identifying different versions of the table for different analytics requirements

Catalog branching and tagging are crucial features of Apache Iceberg and Project Nessie, providing a robust and efficient way to manage and control your data tables at the catalog level. With these tools, you can ensure accurate, reliable data ingestion and easy reproduction of historical data for analytics.

Multitable Transactions

Multitable transactions are a fundamental concept in databases that support consistency and atomicity of operations spanning multiple tables. In a *multitable transaction*, multiple operations, possibly involving different tables, are treated as a single atomic unit of work. This means that either all operations in the transaction succeed, or if any operation fails, all the changes made within that transaction are rolled back, thereby leaving the database in a consistent state.

The importance of multitable transactions primarily lies in their ability to maintain data consistency, which is a crucial aspect of database management systems. Consider a supply chain management system where an order placement involves updating an Orders table and decrementing the stock in an Inventory table. If these operations were not part of a single transaction, a failure in updating the Inventory table after the Orders table was updated could lead to data inconsistency—the system would show an order that was placed, but the inventory would not reflect the decrease in stock.

With multitable transactions, the entire process is treated as a single atomic operation. This means that if updating the Inventory table fails, the changes made to the Orders table would also be rolled back, thus ensuring that the data remains consistent.

Furthermore, multitable transactions are also essential for isolation, another key property of reliable database systems. They ensure that concurrent transactions do not interfere with each other, thereby avoiding potential data inconsistencies and conflicts.

In summary, multitable transactions are vital for maintaining data consistency and isolation in database systems. They allow multiple operations, possibly involving different tables, to be treated as a single atomic unit of work, ensuring that either all operations succeed or all changes are rolled back in the event of a failure. This is especially crucial in complex systems such as supply chain management where data integrity and consistency are paramount.

You can achieve multitable transactions using a Project Nessie catalog by branching the catalog and then running transactions on multiple tables from the branch. All operations from the branch, regardless of which tables, engine, or user is running the transaction, will be isolated from the main production branch.

Once you are happy with the state of the branch and all the catalog tables, you can then merge those changes back into the main branch as shown in the following code. Or, if you're not happy with all of that, you can drop the branch so that none of the changes is seen by anyone else:

```
-- Create a Branch
CREATE BRANCH IF NOT EXISTS etl IN catalog;

-- Switch to Branch (Spark SQL)
USE REFERENCE ingest IN catalog;

-- Run transactions on multiple tables
INSERT INTO catalog.db.tableA ...;
INSERT INTO catalog.db.tableB ...;

-- When done, merge all the transaction simultaneously in production branch
MERGE BRANCH etl INTO main IN catalog;
```

Rolling Back Changes

Catalog- and table-level rollbacks are crucial concepts in data management that greatly contribute to maintaining high data quality.

Table-level rollbacks are a specific data management technique that allows changes to a table to be reversed or "rolled back" to a previous state. This can be particularly useful in situations where an error has occurred during data processing or when a change has led to unexpected results. With the ability to roll back changes, it's possible to revert the data to a state of known good quality, thereby mitigating the impact of errors or problematic changes.

Together, catalog- and table-level rollbacks offer a safeguard against errors and changes that might adversely affect data quality. This combination makes it easier to maintain high-quality, reliable data, which is especially important in data-intensive fields such as data science, machine learning, and business analytics. Data quality directly impacts the reliability of insights drawn from the data, making these concepts critical for ensuring accurate, reliable decision making based on data.

Rolling Back at the Table Level

Rollbacks allow a table in an undesirable state due to a bad ingestion job to have essentially an undo button. This capability is critical in scenarios where an erroneous data update has occurred and you need to revert the table to its previous consistent state. Apache Iceberg has four Spark procedures that can be used to manage the current state of the table: `rollback_to_snapshot`, `rollback_to_timestamp`, `set_cur rent_snapshot`, and `cherrypick_snapshot`. The metadata tables are a great tool for discovering what snapshots you'd want to roll back to using many of the metadata table queries we discussed earlier.

rollback_to_snapshot

Apache Iceberg provides a procedure called `rollback_to_snapshot` to roll back a table based on a snapshot ID. To run the `rollback_to_snapshot` procedure you need to provide it with two pieces of information: the name of the table and the ID of the snapshot you want to roll back to. For example, if you have a table called `orders` and you want to roll back to snapshot 12345, you would use the following command:

```
spark.sql("CALL catalog.database.rollback_to_snapshot('orders', 12345)")
```

When this procedure is invoked, the current table state is changed to point to the provided snapshot ID. The metadata and datafiles of the table and its snapshot remain unchanged, which means this operation is nondestructive. It is designed to be safe to run concurrently with other operations on the table, preventing any potential conflicts.

As an example, let's consider a situation where you have made some updates to your `orders` table, and you realize that an error in the update logic has introduced incorrect values for some of the records. If you have a snapshot of the table taken before the erroneous update, you can roll back the table to this snapshot, thereby restoring the correct state of your data:

```
# Assume the snapshot before the erroneous update was 12345
spark.sql("CALL catalog.database.rollback_to_snapshot('orders', 12345)")
```

It is also possible to adjust the behavior of rollback operations by altering certain settings in Apache Iceberg. For instance, you can set the `rollback_to_snap shot.expire_snapshots.enabled` property to `false` to prevent the automatic removal of snapshots older than the table's expiration period after a rollback. You can also set the `rollback_to_snapshot.expire_snapshots.snapshot_age_ms` property to control the age threshold for removing snapshots after a rollback:

```
spark.sql("""
CALL catalog.database.alter_table_properties(
    'orders',
    map(
```

```
    'rollback_to_snapshot.expire_snapshots.enabled', 'false',
    'rollback_to_snapshot.expire_snapshots.snapshot_age_ms', '172800000'
  -- 2 days in milliseconds
    )
  )
  """)
```

This setting ensures that snapshots older than one day are not automatically removed after a rollback, giving you more control over the snapshot lifecycle and ensuring that you can still roll back to these older snapshots if needed.

rollback_to_timestamp

Sometimes you don't know the exact ID of the snapshot you want to roll back to, but you do know the moment in time, and this is where the `rollback_to_timestamp` procedure becomes very useful. This procedure requires the name of the table to update and a timestamp to roll back to as arguments. It invalidates all cached Spark plans that reference the affected table, ensuring that any subsequent operations will be based on the updated state of the table. The output of this procedure includes the current snapshot ID before the rollback (`previous_snapshot_id`) and the new current snapshot ID (`current_snapshot_id`).

Consider a scenario where you have a table named `orders` and you want to roll back this table to a state that was current at a specific timestamp, say 2023-06-01 00:00:00. In Apache Spark with Iceberg, you would use the `CALL` statement with the `rollback_to_timestamp` procedure:

```scala
// This code is in Scala

// Use the procedure to rollback the table
spark.sql(s"CALL iceberg.system.rollback_to_timestamp('db.orders', time
stamp('2023-06-01 00:00:00'))")
```

This statement calls the `rollback_to_timestamp` procedure on the `orders` table to roll back the table to the snapshot that was current at 2023-06-01 00:00:00. It's important to note that you need to have the necessary permissions to perform this operation on the table.

set_current_snapshot

The `set_current_snapshot` procedure sets the current snapshot ID for a table. Unlike a rollback, you're setting the table not to a snapshot in its history but to any arbitrary snapshot available, which could be on a different branch or tag. This capability allows users to switch between different versions of the table, even if they aren't sequentially related. Before using the `set_current_snapshot` procedure, you need to provide two pieces of information: the name of the table and the snapshot ID of the snapshot that should be made the "current" snapshot. The output is similar to `rollback_to_timestamp`, providing the snapshot ID before the change and the new current snapshot ID.

Say you have a table named `inventory` and you want to set its current snapshot to a specific snapshot ID; for example, 123456789. In Apache Spark with Iceberg, you would use the `CALL` statement with the `set_current_snapshot` procedure, as shown in the following code:

```scala
// This code is in Scala

// Specify the table to update
val tableName = "db.inventory"

// Specify the snapshot ID to set as current
val snapshotId = 123456789L

// Use the procedure to set the current snapshot
spark.sql(s"CALL iceberg.system.set_current_snapshot('$tableName', $snapshotId)")
```

This statement calls the `set_current_snapshot` procedure on the `inventory` table to set the current snapshot to the ID 123456789. Remember that you need to have the necessary permissions to perform this operation on the table.

cherrypick_snapshot

The `cherrypick_snapshot` procedure creates a new snapshot incorporating the changes from another snapshot in a metadata-only operation (no new datafiles are created). To run the `cherrypick_snapshot` procedure you need to provide two parameters: the name of the table you're updating as well as the ID of the snapshot the table should be updated based on. This transaction will return the snapshot IDs before and after the cherry-pick operation as `source_snapshot_id` and `current_snapshot_id`.

For example, say you have a table named `products` and you want to cherry-pick changes from a snapshot with ID 987654321. In Apache Spark with Iceberg, you would use the `CALL` statement with the `cherrypick_snapshot` procedure. Here's an example:

```scala
// This Code is in Scala

// Use the procedure to cherry-pick the snapshot
spark.sql(s"CALL iceberg.system.cherrypick_snapshot('db.products', 987654321)")
```

This statement calls the `cherrypick_snapshot` procedure on the `products` table to cherry-pick changes from the snapshot with the ID 987654321.

These procedures provide powerful tools to manage and manipulate the state of an Apache Iceberg table. They offer flexibility and control over table versions, allowing users to roll back changes, set specific snapshots as the current state, or cherry-pick changes from one snapshot to another. This facilitates effective data versioning and historical analysis, which are essential in modern data science and analytics workflows.

Rolling Back at the Catalog Level

One of the key benefits of using Nessie as your Apache Iceberg catalog is the ability to roll back data at the catalog level. Just like how version control systems allow software developers to roll back their entire codebase to a previous version, Nessie enables data engineers and data scientists to roll back their entire data environment to a previous state. This functionality is incredibly valuable in a variety of scenarios.

For instance, imagine a scenario where a data engineer runs a batch job that modifies a large number of datasets but later realizes that there was a mistake in the transformation logic. Without a tool like Nessie, rectifying this mistake could require rolling back each Iceberg table one by one. However, with Nessie, the engineer can simply roll back the entire catalog to the state before the faulty batch job was run, effectively undoing the mistake for every table in an instant.

Rollbacks in Nessie can be performed using SQL through integrations with tools such as Apache Hive, Apache Spark, and Dremio's SQL Query Engine. Here is an example of how to roll back data in SQL with Project Nessie. First, you'll need to find the hash of the commit that you want to roll back to. This can be done using the SHOW LOG command:

```
SHOW LOG nessie.main
```

This will display a list of all commits on the main branch, along with their hashes. Once you have identified the commit hash that you want to roll back to, you can use the SET REF command to change the head of the branch to that commit:

```
SET REF nessie.main TO 'commitHash'
```

This command changes the head of the main branch to the specified commit hash from before the bad transaction, effectively rolling back all changes that were made after that commit.

Keep in mind that this command doesn't make a permanent change; it makes the change only for the current session. If you want to make the rollback permanent, you can use the ASSIGN command instead of SET REF:

```
ASSIGN nessie.main AT 'commitHash'
```

This command will permanently roll back the main branch to the specified commit, allowing all users to see the data as it was at that commit.

Nessie's ability to roll back data at the catalog level provides a powerful tool for managing your data. It allows for easier recovery from mistakes, facilitates experimentation with data transformations, and simplifies the process of maintaining consistency across different environments. Catalog-level rollbacks are a great remedy when data recovery in production must occur quickly and across many tables.

Conclusion

The robust capabilities provided by Apache Iceberg metadata tables, branching and tagging for Iceberg tables, multitable transactions, and Iceberg table rollback play a fundamental role in effective production data management, allowing both proactive and reactive approaches. In fact, Apache Iceberg metadata tables are integral to proactive and reactive data management, granting users an in-depth understanding of their data landscape, tracking schema changes and partition evolutions. This critical insight allows teams to make informed decisions, optimize data architecture, and anticipate needs.

Branching and tagging further enhance proactive management by offering safe environments to test changes or new features without disrupting production data, enabling iterative development and constant improvement. These features also aid in maintaining version control and facilitating experiment reproducibility.

On the reactive side, multitable transactions provide a higher level of control and consistency. They ensure that related changes across multiple tables are handled as a single atomic operation, preventing partial updates and ensuring the integrity of the data environment.

Lastly, Iceberg table rollback offers a crucial recovery mechanism in case of errors or unforeseen consequences of changes. This ensures the ability to revert to a previous state, making it an essential tool for risk mitigation and data integrity in a reactive data management strategy.

Together, these features constitute a robust framework for managing production data effectively, balancing forward-thinking strategies with responsive, adaptive measures to maintain the health, integrity, and efficiency of the data ecosystem.

In Chapter 11, we'll explore different ways to handle streaming data with Apache Iceberg.

Streaming with Apache Iceberg

Streaming data refers to the continuous generation and processing of data, often coming from various sources. These sources can include logfiles, sensor data, social media feeds, and financial transactions, among others. The data is sent in small sizes (or packets) to allow real-time insights and reactions. The nature of streaming data is that it is in constant motion and does not have a finite beginning or end.

The concept of streaming data is essential in the current age of digital information, where businesses, research institutions, and government agencies often need to analyze and make decisions based on the freshest data possible. For example, financial institutions may use streaming data to detect fraudulent transactions as they occur. Similarly, social media platforms use streaming data to customize and update user feeds based on real-time engagement metrics.

There are several reasons why one might want to stream data into an Apache Iceberg table:

Scalability and performance
    Apache Iceberg is designed to efficiently store and retrieve information from large datasets. The file management procedures enable it to optimize performance of an ever-changing/growing dataset, making it an excellent choice for streaming analytics.

Schema evolution
    As data changes over time, the structure of the data (the schema) may need to evolve as well. Apache Iceberg allows for schema evolution without interrupting ongoing data streaming processes, making it easier to adapt to changing data requirements.

Reliability
> Apache Iceberg provides snapshot isolation, meaning that each transaction operates on an unchanging snapshot of the table. This feature ensures consistent and reliable data, even in environments with many concurrent operations.

Time travel
> Iceberg stores a full history of the table's metadata, which allows time-travel queries that can access previous versions of the table.

By streaming data into an Apache Iceberg table, organizations can manage and analyze their real-time data more efficiently and flexibly, adapting to changes and maintaining reliability in their data analytics operations.

Streaming with Spark

One of the main features of Apache Spark is its ability to process streaming data. This is managed through Spark Streaming, a Spark component that enables scalable, high-throughput, fault-tolerant stream processing of live data streams. Here are some key features of Spark Streaming:

Fault tolerance
> Spark Streaming is designed to be resilient to failures, with built-in recovery mechanisms. If a node goes down during a computation, the system can recover quickly and continue processing.

Integration
> Spark Streaming integrates seamlessly with other Spark components such as Spark MLlib and Spark SQL, enabling powerful combined use cases. For example, you can use MLlib to build a machine learning (ML) model on a large dataset with Spark and then apply that model to a live data stream with Spark Streaming.

Real-time processing
> Spark Streaming can process live data streams in real time. It divides incoming data into batches, which are then processed by the Spark engine to generate the final stream of results in batches.

Window operations
> Spark Streaming provides windowed computations, where transformations on Resilient Distributed Datasets (RDDs), Spark's fundamental data structure, can be applied over a sliding window of data. This is useful in many scenarios, such as computing trends over the last few hours in a data stream.

High throughput
> Spark Streaming is designed to process a large amount of data, making it suitable for applications that need to process high-volume live data streams.

Multiple data sources
> Spark Streaming can ingest data from various sources, including Kafka, Flume, and Kinesis, among others.

Apache Spark's microbatching approach sets it apart from other streaming engines, making it a compelling choice for real-time data processing. This approach involves processing data in small, discrete batches rather than handling each data point individually. This design decision represents a trade-off between factors such as latency, throughput, and cost.

By breaking data into microbatches, Apache Spark gains several advantages. First, it enhances fault tolerance, as any failures can be more easily managed within each batch. Second, it seamlessly integrates with other Spark components, allowing for a unified ecosystem for both batch and real-time processing. Additionally, this approach enables real-time processing capabilities, as the microbatches are processed continuously at a rapid pace. Lastly, it achieves high throughput, efficiently handling large volumes of data.

Overall, Apache Spark's microbatching approach strikes a balance between responsiveness, data volume handling, and resource efficiency, making it a favored choice in the realm of big data and streaming applications.

In the following section, we provide an example of Apache Spark ingesting data from Kafka into Apache Iceberg using Spark Streaming.

Streaming into Iceberg with Spark

Using Spark's DataSourceV2 API allows data engineers to read and write from tables in a structured and scalable manner.

In Spark Structured Streaming, Spark's SQL-based streaming API, Iceberg is fully compatible with DataFrame reads and writes as of Spark 3. A key feature of this integration is the support for processing incremental data, which starts from a historical timestamp. Only append snapshots are supported in the context of streaming reads from an Iceberg table.

Spark's DataStreamWriter is used to write data into an Iceberg table in a streaming fashion. Iceberg supports two output modes: append, which appends rows of every microbatch to the table; and complete, which replaces the table contents at each microbatch.

When writing against a partitioned table, Iceberg necessitates that the data be sorted as per the partition specification. While explicit sorting is recommended for batch queries, it may not be practical for streaming due to the incurred latency. To bypass this, Iceberg provides a fanout writer option that eliminates the need for sorting, thereby reducing latency. A fanout writer is a technique to optimize performance.

Maintaining streaming tables on Iceberg is crucial. Streaming queries can quickly generate new table versions, leading to a significant amount of table metadata and small datafiles. For effective metadata management, strategies such as tuning the rate of commits, expiring old snapshots, compacting datafiles, and rewriting manifests are recommended.

Tuning the commit rate helps control the number of datafiles, manifests, and snapshots, simplifying table maintenance. If not managed, old snapshots can accumulate rapidly and should be regularly expired and removed. The compaction of datafiles helps to reduce metadata and enhance query efficiency, while rewriting manifests optimizes write latency and compacts small manifest files. These operations on table maintenance and optimization are covered in detail in Chapter 4.

Let's look at an example of streaming financial data into Apache Iceberg tables using Spark Structured Streaming, which allows you to continuously capture real-time market data, transactions, and portfolio updates. We'll walk through a simple example using hypothetical financial data. We'll assume we read the data from a Kafka topic and write it to an Iceberg table.

First, we'll use Scala to set up our Spark Session:

```
val spark = SparkSession.builder()
    .appName("FinancialDataStreaming")
    .getOrCreate()
```

Let's assume we have a Kafka topic, financialData, where every message is a JSON string of financial data that contains the following fields: timestamp, symbol, price, and volume. We use the readStream method to read from Kafka:

```
val df = spark.readStream
    .format("kafka")
    .option("kafka.bootstrap.servers", "localhost:9092")
    .option("subscribe", "financialData")
    .load()
```

Then we convert the Kafka stream into a DataFrame of Stock objects:

```
val financialData = df.selectExpr("CAST(value AS STRING)").as[String]
    .map(Stock.from_json(_))
```

The Stock class can be defined as follows:

```
case class Stock(timestamp: Long, symbol: String, price: Double, volume: Long)
object Stock {
  def from_json(jsonString: String): Stock = {
    val parser = new ObjectMapper()
    parser.registerModule(DefaultScalaModule)
    parser.readValue(jsonString, classOf[Stock])
  }
}
```

Now that we have our data stream, we can start appending the data into our Iceberg table. The append output mode is used since we want to add new data without affecting the existing data:

```
val tableIdentifier = "s3://someBucket/financial_data/stock"

financialData.writeStream
    .format("iceberg")
    .outputMode("append")
    .trigger(Trigger.ProcessingTime(1, TimeUnit.MINUTES))
    .option("path", tableIdentifier)
    .option("checkpointLocation", "/tmp/checkpoints")
    .start()
```

If the Iceberg table is partitioned, say, by symbol, we need to enable the fanout-enabled option to eliminate the requirement for data sorting:

```
financialData.writeStream
    .format("iceberg")
    .outputMode("append")
    .trigger(Trigger.ProcessingTime(1, TimeUnit.MINUTES))
    .option("path", tableIdentifier)
    .option("fanout-enabled", "true")
    .option("checkpointLocation", "/tmp/checkpoints")
    .start()
```

Finally, considering the rapid growth of data, we need to take care of the table's maintenance by tuning the rate of commits, expiring old snapshots, compacting datafiles, and rewriting manifests. This ensures that the table stays performant and manageable. A combination of these strategies will ensure that your streaming data platform remains reliable and robust.

Streaming from Iceberg with Spark

While streaming into Iceberg tables focuses on ingesting real-time data, streaming from Iceberg involves reading this data for various downstream applications and analytics tasks. Using Spark Structured Streaming, data engineers can efficiently read and process data stored in Iceberg tables.

Using the DataSourceV2 API in Spark 3, Iceberg supports processing incremental data starting from a historical timestamp, as shown in the following code:

```
val df = spark.readStream
    .format("iceberg")
    .option("stream-from-timestamp", Long.toString(streamStartTimestamp))
    .load(tableName)
```

For streaming read operations from an Iceberg table, it's essential to note that Iceberg only supports reading data from append snapshots. Moreover, it's important to design the downstream applications to handle the real-time data streamed from Iceberg appropriately. Depending on the use case, this might involve real-time analytics, alerts, or further processing.

Sharing real-time data with partners is a common use case in today's interconnected business environments. When both entities use Iceberg tables, the process can be streamlined using Spark Structured Streaming. Here's an example of how this can be achieved.

Let's assume you want to share your Iceberg table our_database.our_table with a partner, and they want this data streamed into their Iceberg table, partner_data base.partner_table. First, you'll set up the Spark Session for reading from your table:

```
val spark = SparkSession.builder()
    .appName("IcebergDataSharing")
    .getOrCreate()
```

Next, initiate a stream to read from your Iceberg table:

```
val ourDF = spark.readStream
    .format("iceberg")
    .option("stream-from-timestamp", Long.toString(streamStartTimestamp))
    .load(sourceTableName)
```

Now you'll write this data stream to the partner's Iceberg table. Considering the nature of the streaming data, you'll use the append mode:

```
ourDF.writeStream
    .format("iceberg")
    .outputMode("append")
    .trigger(Trigger.ProcessingTime(1, TimeUnit.MINUTES))
    .option("path", destinationTableName)
    .option("checkpointLocation", checkpointPath)
    .start()
```

If the partner's Iceberg table has partitions, say, by a column named region, you'll want to ensure that the data writes are optimized:

```
ourDF.writeStream
    .format("iceberg")
    .outputMode("append")
    .trigger(Trigger.ProcessingTime(1, TimeUnit.MINUTES))
    .option("path", destinationTableName)
    .option("fanout-enabled", "true")
    .option("checkpointLocation", checkpointPath)
    .start()
```

To maintain seamless and efficient real-time data sharing with partners, it is essential to adhere to a set of best practices. First, schema consistency is crucial; ensure that the schema of our_database.our_table matches or is compatible with partner_data base.partner_table to prevent any write errors.

Additionally, in cases where the partner is only interested in a subset of the data, it's advisable to implement data filtering before writing to their table. This not only streamlines the process but also makes it more efficient. Furthermore, robust error handling mechanisms should be in place to manage streaming failures, thereby preventing data loss or duplication. Finally, monitoring and setting up alerts for the streaming job is vital.

This approach will help you keep track of the job's performance and quickly identify potential issues, ensuring that necessary stakeholders are alerted if problems arise. By following these best practices, collaboration is enhanced, and both parties benefit from access to timely and accurate information.

Streaming with Flink

Apache Flink is an open source, unified stream-batch processing engine developed by the Apache Software Foundation. Flink is designed to process large volumes of data at high speeds, making it particularly useful for real-time data processing and analytics.

Flink provides a high-throughput, low-latency streaming engine, as well as support for event time semantics, exactly-once semantics, backpressure control, and more. It excels in processing streaming data while also providing batch processing capabilities, ML libraries, and graph processing capabilities. Here are some key features of Apache Flink's streaming capabilities:

Event time processing
Flink's event time processing feature allows it to handle out-of-order data and provide accurate results, which is crucial for many real-time applications. This is particularly useful in scenarios where the order of events matters, such as in financial transactions and sensor data processing.

Fault tolerance
Like Spark, Flink provides fault tolerance through its checkpointing and savepoint mechanism. These features ensure that data is not lost during processing and allow for recovery from failures without data loss.

Backpressure handling
Flink handles backpressure, which occurs when data is produced more quickly than it can be consumed. This ensures the stability of the system even when facing a large influx of data.

High throughput and low latency
Flink is designed to process large volumes of data with low latency, making it suitable for applications that require real-time insights.

Windowing and complex event processing
Flink provides flexible windowing based on time, count, session, and more. Additionally, it supports complex event processing (CEP), which allows for pattern detection and selection in data streams.

Integration
Flink integrates with a variety of data sources and sinks, including Kafka, the Hadoop Distributed File System (HDFS), and databases such as Cassandra.

Exactly-once semantics
Flink supports exactly-once processing semantics, ensuring that each record will be processed exactly once, thereby delivering accurate results.

In a nutshell, Apache Flink is a powerful stream processing technology that excels in delivering high-speed, accurate, and scalable data processing solutions. Its combination of robust streaming capabilities, fault tolerance features, and integrations with other data systems makes it a strong choice for real-time data processing.

Streaming into Iceberg with Flink

The Apache Iceberg Flink libraries allow you to work with Apache Iceberg tables as data sources or data sinks (destinations) using Flink's DataStream API and Table API. First, we'll explore reading from Iceberg in Flink, and then we'll discuss writing from Iceberg in Flink.

What Are Flink's DataStream and Table APIs?

The Apache Flink platform features two main APIs for data processing, the DataStream API and the Table API, each catering to different needs.

The *DataStream API* is designed for handling continuous, unbounded data streams such as Internet of Things (IoT) sensor data or log streams, offering a lower-level, expressive approach with detailed control over aspects such as event time processing and windowing operations. It is ideal for real-time, event-driven scenarios and boasts extensive connectivity options.

In contrast, the *Table API* focuses on structured, bounded data in table format, suitable for batch processing and analytical tasks. It provides a higher-level abstraction with an SQL-like interface, simplifying the expression of data processing tasks and automating execution plan optimization. While it also supports event time processing, its complex event handling capabilities are more limited than the DataStream API.

The choice between these APIs hinges on the specific requirements of the task, with the DataStream API offering detailed control for real-time applications and the Table API being more apt for structured data and analytical processing.

Flink for stream reading

Apache Iceberg provides robust support for both streaming and batch read operations using Apache Flink's DataStream API and Table API. This support allows users to read data easily and flexibly from Iceberg tables.

In the SQL context, the Flink job's execution mode can be toggled between streaming and batch modes with simple SQL commands. For batch read, users can submit a Flink batch job with a SELECT statement after setting the runtime mode to batch. In contrast, for streaming reads, users first set the runtime mode to streaming and enable dynamic table options. They can then use SELECT with the streaming option set to true and specify the monitor interval.

Let's see an example using batch mode for batch data. First set the execution mode to batch. Then execute a SELECT statement to read data from the sales_data table:

```
TableEnvironment tableEnv = TableEnvironment.create(EnvironmentSettings.new
Instance().build());

// Set the execution mode to 'batch'.
tableEnv.getConfig().getConfiguration().setString("execution.runtime-mode",
"batch");

// Execute a SELECT statement.
TableResult result = tableEnv.executeSql("SELECT * FROM sales_data");
result.print();
```

Here's an example using streaming mode for streaming data. First set the execution mode to streaming and enable dynamic table options. Then execute a SELECT statement with the streaming option set to true and specify the monitor interval:

```
// Set the execution mode to 'streaming' and enable dynamic table options.
tableEnv.getConfig().getConfiguration().setString("execution.runtime-mode",
"streaming");
tableEnv.getConfig().getConfiguration().setBoolean("table.dynamic-table-
options.enabled", true);

// Execute a SELECT statement with the streaming option
and a monitor interval of 1 second.
TableResult result = tableEnv.executeSql(
    "SELECT * FROM sales_data /*+ OPTIONS('streaming'='true',
'monitor-interval'='1s')*/");
result.print();
```

Iceberg even supports reading incremental data starting from a specific historical snapshot ID. Users can set different Flink SQL hint options for the streaming job for further customization, such as the start-snapshot-id option, as shown in the following code. With the Hints pattern, available in many software frameworks, you can submit directions via comments that are processed before running the code itself:

```
TableEnvironment tableEnv = TableEnvironment.create(EnvironmentSettings.new
Instance().build());

// Set the execution mode to 'streaming' and enable dynamic table options.
tableEnv.getConfig().getConfiguration().setString("execution.runtime-mode",
"streaming");
tableEnv.getConfig().getConfiguration().setBoolean("table.dynamic-table-
options.enabled", true);

// Specify the historical snapshot ID from which to start reading.
String startSnapshotId = "3821550127947089987";  // Replace
// with your actual snapshot ID.

// Execute a SELECT statement with the streaming option
and a monitor interval of 1 second.
// Start reading incremental data from the specified snapshot ID.
TableResult result = tableEnv.executeSql(
    "SELECT * FROM sales_data /*+ OPTIONS('streaming'='true',
'monitor-interval'='1s', 'start-snapshot-id'='"
    + startSnapshotId + "')*/");
result.print();
```

In the DataStream context, Iceberg supports both batch and streaming reads, which
we will illustrate in the following examples. For streaming reads, similar steps are
followed, but with the streaming option set to true and the startSnapshotId option
set to a specific snapshot ID.

For batch data:

```
StreamExecutionEnvironment env = StreamExecutionEnvironment.createLocalEnviron
ment();
TableLoader tableLoader = TableLoader.fromHadoopTable("s3://someBucket/retail/
sales_data");

IcebergSource<RowData> source = IcebergSource.forRowData()
    .tableLoader(tableLoader)
    .assignerFactory(new SimpleSplitAssignerFactory())
    .build();

DataStream<RowData> batch = env.fromSource(
    source,
    WatermarkStrategy.noWatermarks(),
    "My Iceberg Source",
    TypeInformation.of(RowData.class));

// Print all records.
batch.print();

// execute batch read job.
env.execute("Iceberg Batch Read");
```

For batch reads, users can use the `TableLoader` and `FlinkSource` classes in the Java API to read all records from an Iceberg table. The data is then printed to stdout.

For streaming data:

```
StreamExecutionEnvironment env = StreamExecutionEnvironment.createLocalEnviron
ment();
TableLoader tableLoader = TableLoader.fromHadoopTable("s3://someBucket/retail/
sales_data");

IcebergSource source = IcebergSource.forRowData()
    .tableLoader(tableLoader)
    .assignerFactory(new SimpleSplitAssignerFactory())
    .streaming(true)
    .streamingStartingStrategy(StreamingStartingStrategy.INCREMENTAL_FROM_LAT
EST_SNAPSHOT)
    .monitorInterval(Duration.ofSeconds(60))
    .build()

DataStream<RowData> stream = env.fromSource(
    source,
    WatermarkStrategy.noWatermarks(),
    "My Iceberg Source",
    TypeInformation.of(RowData.class));

// Print all records.
stream.print();

// execute streaming read job.
env.execute("Iceberg Stream Read");
```

For streaming reads, similar steps are followed, but with the `streaming` option set to `true` and the `startSnapshotId` option set to a specific snapshot ID.

Branches and tags can be read via the DataStream API by specifying options in the `branch` or `tag` method of `FlinkSource.Builder`. Users can set a number of options when configuring the Flink `IcebergSource` or via Flink SQL hints, enabling fine-tuned control over their read operations:

```
DataStream<RowData> batch = FlinkSource.forRowData()
    .env(env)
    .tableLoader(tableLoader)
    .branch("etl-branch")
    .streaming(false)
    .build();
```

Flink for stream writing

Streaming writes to Apache Iceberg with Apache Flink's DataStream API and Table API provide seamless support for real-time data ingestion and processing. Iceberg supports both batch and streaming writes, making it a versatile and powerful option for data streaming pipelines.

In Flink's SQL API, Iceberg supports both INSERT INTO and INSERT OVERWRITE operations. To append new data to an Iceberg table in a Flink streaming job, the INSERT INTO command is used. It allows for easy addition of new records to the table. INSERT OVERWRITE can be used in a batch job to replace the data in the table with the result of a query. Iceberg ensures that overwrites are atomic operations, making data updates safe and reliable.

What Is INSERT OVERWRITE and How Does It Work?

INSERT OVERWRITE replaces existing data in a table with query results or new data, commonly used for batch processing in Iceberg tables. This atomic operation refreshes the table with the latest data in scenarios such as periodic loads or updates, ensuring consistency. In partitioned tables, it can target specific partitions. However, for real-time processing in Flink and Iceberg, INSERT INTO is preferred over INSERT OVERWRITE, which is designed for batch updates, guaranteeing data integrity and accuracy.

When working with DataStreams, Iceberg provides convenient APIs to perform various write operations. For appending data, both DataStream<RowData> and Data Stream<Row> can be directly written to the Iceberg table using the FlinkSink.forRow Data() API. For example:

```
StreamExecutionEnvironment env = ...;
DataStream<RowData> input = ...;
Configuration hadoopConf = new Configuration();
TableLoader tableLoader = TableLoader.fromHadoopTable("hdfs://nn:8020/warehouse/
path", hadoopConf);

FlinkSink.forRowData(input)
    .tableLoader(tableLoader)
    .append();

env.execute("Retail Sales Data Example");
```

For more advanced scenarios, Iceberg also supports overwriting and upserting data. Overwriting existing data can be achieved by setting the overwrite flag in the FlinkSink builder. Upserting based on a primary key can be enabled either using a table-level property or as a write option in the builder. Here are examples of both:

```
// Overwriting data
FlinkSink.forRowData(input)
    .tableLoader(tableLoader)
    .overwrite(true)
```

```
    .append();

// Upserting data
FlinkSink.forRowData(input)
    .tableLoader(tableLoader)
    .upsert(true)
    .append();
```

In addition to direct DataStream writes, Iceberg also provides the flexibility to write
a generic DataStream<T> by using a custom mapper, such as AvroGenericRecordTo
RowDataMapper, to convert data to the required format before writing. Here is an
example:

```
// Define the custom AvroGenericRecordToRowDataMapper
        AvroGenericRecordToRowDataMapper mapper = new AvroGenericRecordToRowData
Mapper();

        // Create a generic DataStream<GenericRecord> from a source (e.g., Kafka)
        DataStream<GenericRecord> genericDataStream = ... // your DataStream
source

        // Write the generic DataStream to the Iceberg table using the custom
mapper
        FlinkSink.builderFor(
                genericDataStream,
                mapper,
                // Optionally specify the TypeInfo for RowData if needed
                TypeInformation.of(RowData.class)
        )
        .table(tableName)
        .tableLoader(tableLoader)
        .build();

        env.execute("Iceberg Generic DataStream Example");
```

Streaming writes to Apache Iceberg with Apache Flink offer a robust and efficient
way to handle real-time data ingestion and processing in a retail sales data scenario,
ensuring data consistency and atomicity even in high-velocity streaming environments. The provided code examples demonstrate how to leverage Flink's APIs to
seamlessly interact with Iceberg tables for both batch and streaming writes.

Example of Streaming into Iceberg with Flink

In this scenario, we have two existing tables in the Hive catalog: retail_sales_data
and sales_data_summary. The retail_sales_data table contains raw sales data with
details such as purchase_date, quantity, and price. The sales_data_summary table is
an Iceberg table with a partitioned schema to store monthly aggregated sales data. Our
goal is to perform data processing every hour and update the sales_data_summary table
with the latest aggregated sales data for each month. The sales_data_summary table is

partitioned by the date column by month. The relevant code follows; to see the full code snippet, visit the book's GitHub repository (*https://oreil.ly/supp-guide-apache-iceberg*):

```
String createCatalogStatement = "CREATE CATALOG " + catalogName +
" WITH (\n" +
                "'type'='" + catalogType + "',\n" +
                "'catalog-type'='hive',\n" +
                "'uri'='" + hiveCatalogUri + "',\n" +
                "'warehouse'='" + warehousePath + "',\n" +
                "'clients'='" + hiveClientConfig + "',\n" +
                "'property-version'='1'\n" +
                ")";

// Register Hive Catalog
tEnv.executeSql(createCatalogStatement);
tEnv.useCatalog(catalogName);

// Define the source and destination table names
String sourceTableName = "retail_sales_data";
String destinationTableName = "sales_data_summary";

// Calculate the current month's partition value (e.g., '2023-08' for
August 2023)
String currentMonthPartition = getCurrentMonthPartition();

// SQL query to process data for the current month
String sqlQuery = "INSERT OVERWRITE " + destinationTableName + " PARTI
TION (month = '" + currentMonthPartition + "') " +
                "SELECT date, SUM(sales_amount) as total_sales " +
                "FROM " + sourceTableName + " " +
                "WHERE month = '" + currentMonthPartition + "' " +
                "GROUP BY date";

// Execute the SQL query
tEnv.executeSql(sqlQuery);

// Sleep for one hour before executing the job again
Thread.sleep(3600000);
```

This job is designed to perform a series of tasks in sequence. Initially, it queries the aggregated state to retrieve the current day's sales data for all dates within the current month. Following this, it executes an INSERT OVERWRITE command on the aggregate table. This step is crucial as it updates the data in the current month's partition with the newly fetched information. After completing the data insertion, the job enters sleep mode for an hour. During this period, no operations are conducted. Once the hour-long break concludes, the task is programmed to restart and repeat the same sequence of operations.

This aggregate table can be used for business intelligence (BI) dashboards on sales data and will be updated on sales up to the hour. We can update the data freshness by tweaking how often the job runs. If the job typically takes 30 seconds to complete, we can reduce the job frequency to 30 seconds to improve the data freshness of dashboards fueled by the aggregate table (a more frequent job may run more quickly, enabling even shorter intervals).

Streaming with Kafka Connect

Apache Kafka Connect is an open source component of the Apache Kafka platform that provides a scalable and reliable way to move data into and out of Kafka. Thousands of companies use Kafka Connect for integrating various systems with Apache Kafka to stream data in real time.

Here are some key features of Apache Kafka Connect's capabilities:

High throughput
> Kafka Connect can facilitate the transfer of vast volumes of data effectively. It is designed to work seamlessly with Apache Kafka to ensure efficient data streaming between systems.

Fault tolerance
> Kafka Connect is built to be resilient. It can automatically manage failures, ensuring uninterrupted data flow between different systems and Apache Kafka.

Real-time integration
> With Kafka Connect, data can be integrated in real time, enabling systems to remain synchronized and up to date.

Durability
> Kafka Connect works with Kafka topics, where each record is stored on disk and replicated for fault tolerance. This ensures that even if there's a hiccup, data remains consistent and intact.

Wide integration
> Kafka Connect supports a vast ecosystem of connectors, making it easy to integrate with various systems, databases, and applications. Whether you need to pull data from a database into Kafka or push data from Kafka into a cloud storage solution, there's likely a connector that fits your needs.

Exactly-once semantics
> Just like Apache Kafka, Kafka Connect supports exactly-once processing semantics, ensuring that each record is delivered exactly once, avoiding data duplication or loss.

Connector framework
Kafka Connect provides a framework for building and running reusable connectors, which can be used to stream data between Apache Kafka and other systems, without requiring any code changes to Kafka itself.

Apache Kafka Connect is a robust integration tool within the Apache Kafka ecosystem, providing seamless, real-time integration capabilities. Its extensive features make it the go-to choice for businesses looking to integrate various systems with Apache Kafka in a scalable and reliable manner.

The Iceberg Kafka Sink

A Kafka sink is a component in Apache Kafka that allows data to be consumed from Kafka topics and written to external systems or databases. It plays a crucial role in data integration and data flow by enabling seamless transfer of data from Kafka to various data stores, databases, or analytics platforms.

The Apache Iceberg Sink Connector is a specialized Kafka sink connector that is used for writing data from Kafka into Iceberg tables. It provides various features and capabilities, making it a powerful tool for data integration and storage. There are many features of the Apache Iceberg Sink Connector:

Commit coordination
Centralized Iceberg commits ensure consistency and atomicity in data writes.

Exactly-once delivery semantics
Exactly-once delivery semantics ensure that data is processed and written to Iceberg tables exactly once, even in the presence of failures.

Multitable fanout
Writing data to multiple Iceberg tables based on specific routing criteria allows for flexible data distribution.

Row mutations
Support for row mutations enables update and delete operations on existing rows in Iceberg tables.

Upsert mode
Upsert mode allows for efficient updates of data in Iceberg v2 tables with identity fields defined.

Configuring the Apache Iceberg Kafka sink

The connector offers various configuration options to customize the behavior and ensure smooth data transfer. Let's explore the different configuration properties and their significance:

`iceberg.tables`

This property allows you to specify a comma-separated list of destination tables where data from Kafka will be written to Iceberg.

`iceberg.tables.routeField`

For multitable fanout, this property defines the field used to route records to different destination tables based on their values.

`iceberg.tables.<table name>.routeRegex`

This property is used in multitable fanout mode to specify for the mentioned `<table name>` the regex pattern used to match the `routeField` value to a specific destination table.

`iceberg.tables.dynamic.enabled`

Setting this property to `true` enables dynamic routing of records to different destination tables based on the value in `routeField`.

`iceberg.tables.cdcField`

If specified, this property designates the field that contains change data capture (CDC) operation codes, such as I for insert, U for update, and D for delete.

`iceberg.tables.upsertModeEnabled`

When set to `true`, this property enables upsert mode, which ensures efficient updates to existing data by preceding appends with an equality delete.

`iceberg.control.topic`

This property defines the name of the control topic used for managing connector offsets and committing transactions.

`iceberg.control.group.id`

This property specifies the consumer group ID used to store offsets in the sink-managed consumer group.

`iceberg.control.commitIntervalMs`

This specifies the commit interval in milliseconds, which determines how frequently the connector commits transactions.

`iceberg.control.commitTimeoutMs`

This specifies the commit timeout interval in milliseconds. If a commit takes longer than this duration, it is considered failed.

`iceberg.control.commitThread`

This specifies the number of threads used for committing transactions. The default is twice the number of CPU cores.

`iceberg.catalog`

> This is the name of the catalog used for connecting to the Iceberg table storage. The default is "iceberg."

`iceberg.catalog.*`

> This is for additional properties passed through to the Iceberg catalog initialization. Different catalog types, such as REST, Hive, and Hadoop, may require specific configuration properties.

`iceberg.kafka.*`

> This is for additional properties passed through to the Kafka client used to connect to the control topic. This allows you to set custom Kafka client settings.

Setting up Kafka Connect with Apache Iceberg

To set up Kafka Connect with Apache Iceberg, start by ensuring that Kafka Connect is installed and running on your system. You can download Kafka from the official Apache Kafka website and follow the installation instructions provided in the documentation.

Build the Apache Iceberg Sink Connector for Kafka Connect. You can either use the prebuilt connector JAR or build it yourself from the source code (located in the book's GitHub repository (*https://github.com/tabular-io/iceberg-kafka-connect*)). If you want to build it yourself, clone the Iceberg repository from GitHub and run the following command inside the `kafka-connect-iceberg` module:

```
./gradlew -xtest clean build
```

Open the Kafka Connect worker properties file (usually named *worker.properties*) and add the necessary Kafka client properties related to your Kafka setup. For example, if you want to enable SSL communication with the Kafka broker, you may add the following properties:

```
# Worker properties (worker.properties)
bootstrap.servers=kafka-broker1:9092,kafka-broker2:9092
security.protocol=SSL
ssl.truststore.location=/path/to/truststore.jks
ssl.truststore.password=truststore_password
```

In the same worker properties file (*worker.properties*), you can set the Apache Iceberg Kafka sink properties. For example:

```
# Apache Iceberg Sink properties
connector.class=io.tabular.iceberg.connect.IcebergSinkConnector
tasks.max=2
topics=events
iceberg.tables=default.events
iceberg.catalog.type=rest
iceberg.catalog.uri=https://localhost
```

```
iceberg.catalog.credential=<credential>
iceberg.catalog.warehouse=<warehouse name>
```

You can modify the properties according to your setup. Make sure to set the correct values for `iceberg.catalog.uri`, `iceberg.catalog.credential`, and `iceberg.cata log.warehouse` to connect to your Iceberg catalog.

Start the Kafka Connect service, specifying the *worker.properties* file as a command-line argument:

```
bin/connect-distributed.sh config/worker.properties
```

Alternatively, you can run Kafka Connect in standalone mode:

```
bin/connect-standalone.sh config/worker.properties connector.properties
```

Note that the *connector.properties* file should contain the Apache Iceberg Sink Connector properties mentioned earlier.

Once Kafka Connect is running, it will automatically start the Apache Iceberg Sink Connector and begin writing data from the specified topics to the Iceberg tables. Check the logs to ensure that the connector has started successfully and is processing data as expected.

Monitor the Apache Iceberg sink's performance and check for any errors or warnings in the logs. You can use tools such as the Kafka Connect REST API or Kafka Connect UI to monitor the connector's status and performance.

That's it! You have now set up the Apache Iceberg sink with the Kafka client configuration. The sink connector will take care of writing data from Kafka topics to the specified Iceberg tables, while the Kafka client will handle the communication with the Kafka broker based on the configured properties. Remember to review the Kafka documentation and the Apache Iceberg documentation for more details on available Kafka client properties and the Iceberg sink connector configuration options.

Streaming with AWS

Amazon Web Services (AWS) offers a suite of real-time data streaming services that enable developers to collect, process, analyze, and deliver continuous streaming data at scale for real-time applications and analytics solutions. AWS's data streaming services are secure, highly available, durable, and fully managed, making it easier for developers to build real-time applications.

The AWS data streaming ecosystem consists of the following components:

Source
> Data is produced at a high volume and velocity by thousands of devices or applications, such as mobile devices, web applications, application logs, IoT sensors, smart devices, and gaming applications.

Stream ingestion

AWS provides simple integration with more than 15 AWS services that capture continuous data in a durable and secure manner.

Stream storage

AWS offers solutions such as Amazon Kinesis Data Streams, Amazon Kinesis Data Firehose, and Amazon Managed Streaming for Apache Kafka (Amazon MSK) to meet your storage needs based on scaling, latency, and processing requirements.

Stream processing

AWS provides a range of services for data transformation and delivery. Services range from Amazon Kinesis Data Firehose to custom-built real-time applications and ML integration using services such as Amazon Kinesis Data Analytics and AWS Lambda.

Destination

AWS delivers streaming data to a selection of fully integrated data lakes, data warehouses, and analytics services for further analysis or long-term storage.

Following are some of the key AWS services for real-time data streaming:

Amazon Kinesis Data Streams

A scalable and durable real-time data streaming service that can continuously capture gigabytes of data per second from hundreds of thousands of sources

Amazon Kinesis Data Firehose

Captures, transforms, and loads data streams into AWS data stores for near-real-time analytics with existing BI tools

Amazon Kinesis Data Analytics

Allows you to process data streams in real time with SQL or Java (using Apache Flink) without having to learn new programming languages or processing frameworks

Amazon MSK

A fully managed service that makes it easy to build and run applications that use Apache Kafka to process streaming data

AWS data streaming services support a wide variety of use cases, including real-time data movement, real-time analytics, and event stream processing. This allows users to analyze data as soon as it is produced, store the data for further analysis, enable real-time decisions across an organization, capture and respond to events as they happen in real time across multiple applications, and maintain a system of record via CDC.

Using AWS Glue Studio with Apache Iceberg to ingest data into Iceberg tables provides a powerful and efficient way to manage and process data in data lakes. AWS Glue 3.0 and later support Apache Iceberg. This integration allows users to perform read and write operations on Iceberg tables in Amazon Simple Storage Service (Amazon S3) and leverage the AWS Glue Data catalog for additional operations, including inserts, updates, and Spark reads and writes.

One of the key advantages of using AWS Glue Studio with Apache Iceberg is the support for both AWS Kinesis Stream and Kafka Stream as data sources. Users can seamlessly ingest data from these streaming sources into Iceberg tables in Amazon S3 for further processing and analysis.

To enable Iceberg for AWS Glue, you need to specify `iceberg` as the value for the `--datalake-formats` job parameter. Additionally, you must set specific Spark configurations to handle Iceberg tables correctly. These configurations include setting `spark.sql.extensions` to `org.apache.iceberg.spark.extensions.Iceberg SparkSessionExtensions` and configuring the `glue_catalog` properties such as `ware house`, `catalog-impl`, and `io-impl`. For more details on these settings, refer to Chapters 5 and 8.

If you are using AWS Glue 3.0 with Iceberg 0.13.1, you must also set the additional configurations for using the Amazon DynamoDB lock manager to ensure atomic transactions. AWS Glue 4.0, on the other hand, uses optimistic locking by default (meaning you don't have to configure the lock manually).

To use a different version of Iceberg that is not natively supported by AWS Glue, you can specify your own Iceberg JAR files using the `--extra-jars` job parameter.

Once you have enabled Iceberg and set up the configurations, you can easily create and register Iceberg tables from DataFrames in AWS Glue Studio. For example, you can create an Iceberg table from a DataFrame and register it in the AWS Glue Data catalog using SQL queries. Similarly, you can read data from an Iceberg table in Amazon S3 using the Glue Data catalog and perform insert operations to add data to the Iceberg table.

Here is an example of how to write an Iceberg table to Amazon S3 and register it in the AWS Glue Data catalog using Python:

```
# Example: Create an Iceberg table from a DataFrame and register the table to
Glue Data Catalog
dataFrame.createOrReplaceTempView("incoming_data")

# Insert Data into an existing Iceberg table in Glue Catalog
query = f"""
INSERT INTO glue.db.destination_table SELECT * FROM incoming_data
"""

spark.sql(query)
```

In this example, the DataFrame `dataFrame` is created, and a temporary view is assigned to it. The Iceberg table is then created using SQL query syntax, and the table is registered in the AWS Glue Data catalog.

Overall, using AWS Glue Studio with Apache Iceberg for ingesting data into Iceberg tables provides a seamless and efficient way to manage and analyze data in data lakes. Whether the data is sourced from AWS Kinesis Stream or from Kafka Stream, users can leverage the powerful features of Iceberg and AWS Glue to process and analyze their data effectively.

Conclusion

There are many tools that can be used to help process streaming real-time data into and from Apache Iceberg tables, including Apache Spark, Apache Flink, AWS Kinesis, and Kafka Connect. The book's GitHub repository (*https://oreil.ly/supp-guide-apache-iceberg*) includes a chart summarizing many of the features of the tools covered in this chapter.

In Chapter 12, we will discuss governance and security for your Apache Iceberg tables.

CHAPTER 12
Governance and Security

As organizations increasingly embrace modern data lakehouse architectures such as Apache Iceberg lakehouses, they benefit from their flexibility, scalability, and performance improvements. However, these advantages bring forth new challenges concerning data security and governance.

This chapter delves deep into the multifaceted world of securing and governing Apache Iceberg tables. Apache Iceberg serves primarily as a standard for how metadata defines a dataset and doesn't have any security aspects built into it for purposes of security outside of some table properties to select a file encryption type. Securing your Apache Iceberg tables is primarily handled by the storage, access, and compute layers you use to work with your tables.

As you embark on this journey, you'll discover three critical angles for safeguarding your data lakehouse:

- Securing your datafiles
- Security and governance via a semantic layer
- Security and governance at the catalog level

Organizations must adopt a comprehensive approach to secure and govern their Apache Iceberg tables effectively. By examining these three angles—securing data files, implementing security and governance via a semantic layer, and ensuring catalog-level security—you'll be well equipped to navigate the complexities of data protection in your modern data lakehouse. So, let's embark on this journey to fortify your data assets and harness the full potential of Apache Iceberg.

Keep in mind that governance and security are deep topics to which several books are already devoted. In this chapter, we'll cover a handful of examples of using tools to secure Apache Iceberg tables. This chapter isn't meant to offer an exhaustive list of tools or approaches.

Securing Datafiles

At the core of every data lakehouse lies a vast repository of datafiles. Securing these files is the first defense against unauthorized access and data breaches. This section explores various tools and best practices for securing the underlying datafiles within an Apache Iceberg table, from encryption and access controls to data masking and auditing.

Securing your datafiles at the storage level is paramount, as these files form the bedrock of your data infrastructure. In an age where cyber threats loom, organizations must fortify their data against many vulnerabilities. The potential pitfalls are numerous, from external threats such as hacking attempts and data breaches to internal risks such as data leakage and unauthorized access. By addressing these vulnerabilities proactively, organizations can safeguard their data's integrity, confidentiality, and availability, ensuring compliance with data protection regulations and fostering trust with their customers. In this section, we will explore various storage platforms and their diverse security options for safeguarding your datafiles, providing you with the tools and knowledge needed to make informed decisions about the security measures best suited to your organization's needs.

Securing Files: Best Practices

Securing your Apache Iceberg table's datafiles, regardless of your chosen storage platform, requires adherence to fundamental principles and best practices to ensure comprehensive data protection. Here are some overarching principles and best practices to consider:

Least privilege access
> Limit access to datafiles to only those individuals and processes that require it for their specific tasks. Grant the minimum level of permissions necessary to perform these tasks.

Encryption at rest and in transit
> Enforce encryption of datafiles both at rest and in transit. Utilize the encryption mechanisms provided by your storage platform to safeguard data integrity and confidentiality.

Strong authentication and identity management
> Implement robust identity and access management practices. Leverage multifactor authentication (MFA) and strong password policies to verify user identities.

Audit trails and logging
> Enable auditing and logging features provided by your storage platform. Maintain comprehensive audit trails to monitor and investigate access to and changes to data files.

Data retention and disposal policies
> Define data retention and disposal policies to manage the lifecycle of datafiles. Safely delete or archive files that are no longer needed to reduce risk exposure.

Continuous monitoring
> Implement continuous monitoring and alerting systems to detect and respond to security incidents in real time.

In the context of file-level security for Apache Iceberg tables, there are both advantages and disadvantages to consider. On the positive side, it offers granular control, allowing for precise permissions and encryption settings for individual datafiles. This level also supports data encryption at rest, ensuring the security of sensitive information, and it enables strict data isolation to minimize unauthorized access risks. However, there are drawbacks, including the complexity of managing security at the file level, particularly as the volume of files increases. Additionally, it may need more abstraction to provide a unified and simplified data view to end users and tools. Lastly, scalability can be challenging when managing permissions for a growing data lakehouse, potentially leading to errors and inefficiencies.

Hadoop Distributed File System

Securing your datafiles within Apache Iceberg tables when stored on the Hadoop Distributed File System (HDFS) demands a comprehensive approach to protect against vulnerabilities and ensure data confidentiality and integrity. Three key components are pivotal in this endeavor.

Access control lists

Access control lists (ACLs) in HDFS allow you to exert fine-grained control over who can access specific files and directories within your Iceberg data lakehouse. With ACLs, you can precisely define permissions for individual users or groups, going beyond the standard read, write, and execute permissions. This level of granularity ensures that only authorized personnel can access sensitive data, minimizing the risk of unauthorized access or data breaches.

To set ACLs for a file or directory, you can use the following commands:

```
# Set an ACL to grant read and write access to a specific user
hdfs dfs -setfacl -m user:username:rwx /path/to/your/file_or_directory

# Grant read access to a specific group
hdfs dfs -setfacl -m group:groupname:r-x /path/to/your/file_or_directory
```

Encryption

Encrypting data at rest is paramount to safeguarding your datafiles. HDFS offers robust encryption options, including transparent data encryption (TDE) and encryption zones. TDE encrypts data blocks on disk, rendering data unreadable to unauthorized entities even if the physical storage media is compromised. Encryption zones allow you to specify specific directories or files that require encryption, enabling you to focus encryption efforts on the most critical data.

To enable TDE for an HDFS cluster, you can use the following commands:

```
# Enable Transparent Data Encryption (TDE) for HDFS
hdfs crypto -createZone -keyName myEncryptionKey -path /path/to/encryption/zone
```

Permissions

HDFS adopts a permission system akin to traditional filesystems, empowering you to manage datafile access systematically. Through commands such as chmod and chown, you can allocate specific permissions to users and groups, dictating who can read, write, or execute files and directories. Properly configuring permissions ensures that only the right individuals or processes can access the data, mitigating the risk of data misuse.

To set permissions for a file or directory, you can use the following commands:

```
# Change the owner of a file or directory
hdfs dfs -chown newowner:newgroup /path/to/your/file_or_directory

# Change permissions to grant read, write, and execute to the owner
hdfs dfs -chmod 700 /path/to/your/file_or_directory
```

Securing your Apache Iceberg data on HDFS necessitates combining these robust security measures tailored to your specific requirements. You can fortify your data lakehouse's defenses by emphasizing ACLs for precise access control, encryption for data confidentiality, and permissions for structured access rights management. This multifaceted security approach ensures that your data remains confidential and tamperproof, fortifying your data assets' integrity and trustworthiness.

Amazon Simple Storage Service

Securing the datafiles of an Apache Iceberg table on Amazon Web Services (AWS) involves using various security features offered by Amazon Simple Storage Service (Amazon S3). This section will guide you in using some of the most important features of file-level security, which generally revolves around encrypting and controlling access to your files' security.

Encryption

Amazon S3 provides three server-side encryption (SSE) options to safeguard data at rest. Choose the one that best fits your security requirements.

SSE-S3 (SSE with S3-managed keys).   This option is straightforward and suitable for most use cases. Amazon S3 automatically manages encryption keys. Use the following code to enable SSE-S3 for your S3 bucket using the AWS CLI:

```
aws s3api put-bucket-encryption --bucket YOUR_BUCKET_NAME --server-side-
encryption-configuration '{"Rules": [{"ApplyServerSideEncryptionByDefault":
{"SSEAlgorithm": "AES256"}}]}'
```

SSE-KMS (SSE with the AWS Key Management Service).   This option leverages the AWS Key Management Service (KMS) for advanced key management. It's ideal for scenarios involving regulatory compliance or strict corporate security policies.

To enable SSE-KMS for your S3 bucket, you can use the AWS CLI with your KMS key ID:

```
aws s3api put-bucket-encryption --bucket YOUR_BUCKET_NAME --server-side-
encryption-configuration '{"Rules": [{"ApplyServerSideEncryptionByDefault":
{"SSEAlgorithm": "aws:kms", "KMSMasterKeyID": "YOUR_KMS_KEY_ID"}}]}'
```

SSE-C (SSE with customer-provided keys).   SSE-C provides the highest level of control. You supply your encryption keys for data encryption and decryption, and Amazon S3 has no access to or storage of the keys.

To enable SSE-C for your S3 bucket, you can specify the customer-provided key in the AWS CLI:

```
aws s3api put-bucket-encryption --bucket YOUR_BUCKET_NAME --server-side-
encryption-configuration '{"Rules": [{"ApplyServerSideEncryptionByDefault":
{"SSEAlgorithm": "AES256"}}], "CustomerAlgorithm": "AES256"}'
```

To configure server-side encryption for an Apache Iceberg table on AWS S3, you can utilize the following table configuration properties (these are Iceberg table settings, not AWS settings):

- Property: s3.sse.type

  Default: none

  Description: This specifies the type of SSE to use. You can choose from none, S3, KMS, or custom.

- Property: s3.sse.key

  Default: aws/s3 for the KMS type, null otherwise

  Description: For the KMS type, this property should be set to the KMS key ID or Amazon resource name (ARN). For other types, such as custom, you can provide a custom base-64 AES-256 symmetric key.

- Property: s3.sse.md5

  Default: null

  Description: This property is relevant when the SSE type is set to custom. It should be set as the base-64 MD5 digest of the symmetric key to ensure data integrity.

Bucket policies

To control access at the bucket level using Amazon S3 bucket policies, follow these steps:

1. Create a bucket policy in JSON format with specific rules.
2. Attach the policy to your S3 bucket using the AWS Management Console or AWS CLI.

Here's an example policy that allows access only from a specific IP address:

```
{
    "Version": "2012-10-17",
    "Statement": [
        {
            "Sid": "AllowSpecificIP",
            "Effect": "Allow",
            "Principal": "*",
            "Action": "s3:GetObject",
            "Resource": "arn:aws:s3:::YOUR_BUCKET_NAME/*",
            "Condition": {
                "IpAddress": {
                    "aws:SourceIp": "YOUR_IP_ADDRESS"
                }
            }
        }
    ]
}
```

Attach this policy to your S3 bucket using the AWS Management Console or AWS CLI:

```
aws s3api put-bucket-policy --bucket YOUR_BUCKET_NAME --policy '{
    "Version": "2012-10-17",
    "Statement": [
        {
            "Sid": "AllowSpecificIP",
```

```
        "Effect": "Allow",
        "Principal": "*",
        "Action": "s3:GetObject",
        "Resource": "arn:aws:s3:::YOUR_BUCKET_NAME/*",
        "Condition": {
            "IpAddress": {
                "aws:SourceIp": "YOUR_IP_ADDRESS"
            }
        }
    }
  ]
}'
```

Identity and Access Management

To use AWS Identity and Access Management (IAM) to create and manage user roles and permissions for accessing your S3 resources, follow these steps:

1. Create IAM users, roles, or groups based on your organization's needs.

2. Define policies that specify the actions and resources users can access (e.g., s3:GetObject, s3:PutObject).

3. Attach policies to IAM users, roles, or groups to grant them access to specific S3 buckets or objects.

IAM policies can be highly granular, allowing for precise control over actions and resources.

Here's an example of a CLI command to attach an IAM policy to a particular IAM user, allowing them to read (s3:GetObject) and write (s3:PutObject) to a specific S3 bucket:

```
aws iam put-user-policy --user-name YOUR_IAM_USER_NAME --policy-name S3Access
Policy --policy-document '{
  "Version": "2012-10-17",
  "Statement": [
    {
      "Effect": "Allow",
      "Action": [
        "s3:GetObject",
        "s3:PutObject"
      ],
      "Resource": "arn:aws:s3:::YOUR_BUCKET_NAME/*"
    }
  ]
}'
```

In this example, you can use the AWS CLI command aws iam put-user-policy to attach a policy to a specific IAM user. To execute this command, you need to replace YOUR_IAM_USER_NAME with the actual username of the IAM user to which you want to attach the policy. The `--policy-name` option allows you to provide a name for the policy, which can be chosen to suit your requirements.

The crucial part of this process is `--policy-document`, where you define the permissions using a JSON policy document. In this particular case, the policy grants the IAM user the permissions to perform `s3:GetObject` (read) actions and `s3:Put Object` (write) actions on objects located within a specified S3 bucket. To specify the S3 bucket and objects, you use the `Resource` parameter, which contains the ARN of the S3 bucket and its contents. Be sure to replace `YOUR_BUCKET_NAME` in the ARN with the actual name of the S3 bucket you want to grant access to.

By executing this command, you grant the IAM user permission to read and write objects in the specified S3 bucket. Remember to replace placeholders with your actual username and bucket name.

Object ACLs

Configuring object ACLs for individual datafiles or directories within your S3 bucket allows you to set fine-grained permissions. This section provides details on how to use this feature.

To access the properties of an object, you can follow these steps within the AWS Management Console. Log in to your AWS Management Console and then navigate to the S3 service. Next, click the bucket that houses the object for which you want to configure ACLs. To pinpoint the specific object, click its name or navigate the directory structure. Once you've located the object, select it to access its properties and make the necessary ACL configurations.

Alternatively, you can follow these steps to access the object's properties using the AWS CLI. Begin by opening your terminal or command prompt. Then utilize the AWS S3 CLI commands to gain access to the object's properties. Here is a practical example:

```
aws s3api put-object-acl --bucket your-bucket-name --key path/to/your-object --
acl private --grant-read id="YOUR_IAM_USER_ID"
```

In this scenario, you can use the AWS CLI command `aws s3api put-object-acl` to make adjustments to the ACL of an object stored in an AWS S3 bucket. By specifying `--bucket your-bucket-name`, you indicate the name of the S3 bucket where the object is located. The `--key path/to/your-object` parameter denotes the precise path to the object within the bucket that you intend to modify. Setting `--acl private` ensures that the ACL is configured as private, thereby restricting access to the object to its owner by default. Furthermore, using `--grant-read id="YOUR_IAM_USER_ID"` allows you to grant read permissions to a specific IAM user, identified by their unique IAM user ID or ARN. It's essential to replace the placeholder `"YOUR_IAM_USER_ID"` with the actual IAM user ID or ARN to specify who should have read access to the object.

By running this command, you restrict access to the specified object, allowing only the IAM user with the provided ID to read it. You can adapt this example to grant different permissions or specify different IAM entities.

Object ACLs can become complex to manage at scale, especially when dealing with numerous objects and varying access requirements. It's important to have a well-defined and documented access control strategy to avoid unintended permissions and potential security risks. Also keep in mind the pros and cons of using IAM roles and ACLs (*https://oreil.ly/wPnGI*).

Azure Data Lake Storage

Securing datafiles in Azure Data Lake Storage (ADLS) for Apache Iceberg tables involves using various security features primarily around encrypting your files and controlling access to them. This section discusses how to take advantage of these security features.

ADLS encryption

Securing your datafiles in ADLS involves encrypting data at rest, and you can choose between default encryption and customer-managed keys for enhanced security. Following are detailed steps, including relevant CLI commands, for enabling customer-managed keys in ADLS.

An Azure Key Vault is a secure way to manage and control access to your encryption keys. Follow these steps to create and configure an Azure Key Vault.

Start by using the Azure portal, Azure CLI, or Azure PowerShell to create an Azure Key Vault:

```
az keyvault create --name YourKeyVaultName --resource-group YourResourceGroup
--location YourLocation
```

Replace `YourKeyVaultName`, `YourResourceGroup`, and `YourLocation` with appropriate values. You can then either generate your encryption keys within the Key Vault or import existing keys:

```
az keyvault key create --vault-name YourKeyVaultName --name YourKeyName --kty RSA
```

Replace `YourKeyVaultName` and `YourKeyName` with appropriate values.

Now that you have set up your Azure Key Vault and created or imported your encryption keys, you can configure ADLS to use these customer-managed keys. Ensure that the Azure ADLS account or the service principal you plan to use has the necessary permissions to access the keys in your Azure Key Vault.

Now use the Azure portal or Azure CLI to link your ADLS account to your Azure Key Vault:

```
az storage account update --name YourStorageAccountName --resource-group Your
ResourceGroup --assign-identity [system] --keyvault YourKeyVaultName
```

Replace YourStorageAccountName, YourResourceGroup, and YourKeyVaultName with appropriate values.

To maintain security, only authorized personnel should have access to the Azure Key Vault for key management. To configure access policies within the Key Vault, use the Azure portal, Azure CLI, or Azure PowerShell to add an access policy that grants appropriate permissions to individuals or applications:

```
az keyvault set-policy --name YourKeyVaultName --resource-group YourResourceGroup
--spn YourServicePrincipalName --key-permissions get list
```

Replace YourKeyVaultName, YourResourceGroup, and YourServicePrincipalName with appropriate values and specify the required permissions.

Role-Based Access Control

Role-based access control (RBAC) in Azure allows you to define and manage who can perform actions on your ADLS resources. Here are detailed steps, along with relevant Azure CLI commands, to implement RBAC in Azure for ADLS.

Before implementing RBAC, ensure that you have ADLS resources created and configured appropriately. Now you can create an ADLS account using the Azure portal, Azure CLI, or Azure PowerShell:

```
az dls account create --name YourADLSAccountName --resource-group YourResource
Group --location YourLocation --tier TierName --encryption-type ServiceManaged
```

Replace YourADLSAccountName, YourResourceGroup, YourLocation, and TierName with appropriate values.

Azure offers predefined roles suitable for ADLS resources, such as "Storage Blob Data Contributor." However, you can create custom roles with specific permissions tailored to your organization's needs.

Use the Azure CLI to list existing built-in roles for ADLS:

```
az role definition list --resource-type Microsoft.DataLakeStore/accounts
```

If predefined roles don't meet your requirements, you can create a custom role. Define the permissions required for your custom role:

```
az role definition create --role-definition CustomRoleDefinition.json
```

Replace CustomRoleDefinition.json with the JSON file containing your custom role definition.

Once you have defined the appropriate roles, you can assign them to users, groups, or service principals to control access to your ADLS resources.

Use the Azure CLI to assign a predefined role to a user, group, or service principal:

```
az role assignment create --assignee YourPrincipalName --role "Storage Blob
Data Contributor" --scope /subscriptions/YourSubscriptionId/resourceGroups/Your
ResourceGroup/providers/Microsoft.DataLakeStore/accounts/YourADLSAccountName
```

Replace `YourPrincipalName`, `YourSubscriptionId`, `YourResourceGroup`, and `Your ADLSAccountName` with appropriate values.

If you created a custom role, use a similar command to assign it. If you need to revoke access, you can remove a role assignment:

```
az role assignment delete --assignee YourPrincipalName --role "Storage Blob
Data Contributor" --scope /subscriptions/YourSubscriptionId/resourceGroups/Your
ResourceGroup/providers/Microsoft.DataLakeStore/accounts/YourADLSAccountName
```

To maintain security and compliance, regularly review and audit access permissions assigned through RBAC. Ensure that users, groups, and service principals have the appropriate level of access according to the principle of least privilege.

ACLs

ACLs in ADLS provide fine-grained control over access permissions for individual users, groups, or service principals at both the directory and file levels. Here are detailed steps, including relevant Azure CLI commands, for configuring ACLs in ADLS.

To configure ACLs, you can use either the Azure portal or Azure CLI to access your ADLS account. Log in to the Azure portal (*https://portal.azure.com*) and navigate to your ADLS account.

Open your terminal or command prompt:

```
az login
```

Use the following Azure CLI command to set the default subscription (if it's not already set):

```
az account set --subscription YourSubscriptionName
```

Once you've accessed your ADLS account, navigate to the specific directory or file for which you want to set ACLs. Use the Azure portal's user interface to browse and select the desired directory or file.

With the Azure CLI, list the contents of a directory or get information about a specific file:

```
az dls fs list --account YourADLSAccountName --path /your/directory/path
```

You can use the following Azure CLI command to get file information:

```
az dls fs show --account YourADLSAccountName --path /your/file/path
```

Replace `YourADLSAccountName`, `/your/directory/path`, and `/your/file/path` with appropriate values.

You can configure ACLs by defining access permissions for users, groups, or service principals. Within the Azure portal, navigate to the directory or file and access the "Access control (IAM)" or Permissions section. Next, add or modify the permissions for specific users, groups, or service principals.

Use the Azure CLI to set ACLs for a specific directory or file:

```
az dls fs access set --account YourADLSAccountName --path /your/directory/path
--acl-spec "user::rwx,group::r--,other::---"
```

Here is the Azure CLI command to set the ACL for a file:

```
az dls fs access set --account YourADLSAccountName --path /your/file/path
--acl-spec "user::rw-,group::r--,other::---"
```

Replace `YourADLSAccountName`, `/your/directory/path`, and `/your/file/path` with appropriate values. Adjust the ACL specification (`--acl-spec`) as needed to grant or deny permissions.

When configuring ACLs, ensure that the permissions granted align with your organization's security policies. Regularly review and audit ACL settings to maintain security and compliance.

By following these steps and utilizing the provided Azure CLI commands, you can effectively configure ACLs in ADLS to manage fine-grained access permissions for directories and files, ensuring data security and compliance with organizational policies.

Google Cloud Storage

Google Cloud Storage (GCS) offers security features to protect your datafiles, including encryption, identity and access management, bucket policies, and object ACLs. In this section, we provide the steps with CLI commands on how to use these security features.

Encryption at rest and in transit

GCS automatically encrypts your data at rest using SSE with Google-managed keys. To add an extra layer of control, you can opt for customer-managed encryption keys (CMEK), where you manage the encryption keys.

Start by creating a cloud KMS keyring and key:

```
gcloud kms keyrings create your-keyring --location global
gcloud kms keys create your-key --location global --keyring your-keyring
--purpose encryption
```

Now assign the CMEK to a bucket:

```
gsutil kms authorize -k projects/your-project/locations/global/keyRings/your-
keyring/cryptoKeys/your-key
gsutil defacl set private gs://your-bucket-name
```

GCS ensures that data is encrypted during transit using industry-standard protocols such as HTTPS.

Identity and access management

Google cloud identity and access management (IAM) allows you to control who can access your GCS resources and define the actions they can perform. IAM roles are used to assign fine-grained access control.

Here is the code to create a service account and grant it a role with the necessary permissions:

```
gcloud iam service-accounts create your-service-account
gcloud projects add-iam-policy-binding your-project --member serviceAccount:
your-service-account@your-project.iam.gserviceaccount.com --role roles/
storage.objectAdmin
```

Now use this code to authenticate as the service account to access GCS:

```
gcloud auth activate-service-account --key-file=your-service-account-key.json
```

Bucket policies

GCS allows you to configure bucket-level access controls using bucket policies, which let you set rules for access based on factors such as IP addresses, requesters, or conditions.

Start by defining a JSON bucket policy specifying the access rules:

```
{
  "bindings": [
    {
      "role": "roles/storage.objectViewer",
      "members": ["user-email@example.com"]
    }
  ]
}
```

Now apply the bucket policy to your bucket:

```
gsutil iam set your-policy.json gs://your-bucket-name
```

Object ACLs

GCS supports ACLs for individual objects within a bucket, allowing you to specify who can read, write, or delete specific objects.

Configure the ACL for a specific object using the following code:

```
gsutil acl ch -u user-email@example.com:READ gs://your-bucket-name/your-object
```

By following these steps and using the provided CLI commands, you can effectively leverage the security features of GCS object storage to safeguard your Apache Iceberg table's datafiles, ensuring confidentiality, integrity, and controlled access to meet your organization's security requirements.

Securing and Governing at the Semantic Layer

A semantic layer is a virtual abstraction atop your data lakehouse, providing a structured and business-friendly view of the underlying data. It acts as a translation layer, allowing users and applications to interact with data in a way that's intuitive and meaningful to them without needing to understand the complexities of the data's storage or schema. This layer enables governance and security by centralizing control over data access, defining fine-grained permissions, and applying data masking and transformation rules. It simplifies data management, ensuring data consistency, quality, and compliance with organizational policies, all while shielding users from the underlying data intricacies. A semantic layer empowers organizations to manage and secure their data lakehouse efficiently.

Semantic layers enable performance to make the data useful, so they often contain features to precompute aggregation metrics such as Dremio's aggregate reflections. Let's look at some semantic layer solutions that may work with Apache Iceberg tables.

Semantic Layer Best Practices

A well-designed and secure semantic layer is the cornerstone of effective data governance in a data lakehouse environment. Here are some best practices to consider when crafting such a layer:

Understand your data

Start by deeply understanding the data sources in your data lakehouse. Identify the types of data, data owners, and sensitivity levels. This understanding will inform your data governance and security decisions. Semantic layer platforms will enable you to label and tag your data to help make this classification more explicit.

Define clear access control policies

Develop a comprehensive access control policy that defines who can access what data and what actions they can perform. Use RBAC and attribute-based access control (ABAC) to ensure that only authorized users can access sensitive data.

Implement data masking

Data masking protects sensitive data. Implement masking rules to ensure that sensitive information is obfuscated when accessed by unauthorized users. Consider column-level masking for sensitive attributes such as personal identifiable information (PII).

Maintain data lineage

Keep track of the data flow within your semantic layer. Data lineage helps you understand how data is transformed and consumed, which is crucial for ensuring data quality and compliance.

Document everything

Maintain detailed documentation of your data governance and security policies, access controls, catalogs, and lineage. Documentation is essential for transparency, compliance, and troubleshooting.

When securing your Apache Iceberg tables at the semantic layer level, there are advantages and disadvantages to consider. On the positive side, this layer offers unified access to data, serving as a consistent entry point for queries and enabling standardized data governance and security policies. It also provides data abstraction, simplifying the data view for end users and tools, thus facilitating easier querying and analysis. However, there are drawbacks, including the risk of a single point of failure when relying solely on the semantic layer, potentially impacting query availability.

Dremio

The Dremio semantic layer offers a robust solution for governing, monitoring, and securing your data within a data lakehouse environment. Dremio provides several features for governing and securing your data lakehouse.

Data lineage of virtual datasets

Dremio's semantic layer allows you to create virtual datasets that abstract the underlying data complexity. It provides a clear and intuitive way to visualize the data lineage, helping users understand how different virtual datasets are derived from the raw data. This lineage tracking is invaluable for auditing, compliance, and understanding the transformation history of your data. Figure 12-1 provides an example.

Figure 12-1. Viewing data lineage from the Dremio semantic layer (in the book's GitHub repository (https://oreil.ly/supp-guide-apache-iceberg), a larger version of this image is available)

Built-in wiki for documentation

The semantic layer includes a built-in wiki feature, making it easy to document your catalogs, virtual datasets, and folders. Documentation is crucial for data governance, as it helps users understand data semantics, business logic, and data source information. With Dremio's wiki, you can create and maintain rich documentation alongside your data, ensuring clarity and transparency. You can see an example of a wiki entry for a particular dataset in Figure 12-2.

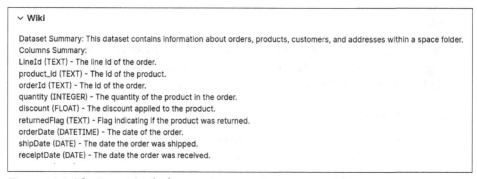

Figure 12-2. The Dremio wiki feature

Role-, column-, and row-based access rules

Dremio's semantic layer empowers you to enforce fine-grained access control over your data. You can define access rules at multiple levels.

Role-based access control. At the RBAC layer, you can create roles that represent different user categories. For example, you can create roles such as analyst, manager, and admin:

```
CREATE ROLE analyst;
CREATE ROLE manager;
CREATE ROLE admin;
```

You also can specify which roles should have access to specific datasets or virtual datasets:

```
GRANT SELECT ON VDS_sales_data TO analyst;
GRANT SELECT, UPDATE ON VDS_employee_data TO manager;
```

And you can map individual users or groups to the defined roles:

```
GRANT analyst TO user1;
GRANT manager TO user2;
```

With RBAC, only users belonging to authorized roles can interact with datasets. For example:

- User1, assigned the analyst role, can access VDS_sales_data.
- User2, assigned the manager role, can access and update VDS_employee_data.

Column-based access control. Column-based access controls allow masking the content in a particular column when different conditions are true, such as the user having a particular role. This can be used to help hide sensitive PII from those who shouldn't have access to it but can use other columns for analytics. In Dremio, these controls are achieved by applying user-defined functions (UDFs) that test certain conditions and return what the user should see:

```
-- Create the mask_salary UDF
CREATE FUNCTION mask_salary(salary VARCHAR)
RETURNS VARCHAR
RETURN SELECT CASE
    WHEN query_user()='user@example.com' OR is_member('HR') THEN salary
    ELSE 'XXX-XX'
END;

-- Create the employee_salaries table with the column masking policy
CREATE TABLE employee_salaries (
    id INT,
    salary VARCHAR MASKING POLICY mask_salary (salary),
    department VARCHAR
);
```

Row-based column access. Row-based column access allows masking the content in a particular row when different conditions are true, such as the user having a particular role. This can be used to hide records from those who shouldn't have access to it but can use other rows for analytics. In Dremio, these controls are achieved by applying UDFs that test certain conditions and return what the user should see:

```
-- Create the restrict_region UDF
CREATE FUNCTION restrict_region(region VARCHAR)
RETURNS BOOLEAN
RETURN SELECT CASE
    WHEN query_user()='user@example.com' OR is_member('HR') THEN true
    WHEN region = 'North' THEN true
    ELSE false
END;

-- Create the regional_employee_data table with the row access policy
CREATE TABLE regional_employee_data (
    id INT,
    role VARCHAR,
    department VARCHAR,
    salary FLOAT,
    region VARCHAR,
    ROW ACCESS POLICY restrict_region(region)
);
```

By leveraging these access control mechanisms, you can ensure that data is accessed, transformed, and presented in compliance with your organization's security and governance policies.

Trino

Trino, formerly known as PrestoSQL, is an open source distributed SQL query engine designed for high-performance data processing across various data sources. Trino enables the creation of a semantic layer with its ability to create layers of logic views over your federated data sources, with controls on access to those views.

There are two security modes to choose from when creating views, DEFINER and INVOKER:

DEFINER

In this security mode, tables referenced in the view are accessed using the permissions of the view owner, which is the creator or definer of the view. This mode allows you to provide restricted access to the underlying tables, even if the user executing the query may not have direct access to those tables.

INVOKER

When you create a view in this security mode, tables referenced in the view are accessed using the permissions of the user executing the query, known as the invoker of the view. In this mode, the view essentially acts as a stored query. It provides a way to ensure that access to the underlying data is determined by the user running the query.

Regardless of the security mode chosen, you can always use the current_user function within views to identify the user executing the query. This allows you to implement row-level filtering or other access restrictions within your views.

Trino provides RBAC as a critical component of its security model. RBAC enables organizations to manage and control access to data by assigning roles to users and granting specific privileges to those roles. This ensures that only authorized users can perform specific actions on data, helping to enforce data security and compliance with organizational policies.

To begin using Trino's RBACs, you need to create roles. Roles are essentially named groups that you can assign to users or other roles. Use the CREATE ROLE command to create roles:

```
CREATE ROLE analyst;
CREATE ROLE data_scientist;
```

In the preceding example, we created two roles: analyst and data_scientist.

After creating roles, you can assign them to users or other roles using the GRANT command. This allows you to define who belongs to each role:

```
GRANT analyst TO USER alice;
GRANT data_scientist TO USER bob;
```

Here, we assigned the analyst role to the user alice and the data_scientist role to the user bob.

Roles in Trino can be associated with specific privileges that define what actions users in those roles can perform. You can use the GRANT command to grant privileges on tables, schemas, or other objects to roles:

```
GRANT SELECT ON orders TO analyst;
GRANT INSERT, SELECT ON customer_data TO data_scientist;
```

In this example, we granted the analyst role the privilege to perform SELECT queries on the orders table and the data_scientist role the privilege to perform both INSERT and SELECT operations on the customer_data table.

You can also use the REVOKE command to remove privileges from roles or revoke roles from users:

```
REVOKE SELECT ON orders FROM analyst;
REVOKE data_scientist FROM USER bob;
```

These commands allow you to refine and modify access control as needed.

Trino also allows you to specify role administrators who have the authority to grant or revoke roles. You can use the WITH ADMIN clause when creating roles or the GRANTED BY clause when granting roles:

```
CREATE ROLE admin WITH ADMIN USER admin_user;
GRANT admin TO USER alice GRANTED BY admin_user;
```

In this example, the `admin_user` is designated as the role admin for the `admin` role, and `admin_user` can grant the `admin` role to `alice`.

RBACs are particularly valuable for controlling access to sensitive data within your organization. By carefully defining roles and their associated privileges, you can ensure that only authorized users have access to critical information.

Trino's RBACs provide a way to manage access to data, making it easier to enforce security policies and meet compliance requirements within your organization.

Securing and Governing at the Catalog Level

Your data catalog is the backbone of your data lakehouse architecture, managing metadata and enabling efficient query execution. This section explores strategies for securing and governing the Apache Iceberg catalog so that you can maintain control over data assets.

Some Apache Iceberg catalogs go beyond merely tracking your Apache Iceberg metadata; they also offer robust security features that provide a mechanism for securing your Iceberg tables effectively. These security features enhance data protection and access control within your data lakehouse environment.

What makes these security features particularly valuable is their potential for portability between different query engines. This means that the security policies and access controls you define within the Iceberg catalog can be enforced consistently across various query engines, ensuring a uniform layer of data security regardless of how you query and analyze your data. This portability simplifies the management of security policies and minimizes the risk of security gaps when transitioning between query engines or integrating multiple tools within your data ecosystem. Let's examine some of the possible security features of some Apache Iceberg catalogs.

When it comes to securing your Apache Iceberg tables at the catalog level, several advantages and disadvantages come into play. On the positive side, catalogs offer centralized metadata management, enabling the enforcement of consistent governance policies and metadata-driven security measures. They also support fine-grained access control at this level, granting comprehensive authority over who can access and manipulate tables and databases. Furthermore, catalogs abstract the underlying file structure, simplifying data access for both users and tools. However, there are drawbacks, including the dependency on the catalog for metadata and access control, which means that any catalog issues can impact data access. Additionally, managing intricate access control policies at the catalog level can be challenging depending on the chosen solution. As the catalog grows, handling permissions and metadata can become more intricate, affecting scalability.

Nessie

Nessie's metadata authorization feature is crucial in creating portable governance and security for your Apache Iceberg data lakehouse. While Nessie primarily manages metadata, it offers a powerful authorization layer that controls access to this metadata. It's important to note that Nessie doesn't directly store data but manages data location and metadata. Therefore, its authorization layer primarily focuses on controlling access to this metadata, ensuring that only authorized users or roles can interact with the metadata stored in Nessie.

The authorization scope of Nessie is centered on controlling access to references (branches and tags) and paths within the metadata. Users and roles can be granted specific permissions for various reference operations, such as viewing, creating, and assigning a hash, or deleting references. Similarly, access control is applied to paths, enabling operations such as creating, deleting, and updating entities' content within a specific reference.

Access to historical data is a key feature of Nessie, allowing users to view data at different times. However, it's important to note that Nessie's authorization primarily covers metadata, and additional security measures should be in place to prevent unauthorized access to data stored in the data lake. For example, sensitive data should be removed or masked from tables, and appropriate access controls should be enforced on the datafile itself.

Nessie's access control model is designed around references and paths, allowing for fine-grained control over metadata operations. Users can define authorization rules using a Common Expression Language (CEL) expression, which provides flexibility in specifying access control conditions. These rules are defined in the *application. properties* file and are associated with specific operations, roles, references, and paths. For example, rules can be created to grant or deny permissions for viewing, creating, deleting, or updating references and entities based on various conditions, including roles and reference names.

Let's look at some examples of managing permissions to Nessie branches through *application.properties*.

In this example code, users with the roles analyst and viewer can view (list) branches and tags:

```
nessie.server.authorization.rules.allow_branch_listing=op=='VIEW_REFERENCE' &&
role in ['analyst', 'viewer']
```

Here, users with the `data_admin` role can create branches that match the regex pattern `.*prod.*`. This allows them to create branches with names containing "prod":

```
nessie.server.authorization.rules.allow_branch_creation=op=='CREATE_REFERENCE' &&
role=='data_admin' && ref.matches('.*prod.*')
```

With this code, users with the roles `data_admin` and `super_admin` can delete branches and tags:

```
nessie.server.authorization.rules.allow_branch_deletion=op=='DELETE_REFERENCE' &&
role in ['data_admin', 'super_admin']
```

With the following code, users with the roles `analyst` and `viewer` can read entity values if the path starts with `'data/'`:

```
nessie.server.authorization.rules.allow_reading_
entity_value=op=='READ_ENTITY_VALUE' && role
in ['analyst', 'viewer'] && path.startsWith('data/')
```

Here, users with the `data_admin` role can update or delete the entity with the path `'data/sensitive'`:

```
nessie.server.authorization.rules.allow_updating_specific_entity=op in ['UPDATE_
ENTITY', 'DELETE_ENTITY'] && role=='data_admin' && path=='data/sensitive'
```

In essence, Nessie's metadata authorization feature serves as a critical layer of governance and security for your Apache Iceberg data lakehouse by controlling access to metadata. By defining and enforcing authorization rules, organizations can ensure that only authorized users and roles can interact with the metadata, helping to maintain data integrity and security. However, it's essential to complement Nessie's metadata authorization with broader data lake security measures to safeguard the actual data stored in the lakehouse.

Tabular

Tabular is a cloud-native *headless warehouse* (a layer for storage management decoupled from any particular query engine or compute) and automation platform offering a unified solution for managing analytic data with Apache Iceberg tables. It is a centralized hub for Apache Iceberg data storage and cataloging, focusing on versatility and efficiency. Tabular features an access control framework designed to govern and secure access to platform resources. We will outline its key elements.

Tabular adopts an RBAC model, where access privileges are assigned to roles, and roles are subsequently assigned to individuals or other roles.

Roles are entities to which access privileges are granted and can be assigned to individuals and other roles. Privileges, conversely, define the level of access to a resource, including LIST, SELECT, UPDATE, and more. Users receive a cumulative set of privileges based on their roles. There are three system-defined roles that exist out of the box that can be used for defining access:

`ORG_ADMIN` *(organization administrator)*
    Responsible for overseeing organizational-level operations, including renaming and deleting the organization, managing users within the `SECURITY_ADMIN` role, and accessing usage and billing information.

`SECURITY_ADMIN`
    Manages global resource grants and creates, monitors, and manages users and roles. This role implicitly holds the `MANAGE GRANTS` security privilege.

`EVERYONE`
    Automatically granted to all individuals and roles in the organization. This role carries inherent privileges on resources and is typically utilized when explicit access control is not required.

Users can define additional roles without necessitating special privileges. These roles can be equipped with specific privileges to regulate resource access.

AWS Glue and Lake Formation

The AWS Glue catalog enables managing metadata for your data lakehouse on AWS. In addition to its metadata management capabilities, the AWS Glue catalog offers robust security features, mostly through the AWS Lake Formation service, that empower organizations to govern and secure their data lakes.

AWS Lake Formation's tag-based access control (TBAC) is a valuable feature that allows you to control access to tables and data stored in your AWS Glue Data catalog based on the tags associated with those resources. With TBAC, you can enforce fine-grained access control policies by using tags to categorize and restrict access to specific datasets. Here is how to use Lake Formation's TBAC to control access to tables in your AWS Glue catalog.

Define data categories with tags

Start by categorizing your data resources by assigning tags to tables or other metadata objects in your AWS Glue Data catalog. Tags can represent various data attributes, such as sensitivity levels, data owners, or project names. For example, you might tag a table with "Confidential," "Finance," or "ProjectA."

To assign tags to a table, you can use the AWS Glue Console, AWS CLI, or AWS SDKs. Here is an example using the AWS CLI:

```
aws glue update-table --database-name mydatabase --table-input '{
    "Name": "mytable",
    "Parameters": {
```

```
        "TAGS": {
            "sensitivity": "Confidential",
            "project": "ProjectA"
        }
    }
}'
```

Define data access policies with TBAC

Once you've tagged your tables, you can define data access policies based on those tags using AWS Lake Formation. Access policies specify which users or groups are allowed or denied access to tables based on the tags associated with the resource.

For example, you can create a policy that grants read access to tables tagged as "ProjectA" only to members of the "ProjectA-Team" IAM group:

```
{
    "Version": "2012-10-17",
    "Statement": [
        {
            "Effect": "Allow",
            "Action": "lakeformation:GetDataAccess",
            "Resource": "*",
            "Condition": {
                "StringEquals": {
                    "glue:ResourceTag/project": "ProjectA"
                }
            },
            "Principal": {
                "AWS": "arn:aws:iam::123456789012:group/ProjectA-Team"
            }
        }
    ]
}
```

You can create such policies using the AWS Lake Formation Console, AWS CLI, or AWS SDKs.

Apply policies to datasets

After defining your access policies, you can apply them to datasets in your AWS Glue Data catalog. These policies are associated with specific tags, so tables with matching tags inherit the policies.

AWS Lake Formation will evaluate access requests based on these policies and tags. Users or groups that match the policies will be granted access to the corresponding tables, while others will be denied access.

Monitor and audit access

AWS Lake Formation provides tools for monitoring and auditing access to your data resources. You can use AWS CloudTrail to capture API calls related to data access, allowing you to review who accessed your data and what actions were performed.

Review and revise policies as needed

Over time, your data access requirements may change. AWS Lake Formation allows you to easily modify and update your access policies and tags as needed. You can adapt your policies to accommodate new data categories or access requirements.

Leverage integration with other AWS services

AWS Lake Formation integrates seamlessly with other AWS services, such as AWS IAM and AWS KMS, to provide additional security and encryption options for your data lake.

By implementing TBAC in AWS Lake Formation, you can enforce strict data access controls based on the tags associated with your data resources. This approach ensures that only authorized users and groups can access sensitive data, helping you maintain data security and compliance in your organization.

Additional Security and Governance Considerations

Securing and governing Apache Iceberg tables within your data lakehouse can be approached at different levels, each with its own set of pros and cons. Here, we'll explore the advantages and drawbacks of focusing on security and governance at the file store level, semantic layer level, and catalog level.

When deciding where to focus your Apache Iceberg table security and governance efforts, consider the following:

Use case
> Different use cases may benefit from different levels of security and governance. For example, highly sensitive data might require catalog-level control, while less sensitive data could rely on the semantic layer.

Scalability
> Consider the scalability of your data lakehouse. As your data grows, managing permissions and governance policies may become more challenging at the file store level.

Performance
> Evaluate the performance requirements of your organization. A semantic layer can optimize query performance, but it may introduce overhead.

Data abstraction
   Think about how abstracted and simplified you want data access to be for end users and tools.

Operational overhead
   Assess the operational overhead associated with each level of governance and security.

Redundancy and failover
   Consider redundancy and failover mechanisms to ensure availability and reliability.

Conclusion

There is no one-size-fits-all approach to securing and governing Apache Iceberg tables within a data lakehouse. The choice of focusing on the file store level, semantic layer level, or catalog level should align with your organization's specific requirements, use cases, and priorities. In many cases, a combination of these levels may be the most effective way to achieve comprehensive security and governance.

In Chapter 13, we will explore how to move your existing data into Apache Iceberg tables.

Migrating to Apache Iceberg

Organizations are constantly seeking innovative solutions to manage their data more efficiently and effectively. Apache Iceberg has emerged as a powerful framework for data lakes, offering a high-performance table format that operates like a relational database management system (RDBMS) table. This chapter delves into the process of migrating your data architecture to leverage the benefits of Apache Iceberg.

Why would you migrate to Apache Iceberg?

You don't have a data lakehouse or are using the Hive table format
> Apache Iceberg will supercharge the data on your data lake with ACID transactions, schema/partition evolution, time travel, and more, effectively turning your data lake into a data lakehouse that gives you the flexibility of data lakes with the performance/features of data warehouses.

Iceberg offers unique benefits over other table formats
> Apache Iceberg's unique features include an open specification, open source libraries, transparent project governance, diversity in project governance, no vendor lock-in, and a diverse ecosystem.

While migrating to Apache Iceberg promises a more streamlined data architecture, the process itself, as with any migration, can be intricate and demanding. The transition involves adapting existing data structures, modifying data ingestion pipelines, and updating data processing workflows. Moreover, organizations may need to refactor existing data models and restructure data storage in Iceberg-compatible formats. Migrating also requires addressing backward-compatibility concerns and ensuring that existing data seamlessly integrates with the new architecture. Throughout this chapter, we will explore best practices and strategies to overcome these challenges effectively. We divided the chapter into several sections, each addressing a specific aspect of the migration process.

Migration Considerations

Data migration requires careful planning and adherence to best practices to ensure a seamless and reliable process. This section serves as an essential foundation, outlining the key factors to consider before embarking on the migration journey. We will discuss best practices, common pitfalls, and how to approach data migration in a structured manner. Here are some key considerations:

Adapting data structures

Before migrating data to Apache Iceberg, assess your existing data structures and adapt them to align with Iceberg's table format. This may involve restructuring data, renaming columns, or adjusting data types to fit Iceberg's requirements. Ensuring data compatibility is crucial for a successful migration. Apache Iceberg should be flexible enough for all kinds of data, but when it comes to complex types, Iceberg offers lists, structs, and maps. So, for something like JSON data, which may have its own field type in other platforms, you'll have to decide whether you want to convert the data into a map or save it as a string.

Adapting pipelines

Update your data pipelines to support writing data to Iceberg tables. This may involve modifying your ETL processes and ensuring that data is correctly partitioned. Fortunately, Apache Iceberg has many utilities to make moving things such as Hive, Delta Lake, and Hudi tables pretty straightforward.

Adapting workflows

Review and adjust your data workflows to accommodate Iceberg. This includes considering how data dependencies, scheduling, and data access will change with the new data storage format. For example, if you are denormalizing multiple datasets into an Apache Iceberg table, you'll want to check that tables are up to date and that any directed acyclic graphs (DAGs) make ingestion dependent on any work on the source tables so that they finish before the ingestion job begins.

You will also need to consider whether to perform an in-place migration or a shadow migration. *In-place migration* uses your existing datafiles to construct your Apache Iceberg tables, while *shadow migration* involves creating a duplicate dataset in Apache Iceberg and then transitioning off the old dataset. Table 13-1 lists the pros and cons of each approach.

Table 13-1. Pros and cons of in-place migration and shadow migration

	In-place migration	Shadow migration
Pros	Simplicity Potentially lower initial storage costs	Safe, as it preserves the original data and allows for testing and validation Minimal impact on existing systems
Cons	Riskier, since data is modified directly and there's no easy rollback option if issues arise Only works for tables using Iceberg-supported file formats	Increased complexity Potentially higher storage costs during migration

Three-Step In-Place Migration Plan

As you'll see throughout this chapter, several utilities are available for conducting in-place migration, including the `migrate` and `add_files` procedures. Since there is no need to write new files, the questions to consider are:

- Do I want to migrate an entire table in one transaction or incrementally by partition?
- When should I change all my read and write mechanisms to use the new tables instead of the old ones?

Small to medium-sized datasets can easily be migrated in one transaction, but it makes more sense to migrate larger tables incrementally, adding one partition to the Apache Iceberg table at a time until all the partitions have been added. When doing incremental migrations, running record number and file number checks in between each job will assist in making sure that the new Iceberg table has accurately replicated the old table using the existing datafiles. With that said, essentially an in-place migration plan would comprise the following steps:

1. Determine the number of files and records in the partition from the old table.
2. Migrate the partitions' existing files into an existing Apache Iceberg table.
3. Determine the number of files and records in the same partition within the Iceberg table to make sure it matches.

Just repeat these steps until all the partitions have been added. Then you can move all read and write operations to the Apache Iceberg table.

Four-Phase Shadow Migration Plan

When assembling a plan for a shadow migration where the table's datafiles are rewritten into a new Apache Iceberg table, you'll want to take a multiphase approach to give yourself time to gradually adopt the new systems. Following is an outline of what such a plan may look like at a high level (see Figure 13-1 for a summary):

Phase 1: Write to the old system, read from the old system
> Initially, keep writing data to your existing system while setting up Iceberg tables. This phase allows you to establish Iceberg infrastructure without affecting ongoing operations. However, you won't benefit from Iceberg's features yet. You should also make sure to write all historical data from the old table to the new Iceberg table before you begin writing new data to Iceberg in Phase 2.

Phase 2: Write to the old and new systems, read from the old system
> In this phase, duplicate data is written to both the old and new systems. This redundancy ensures data consistency but increases storage costs.

Phase 3: Write to the old and new systems, read from the new system
> Once you are confident in the new Iceberg setup, switch your read operations to use the new Iceberg tables. Ensure that data consistency is maintained between both systems during this transition.

Phase 4: Write to the new system, read from the new system
> Gradually phase out the old system and start writing data exclusively to the new Iceberg tables. Monitor the transition carefully to catch any potential issues.

By following these best practices and adopting a structured shadow migration plan, you can minimize disruptions, reduce risks, and ensure a successful data migration to Apache Iceberg while maintaining data integrity and availability.

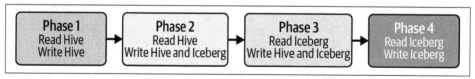

Figure 13-1. Four-phase shadow migration plan

Migrating Hive Tables to Apache Iceberg

Migrating from Hive tables to Apache Iceberg tables using Iceberg's native procedures can greatly enhance data management and provide more robust capabilities for your analytics workflows. In this section, we'll explore the process of migrating Hive tables to Iceberg using Spark and Dremio, enabling users to leverage the full potential of Iceberg's performance and reliability features. Iceberg's Spark extensions offer two primary procedures, snapshot and migrate, each serving a specific purpose in the migration process for Hive tables.

The Snapshot Procedure

When migrating from Hive tables to Apache Iceberg, the snapshot procedure is handy for creating a temporary Iceberg copy of a table specifically for testing purposes. It's a safe way to experiment with data without impacting the source table. The snapshot is created using the original table's datafiles.

To demonstrate, consider the following example code:

```
-- Create a snapshot of the 'db.tableA' table named 'db.tableAsnapshot'
CALL catalog.system.snapshot('hive.db.tableA', 'db.tableAsnapshot')

-- Alternatively, specify a custom location for the snapshot
CALL catalog.system.snapshot('hive.db.tableA', 'db.tableAsnapshot', 's3://
bucket/location')
```

In the first example, we take a Hive table, `tableA`, and create an Apache Iceberg snapshot called `tableAsnapshot`, so now we have a Hive table and an Apache Iceberg table using the same datafiles. By default, this will create a folder based on the table path to house the metadata and any datafiles created later. If we want to customize this location, we can specify a custom location as a third argument, as shown in the preceding code's second example.

The Migrate Procedure

The migrate procedure facilitates the transition from a Hive table to an Apache Iceberg table, retaining the source's datafiles. It copies the table schema, partitioning, properties, and location from the source table to the new Iceberg table. This procedure is a powerful tool for data migration. If your source table's datafiles are in supported formats such as Avro, Parquet, or ORC, this process is particularly effective.

Here's how to use the migrate procedure:

```
-- Migrate the 'hive.db.sample' table to an Iceberg table with additional
properties
CALL catalog.system.migrate('hive.db.sample', map('foo', 'bar'))
```

In this example, we are migrating a Hive table called `sample` into our Apache Iceberg catalog. The new table metadata is written around the existing datafiles, but accessing the table through the old Hive table is eliminated. It must now be accessed as an Apache Iceberg table. If you have custom properties you'd like to specify in the new table, you can optionally pass a map as a second argument with these properties.

When using the migrate procedure, you should carefully plan for schema compatibility, consider whether to retain the original table, and provide any necessary additional properties:

Compatibility
Ensure that the schema of the source table is compatible with Iceberg's requirements. As noted earlier, supported formats for datafiles include Avro, Parquet, and ORC. If the schema of the source table isn't compatible, you may encounter issues during migration.

Backup retention
When using the migrate procedure, it's crucial to decide whether to retain the original table as a backup. Retaining the backup can be beneficial for rollback or reference purposes. However, doing so may increase storage costs. Setting `drop_backup` to `true` ensures that the original table is not retained (meaning a reference in the Hive Metastore to the table under a backup namespace isn't retained; the datafiles are still being used in the new Apache Iceberg table).

Migrating Delta Lake to Apache Iceberg

Migrating from Delta Lake to Apache Iceberg opens up new possibilities for managing your data while preserving its history and ensuring compatibility with a robust table format. Delta Lake, known for its support for the Parquet file format and time-travel/versioning features, provides valuable capabilities for data management.

When transitioning from Delta Lake to Iceberg, you can use the `snapshotDeltaLake Table` action provided by the `iceberg-delta-lake` module. This action allows you to snapshot an existing Delta Lake table into a new Iceberg table using the original table's datafiles. The newly created Iceberg table mirrors the schema and partitioning of the source Delta Lake table. This migration action provides a seamless transition path while retaining data integrity.

To migrate from Delta Lake to Iceberg, you'll need the minimum required dependencies, including iceberg-delta-lake, delta-standalone-0.6.0, and delta-storage-2.2.0. The migration process supports Delta Lake tables with specific protocol versions, ensuring compatibility during the transition.

The following code example demonstrates the `snapshotDeltaLakeTable` action. It includes specifying the source Delta Lake table's location, the destination table's location, the new Iceberg table's identifier, the catalog to use, the Hadoop configuration for access, and additional table properties:

```
import org.apache.iceberg.catalog.TableIdentifier;
import org.apache.iceberg.catalog.Catalog;
import org.apache.hadoop.conf.Configuration;
import org.apache.iceberg.delta.DeltaLakeToIcebergMigrationActionsProvider;

// location of the original delta lake table
String sourceDeltaLakeTableLocation = "s3://my-bucket/delta-table";

// where the new Apache Iceberg tables should be located
String destTableLocation = "s3://my-bucket/iceberg-table";

// Name of the table
TableIdentifier destTableIdentifier = TableIdentifier.of("my_db", "my_table");

// iceberg catalog to add the table to
Catalog icebergCatalog = ...;

// file system configurations for Delta Lake table
Configuration hadoopConf = ...;

DeltaLakeToIcebergMigrationActionsProvider.defaultActions()
    .snapshotDeltaLakeTable(sourceDeltaLakeTableLocation)
    .as(destTableIdentifier)
    .icebergCatalog(icebergCatalog)
    .tableLocation(destTableLocation)
    .deltaLakeConfiguration(hadoopConf)
    .tableProperty("my_property", "my_value")
    .execute();
```

The snapshotDeltaLakeTable action simplifies the migration process, ensuring that your data's history is preserved while providing the benefits of Iceberg's exclusive features.

Migrating Apache Hudi to Apache Iceberg

Apache Hudi is a popular data lake storage format known for supporting ACID transactions and efficient data management capabilities. However, suppose you are considering migrating from Hudi to Apache Iceberg. In that case, you'll be pleased to know that as of this writing, a procedure similar to the Delta Lake snapshot procedure is being developed for Hudi tables (Pull Request #6642). This procedure allows you to seamlessly transition your data using the datafiles of the existing table.

The migration procedure for Hudi tables to Iceberg tables involves using the HudiTo IcebergMigrationActionsProvider class provided by the iceberg-hudi module. The key action for this migration is snapshotHudiTable, which enables you to snapshot an existing Hudi table into a new Iceberg table. This migration action offers a reliable path for transitioning from Hudi to Iceberg.

Here is an example of how to use the `snapshotHudiTable` action for migrating a Hudi table to an Iceberg table:

```
import org.apache.iceberg.catalog.TableIdentifier;
import org.apache.iceberg.catalog.Catalog;
import org.apache.hadoop.conf.Configuration;
import org.apache.iceberg.hudi.HudiToIcebergMigrationActionsProvider;

// location of existing hudi table
String hudiTablePath = "hdfs://my-hudl-tablet";

// name of new iceberg table
String newTableIdentifier = "my_db.my_table";

// iceberg catalog new table will be registered with
Catalog icebergCatalog = ...;

// File System configs for Hudi Table
Configuration hadoopConf = ...;

HudiToIcebergMigrationActionsProvider.defaultProvider()
    .snapshot AudiTable(hudiTablePath)
    .as(TableIdentifier.parse(newTableIdentifier))
    .hoodieConfiguration(hadoopConf)
    .icebergCatalog(icebergCatalog)
    .execute();
```

In this example, we specify the Hudi table's path, the new Iceberg table's identifier, the Hadoop configuration for access, and the Iceberg catalog to use.

Migrating Individual Files to Apache Iceberg

In some scenarios, you may have datasets stored as individual files, such as pure Parquet datasets (meaning a Hive Metastore is not tracking the partition directories containing these files), and you want to migrate these files into an Apache Iceberg table for improved management, query performance, and schema evolution capabilities. Apache Iceberg provides the `add_files` procedure to facilitate this migration process, allowing you to import files into an existing Iceberg table without creating a new table. Additionally, you can use this procedure to migrate data from Delta Lake and Apache Hudi tables, without preserving history, by expiring all previous snapshots.

Using the add_files Procedure

The `add_files` procedure is a versatile method for adding external datafiles to an Apache Iceberg table. It does not analyze the schema of the files, so it's important to ensure that the files match the schema and partitioning of the target Iceberg table to prevent inconsistencies when reading the Apache Iceberg table. Here is how you can use the add_files procedure:

```
CALL catalog.system.add_files(
  table => 'db.my_table',
  source_table => 's3://my-parquet-tables/tables',
  partition_filter => map('partition_col', 'partition_value'),
  check_duplicate_files => true
)
```

In this example, we tell the engine that all datafiles in the table in a particular folder should be added to my_table. We can use the partition_filter argument to only add files from a particular partition for incremental processing and enable checking for duplicate files to avoid duplicative additions.

This procedure will create metadata for the new files and treat them as part of the Iceberg table's file set (it is assumed that these files match the Iceberg table's partitioning and schema). It's worth noting that subsequent Iceberg operations can physically delete files added using this method.

Migrating from Delta Lake or Apache Hudi Without Preserving History

To migrate data from Delta Lake or Apache Hudi tables into an Apache Iceberg table without preserving history, follow these steps:

1. Expire all previous snapshots in the Delta Lake or Hudi table to retain only the current snapshot's files.

2. Use the add_files procedure to import the files from the current snapshot into the target Iceberg table, as shown in the previous example.

This approach allows you to transition to Apache Iceberg while keeping only the latest version of your data, which can be advantageous when maintaining a simplified version of your data lake.

By leveraging the add_files procedure, Apache Iceberg provides a flexible and efficient way to migrate individual files or data from other storage formats into an Iceberg table.

Migrating from Anywhere by Rewriting Data

Flexibility often stands as a paramount goal. When it comes to migrating data from diverse sources to an Apache Iceberg table, there are two approaches. You can migrate data into a new table using a CREATE TABLE...AS SELECT (CTAS) statement with any engine, including Spark, Dremio, Trino, and Presto. You can also insert data into existing Iceberg tables from other nontable sources, such as JSON/CSV, with the COPY

INTO command (Dremio/Snowflake) and from any other table using an INSERT INTO SELECT command.

Migrating Data to a New Iceberg Table

Migrating data into a new Apache Iceberg table using a CTAS statement is a powerful and versatile method for the following reasons:

Schema evolution
> CTAS allows you to adapt the schema during migration. You can map columns from the source to the target table, rename columns, change data types, and apply expressions for calculated columns.

Partitioning control
> If the source data is not partitioned in the desired way, you can use CTAS to create partitions based on specific columns, dates, or other criteria. This enables better data organization and query performance.

Data transformation
> You can apply data transformations within the CTAS query, making it possible to clean, aggregate, or preprocess data during migration.

This approach allows for fine-grained control over the migration process and enables schema, partitioning, and data alterations to be made during data transfer. Following is a breakdown of how to execute this migration.

First, connect your original data source and the target Iceberg catalog. This typically involves configuring your query engine (e.g., Dremio's SQL Query Engine, Apache Spark, Trino, Presto) to access the source data and the destination Iceberg catalog.

Once the connections are established, you can migrate the data using a CTAS statement. The CTAS statement creates a new Iceberg table and populates it with data from the source. Here's an example using Apache Spark SQL:

```
CREATE TABLE catalog.db.tableA
USING iceberg
PARTITIONED BY (month(ts_field))
AS
SELECT *,
       CAST(old_field AS <data_type>) AS updated_field
FROM my_source_table;
```

In this example, we are creating a new Apache Iceberg table in a catalog called tableA. The table will replicate the results of the SELECT query, which converts the data type of an old field we've meant to update. We also specify a partitioning scheme using the month transform to leverage Iceberg's partitioning features as the new data is written. New datafiles are then written to create this table.

When migrating large datasets to a new Iceberg table, there are a few best practices to consider regarding scalability and performance:

Migrate incrementally
Consider an incremental approach instead of migrating the entire dataset in one go. Start with a CTAS statement that covers a single partition or a subset of data. Afterward, use INSERT INTO SELECT statements to gradually add data for other partitions. This reduces the risk of overloading resources and improves manageability. Make sure to run record number checks by partition as you do this to check for completeness of the data.

Optimize for parallelism
You can optimize performance by leveraging parallel processing depending on your query engine. Ensure that your query engine's parallelism settings are configured appropriately for the migration task.

Conduct monitoring and logging
Keep a close eye on the migration process. Monitor progress, resource utilization, and any potential errors or issues. Logging the migration activities is essential for troubleshooting and auditing purposes.

In summary, using a CTAS statement with query engines provides you with fine-grained control over the migration process into an Apache Iceberg table. This method accommodates schema changes, partitioning strategies, and data transformations, making it suitable for a wide range of migration scenarios. When dealing with large datasets, consider incremental migration and performance optimization for a smooth and efficient data transfer process while preserving table history.

Migrating Data into an Existing Iceberg Table

Migrating data into an existing Apache Iceberg table requires different paths than CTAS, which creates a new table. We'll discuss two common paths here:

- Inserting data from a nontable source (files) using a COPY INTO statement
- Inserting data from another table using an INSERT INTO SELECT statement

The COPY INTO command

The COPY INTO command takes data from a source that is not a cataloged table by the engine and inserts it into a target table (new datafiles are written). There are many benefits to using COPY INTO:

Schema coercion

The COPY INTO command automatically coerces the data in the files coming from schema-less sources such as CSV to match the schema of the target Iceberg table. This means that data types, column names, and structures are adjusted as needed, reducing the risk of data type mismatches.

Efficient data ingestion

The COPY INTO command is optimized for efficient data ingestion. It saves you time in having to stage data as another table.

Incremental data ingestion

You can use the COPY INTO command for incremental data ingestion. If you have new CSV, JSON, or Parquet files to add to the Iceberg table, simply run the command again against the new files.

This can be helpful as it saves the step of needing to stage the data as a table when you only intend to insert the data into another table. Following is an example:

```
-- Example of COPY INTO using Dremio Syntax
COPY INTO catalog.db.my_iceberg_table
FROM '@my_dremio_source/folder'
FILE_FORMAT 'csv';
```

In this example, the intent is to add the data from a folder's CSV files into a table named my_iceberg_table. Dremio will read all the data in the CSV files, apply the schema from the destination table, and write new datafiles that will get added to that table.

There are several considerations for a successful migration using COPY INTO:

Data quality

Ensure that the data in your CSV, JSON, or Parquet files is clean and adheres to the schema of the target Iceberg table. Inconsistent or malformed data may lead to ingestion errors.

File organization

Organize your datafiles in a way that makes sense for your use case. For example, if you're partitioning your Iceberg table by date and ingesting incrementally, organize your files into date-specific folders, making it easy to specify which data is to be ingested at each incremental step.

File format options

Depending on your data's characteristics, you can specify additional options within the FILE_FORMAT clause, such as date and time formats, delimiter characters, and the handling of NULL values.

The Dremio version of the `COPY INTO` statement can perform incremental data ingestion. This means you can add new data to your existing Iceberg table without reloading the entire dataset.

First you must prepare the new data by organizing it into files, placing the files in the source location, and prefixing their names with the target ingestion date. Next, rerun the `COPY INTO` command and filter the files using regular expressions for only the files that are prefixed with the particular date, specifying the same target Iceberg table. Here is an example:

```
-- DremioSQL Syntax
-- Use the COPY INTO command with a regex pattern
COPY INTO my_table
FROM '@my_storage_location'
REGEX '^2023-10-11_.*\.csv'
FILE_FORMAT 'csv';
```

For a Snowflake `COPY INTO`, you can just have different folders representing different ingestion points:

```
-- SnowflakeDB Syntax
-- Use the COPY INTO command to ingest files
COPY INTO '@my_external_stage'
FROM '@s3://my-s3-bucket/path/tablea-2023-10-11'
FILE_FORMAT = (TYPE = 'CSV' FIELD_DELIMITER = ',' SKIP_HEADER = 1)
CREDENTIALS = (AWS_KEY_ID = '<your_aws_key_id>' AWS_SECRET_KEY =
'<your_aws_secret_key>')
VALIDATION_MODE = RETURN_ROWS;
```

The `COPY INTO` command offers a straightforward and efficient method for migrating data into an existing Apache Iceberg table. This approach ensures schema coercion and efficient data ingestion. Also, it supports incremental updates, making it a valuable choice for maintaining table history while keeping your Iceberg table current with new data.

The INSERT INTO SELECT command

Using any query engine, you can insert data from any table into an Apache Iceberg table using `INSERT INTO SELECT`. This is particularly useful with engines that can federate data from several sources, such as Dremio, Trino, and Presto. Simply insert data from another table:

```
INSERT INTO tableB
SELECT * FROM tableA;
```

To update the data, you can use `MERGE INTO` statements, which can be easier if the source table has `updated_at` and `created_at` fields:

```
-- DremioSQL Syntax
MERGE INTO tableB AS target
```

```
USING (
    SELECT *
    FROM tableA
    WHERE created_at >= DATE_DIFF(CURRENT_DATE(), CAST(30 AS INTERVAL DAY))
        OR updated_at >= DATE_DIFF(CURRENT_DATE(), CAST(30 AS INTERVAL DAY))
) AS source
ON target.id = source.id
WHEN MATCHED THEN
    UPDATE SET
        target.column1 = source.column1,
        target.column2 = source.column2,
        target.created_at = source.created_at,
        target.updated_at = source.updated_at
WHEN NOT MATCHED THEN
    INSERT *
```

In the preceding example, we are merging data that was created or updated in the last 30 days. This makes for a more performant job because we aren't merging every record in both tables, just the relevant ones. When working with tables, using the INSERT INTO command allows you to easily take data from one table and insert it into your Apache Iceberg tables. Furthermore, MERGE INTO can make it easy to run comprehensive upserts in platforms supporting that capability.

Conclusion

This chapter provided a comprehensive overview of data migration strategies and best practices when migrating to Apache Iceberg. We began by laying the groundwork, highlighting the critical considerations and structured approaches necessary for a successful migration. Understanding the challenges and pitfalls is paramount to achieving a seamless transition.

We then delved into specific migration scenarios, starting with Hive tables and showing how to use the migrate and snapshot procedures. We explored migrating from Delta Lake and Apache Hudi, and for those working with no table format, we discussed migrating individual files into Apache Iceberg. This flexibility allows for efficient data movement without compromising the power of Iceberg's management and performance capabilities.

Furthermore, we explored how to rewrite data from various sources, including the use of the CTAS statement to populate new Apache Iceberg tables with data or to inject data into existing Iceberg tables using the COPY INTO or INSERT INTO SELECT statement, regardless of the original format. This adaptability allows you to accommodate data from diverse origins seamlessly.

In Chapter 14, we'll walk through the process of using Apache Iceberg in several use cases, including business intelligence dashboards and AI/ML.

Real-World Use Cases of Apache Iceberg

In this chapter, we will dive into some of the real-world applications of Apache Iceberg and provide you with hands-on experience in running different analytical use cases supported by a lakehouse architecture. These use cases will include ensuring data quality in data lakes, building business intelligence (BI) reports, and implementing critical processes such as CDC. Additional use case for building a real-time analytical architecture, running machine learning (ML) workloads, and slowly changing dimensions (SCDs) are available at this supplemental repository (*https://oreil.ly/apache-ice_more-content*). This chapter is a practical introductory guide, showcasing how to tackle essential real-world applications using Iceberg and highlighting its adaptability and importance as a core element in any data architecture.

Ensuring High-Quality Data with Write-Audit-Publish in Apache Iceberg

Maintaining the highest level of data quality is crucial for deriving meaningful insights. If data quality is compromised at any point in a data engineering workflow, it can adversely affect subsequent analyses such as BI and predictive analytics. For example, consider an extract, transform, and load (ETL) process: it takes data from an operational system and transfers it to an analytical system for use in BI reports or ad hoc analyses. If the original data has duplicates or inconsistencies or if such issues are introduced during the ETL process and are not addressed before reaching the production analytics environment, the result can be flawed insights that can lead to incorrect decisions. This highlights the critical importance of data quality in data engineering workflows. It's essential, not just in theory but as a practical necessity, to ensure that data is accurate, consistent, and reliable.

This is where the Write-Audit-Publish (WAP) pattern provides a systematic approach to ensure that data is of good quality. Let's take a look at the process in more detail:

1. Write: Data is first extracted from sources and written to a nonproduction location, isolating production data from potential inconsistencies.

2. Audit: Once staged, the data undergoes a thorough validation process. This could involve inspecting null or duplicate values, validating data types, and checking data integrity.

3. Publish: After validation, the data is atomically pushed to production tables, ensuring that consumers see the entire updated dataset or none of it.

Let's see how we can implement this process with Apache Iceberg. While Iceberg offers the APIs and semantics to implement WAP, the onus of actual pattern implementation falls on the compute engine. Apache Spark supports the implementation of WAP, and we will be using it for our hands-on exercise.

WAP Using Iceberg's Branching Feature

Although there is more than one way to implement WAP in Iceberg, we will focus on an approach using Iceberg's table-level *branching* capabilities. Branching in Iceberg works similarly to Git (*https://git-scm.com/docs/git-branch*) branches where you can create local branches from the production table (main branch) to carry out isolated data work on the table. The core Iceberg component behind a branch is the *snapshot*, which describes the state of an Iceberg table at a certain point in time. Branches are named references to these snapshots. We discuss branching in detail in Chapter 10.

Let's imagine that product sales data from an ecommerce company is regularly extracted from operational systems, such as relational database management systems (RDBMSs) and customer relationship management (CRM) systems, and is then loaded into the company's Amazon Simple Storage Service (Amazon S3) data lake. The data engineering team is responsible for creating and maintaining Iceberg tables in the data lake, which serves as the base dataset to cater to different production applications such as BI reports and predictive models. How can they ensure the quality of the data before pushing it into the production environment?

The first step to implementing WAP in Iceberg is to create a new branch from the production version of the Iceberg table in order to ensure that it has no impact on the main branch. Once the branch is created, they can ingest the new records onto the branch. After conducting data validation checks and ensuring that the data meets the required quality standards, they can publish the new data to the main branch, and if the checks fail, they can drop the branch and reattempt the job without affecting production. This process is illustrated in Figure 14-1.

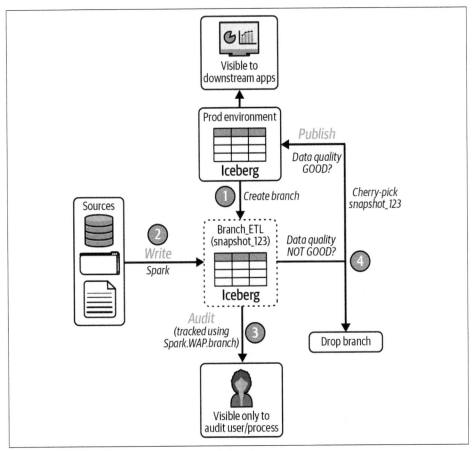

Figure 14-1. The WAP process at the table level

Let's get hands-on and walk through this example using WAP.

Create a branch

First, let's create a new branch named ETL_branch from the existing Iceberg table. This branch will act as the staging area for the new data:

```
# Create a Branch on the Table called 'etl_branch'
spark.sql("ALTER TABLE catalog.db.table CREATE BRANCH etl_branch").show()
```

Let's query this branch to see this dataset's total number of records:

```
# Get a count of all records in the table
spark.sql("SELECT COUNT(*) as total_records FROM catalog.db.table").show()
```

This query will print out the total number of records in the table; this is a good number to have ready for validating our ingestion job after it has run by ensuring that the correct number of records has been added. Let's also confirm the branch we created exists using the following query, which gives us a list of all references in the table, including branches and tags:

```
# List all Table References
spark.sql("SELECT * FROM catalog.db.table.refs").show()
```

We should see our `main` branch and the `etl_branch` we created earlier.

Write the data

A couple of preparatory steps are required before we begin using the WAP method for ingesting new data. First we must adjust the Iceberg table property by turning on `write.wap.enabled=true`. This step prepares our Iceberg table to follow the WAP pattern. After that, to make sure any actions, whether reading or writing, target this specific branch directly, we use the `spark.wap.branch` setting to assign the branch identifier `etl_branch` to the Spark session configuration:

```
# Enabling the Apache Iceberg WAP feature
spark.sql("ALTER TABLE catalog.db.table SET TBLPROPERTIES ('write.wap.ena
bled'='true')")

# Setting the table for WAP
spark.conf.set('spark.wap.branch', 'etl_branch')
```

Now we are ready to run the ETL job to ingest new records to this specific branch of the table:

```
# Insert New Records Into the Table
spark.sql("INSERT INTO catalog.db.table SELECT * FROM new_data")
```

If you query the table's record count now, you'll see the table has additional records:

```
# The Number of Records on the 'etl_branch'
spark.sql("SELECT COUNT(*) as total_records FROM catalog.db.table VERSION AS OF
'etl_branch'").show()
```

Remember that this branch acts as a standalone variant of the production data. Any action taken on this branch affects only this dataset, not the `main` one. You can validate your production table by querying the record count on the `main` branch. You should see that this query returns the same count we had originally, telling us the `main` branch is unchanged:

```
# Count of Records on the Main Branch
spark.sql("SELECT COUNT(*) as total_records FROM catalog.db.table VERSION AS OF
'main'").show()
```

Audit the data

After writing the new data into the isolated local branch, `etl_branch`, it is essential to ensure that this new dataset stands up to the organization's quality standards. The audit phase acts as a checkpoint where we subject our data to rigorous evaluation, ensuring its fitness for purpose.

The audit process offers the flexibility to write native code or incorporate third-party tools tailored to validate data quality checks. We will perform a few basic data quality checks for this exercise.

NULL values. First let's use PySpark to see if there are any null values in the table:

```
# df = dataframe with our "catalog.db.table" table
# Check for nulls in each column
null_counts = df.select([count(when(col(c).isNull(), c)).alias(c) for c in
df.columns])

# Show the result
null_counts.show()
```

The resulting DataFrame will list the number of nulls in each column.

Duplicate records. As part of the next data quality check, let's use PySpark to see if there are any duplicate records in our table and print them:

```
# df = dataframe with our "catalog.db.table" table
# Group by all columns and count
duplicates = df.groupBy(df.columns).count()

# Filter out groups with count > 1, which indicates duplicates
duplicates = duplicates.filter(col("count") > 1)

# Optionally, drop the count column if not needed
duplicates = duplicates.drop("count")

# Show the result (duplicates)
duplicates.show()
```

The output shows which records have duplicates (all columns have the same values).

Date consistency. The final data quality validation we want to perform on this new dataset is date consistency. When dealing with time-series data or records with timestamped entries, it is critical to ensure that every date in the dataset is valid and falls within a predefined, acceptable range. For example, let's assume that the data we ingested represents the period of January 2024. The number of records whose date_column values are in this period should equal the number of records added.

Let's quickly write some code to do this:

```
# df = dataframe with our "catalog.db.table" table
# Define your date range
start_date = datetime(2024, 1, 1)  # for example, Jan 1, 2024
end_date = datetime(2024, 1, 31)  # for example, Jan 31, 2024
```

```
# Convert the date column to date type if it's not already
df = df.withColumn("date_column", col("date_column").cast("date"))

# Filter the DataFrame to find records within the date range
within_range = df.filter((col("date_column") >= start_date) & (col("date_col
umn") <= end_date))

# Count the records that fall within the desired date range
count_within_range = within_range.count()
```

We compare this count to the difference between the count of the records on the main branch and the count on etl_branch. If they don't match, we can inspect whether any records have incorrect dates or null dates causing the inconsistency.

We have gone through three examples of data quality checks we can run on an isolated branch. During these checks, the yet-to-be-validated data was not being scanned by incoming queries that would query the main branch, which will only have validated data. The ability to perform these quality checks flexibly in an isolated branch without impacting anything in production is a critical capability in Apache Iceberg.

By using this approach, we end up with a couple of benefits:

Enhanced data quality
> Production environments are not exposed to unverified data, preventing incorrect results and decisions. This eliminates the rush to correct data errors, reducing the risk of additional mistakes during the fixing process.

Efficient data handling
> Compared to the traditional way of using a staging table for quality checks, the need for data copies is eliminated, saving resources and ensuring efficiency. This enables the easy identification of issues, such as duplicate data, that are often missed when just checking new data.

Applying fixes. At this stage, you can take a couple of actions, such as communicating about the anomalies with the required stakeholders, reviewing the ETL job, determining the origin of the anomalies, and applying some quick fixes. As a basic remediation step, let's create two DataFrames—one with records needing remediation, which we can save to another table or write to a file to give to stakeholders, and another comprising validated records that we can overwrite the table with so that it only has validated records:

```
# 1. Identifying Null Records
# Check for nulls in each column and create a filter condition
is_null_condition = [col(c).isNull() for c in df.columns]
combined_null_condition = is_null_condition[0]
for condition in is_null_condition[1:]:
    combined_null_condition = combined_null_condition | condition
```

```
# 2. Identifying Duplicated Records
# Group by all columns, count occurrences, and filter for counts greater than 1
duplicates_condition = df.groupBy(df.columns) \
                          .count() \
                          .filter(col("count") > 1) \
                          .drop("count") \
                          .distinct()

# 3. Creating DataFrame for Records Needing Remediation
# Union the null and duplicated conditions to find all records needing remedia
tion
records_needing_remediation = df.filter(combined_null_condi
tion).union(df.join(duplicates_condition, df.columns, "inner")).distinct()

# 4. Creating DataFrame for Valid Records
# Use exceptAll to find records that are neither null nor duplicated
valid_records = df.exceptAll(records_needing_remediation)

# Show the records needing remediation
records_needing_remediation.show()

# Show the valid records
valid_records.show()

# Overwrite the table with only the validated records
valid_records.write.format("iceberg").mode("overwrite").save("catalog.db.table")
```

Now our branch has new validated records, and we've shipped off the invalid records to our stakeholders, who can fix them for later backfilling.

Publish the changes

The final operation in the WAP pattern is to publish the changes and make the data available to the production environment so that downstream applications can use it. The publish operation is made possible by the cherry-pick (*https://oreil.ly/416_7*) procedure in Iceberg.

In Spark, the cherrypick_snapshot() procedure produces a new snapshot based on a previous one, all the while preserving the original without any changes or deletions. For our use case, we can select a specific snapshot, the branch (ETL_branch), to form a new snapshot. What sets cherry-picking apart is that it is a metadata-only operation. This implies that the actual datafiles remain untouched and only the metadata references are altered. As a result, we're essentially making the new data available in the production table without the need to relocate any datafiles. One limitation to note is that cherry-picking caters to a single commit.

To run this procedure, we will need to provide the snapshot ID as an argument to the method. Let's find out the snapshot ID associated with etl_branch by querying a metadata table called `refs`, meaning *references* (we discussed all the metadata tables facilitated by Iceberg in Chapter 10):

```
#Query The List of References for the Table
spark.sql("SELECT * FROM catalog.db.table.refs")
```

This will return our list of references (branches and tags), and we can see the current snapshot ID for each branch, which is the information we need. Now let's execute the `cherry_pick()` procedure:

```
#Cherry-picking the snapshot from 'etl_branch' over to 'main'
spark.sql("CALL catalog.system.cherrypick_snapshot('db.table',
2668401536062194692)").show()
```

Once the operation runs successfully, our `main` branch's current snapshot will be made the same snapshot at the current `etl_branch` snapshot. This means we have made the newly inserted records in `etl_branch` available to the `main` branch for production usage.

If we now query the record count on `main` and `etl_branch`, we should see they are identical:

```
# Record count on the 'main' branch
spark.sql("SELECT count(*) FROM catalog.db.table VERSION AS OF 'main'").show();
```

```
# Record count on the 'etl_branch' branch
spark.sql("SELECT count(*) FROM catalog.db.table VERSION AS OF
'etl_branch'").show();
```

To conclude this particular WAP session associated with the branch, we will remove the specific Spark configuration property, `spark.wap.branch`. This ensures that all the subsequent reads and writes do not explicitly happen from this branch but from the `main` branch of the table:

```
#Turn off the WAP feature
spark.conf.unset('spark.wap.branch')
```

In this use case, we reviewed how to leverage the WAP data quality pattern in Apache Iceberg to address the challenges of dealing with data quality at scale. With WAP, before committing data to the production environment, there's a structured mechanism to write, assess for quality concerns, and finalize or discard the data. This method preserves the reliability of the data, ensuring that what drives business decisions is accurate, consistent, and free from anomalies. If you need to isolate changes across multiple tables, catalog-level branches can be created for a similar pattern using the Nessie catalog covered in Chapter 10.

Running BI Workloads on the Data Lake

BI dashboards are the lifeblood of many companies, but making BI dashboards performant can often be easier said than done. As you start creating dashboards on larger and larger datasets, performance begins to deteriorate and the need for engineering kicks in. This would normally come in BI extracts and cubes, independent data structures created from precomputer aggregations over several dimensions and measures. There are several problems with this solution:

- The BI dashboard has to be manually re-created periodically to reflect fresh data.
- BI dashboards can get very large, leading to OOM issues.
- Historical copies add up, causing storage costs or painful maintenance work.
- The user needs to know that their dashboard must work off the BI extract/online analytical processing (OLAP) cube and not the original table.
- A BI dashboard impairs the goal of self-service, as users will need to submit work tickets to have these kinds of structures created to accelerate their dashboards.

Apache Iceberg's use, particularly in the Dremio SQL query engine, eliminates a lot of this work through its aggregate reflections feature. Aggregate reflections are precomputed aggregations stored as an Apache Iceberg table on the user's data lake, providing several benefits:

- Refreshes of the data structure are automated by Dremio.
- Dremio's query engine knows how to handle reflections to avoid OOM errors.
- Dremio automatically cleans up historical copies to avoid storage creep.
- Dashboards can be built on the original table, and Dremio will swap the aggregate reflection when your BI tools send aggregate queries.
- They can be turned on at the flip of a switch or an SQL query, enabling self-service acceleration.
- If the underlying table is an Apache Iceberg table, the aggregate reflection is updated incrementally, allowing for data updates to proliferate in near-real time.

As you can see, Apache Iceberg is the core that powers the acceleration of BI dashboards throughout this story. The workflow would typically go as follows:

1. Raw data is landed as Apache Iceberg tables in the data lake.
2. Virtual data marts and data products are created by creating layers of logical views on these tables.
3. Reflections are enabled on a view that a dashboard will be made from. An Apache Iceberg representation of the aggregates will be created behind the scenes.
4. A dashboard will be created on the source, which will feel performant as aggregate queries are executed against the reflection instead of the raw sources.

Let's look at each step in turn.

Land the Raw Data into the Data Lake

The first step is to land your data into the data lake as Apache Iceberg tables, which can be done using many of the tools discussed in this book. Here are a few of the many possible approaches to getting this done:

- Using tools such as Apache Spark and Apache Flink to ingest batch or stream data into Apache Iceberg tables in the data lake

- Using CREATE TABLE...AS SELECT (CTAS) statements with any query engine to take a data source such as a database and re-create it as an Apache Iceberg table on your data lake

- Using the COPY INTO statement on Dremio to copy data from different datafiles into an existing Apache Iceberg table

- Using data integration tools such as Upsolver, Airbyte, or Fivetran to ingest data into Apache Iceberg tables using their no-code interfaces

Once your data is in the form of Apache Iceberg tables, you just need to connect your data lake storage (Amazon S3, Azure Data Lake Storage [ADLS], Minio) or Apache Iceberg catalog (Hive, Nessie, Amazon Web Services [AWS] Glue) to Dremio to be able to have access to your Apache Iceberg tables, as you can see in Figure 14-2.

Figure 14-2. Apache Iceberg tables in the Dremio UI

Curate Virtual Data Marts/Data Products

In data warehouses, you'll often apply your cleanup, validation, and business logic through layers of copies organized into datasets for different business units; these subwarehouses are known as *data marts*. Dremio enables the creation of virtual data marts on the data lakehouse, so instead of creating more physical tables from our raw

Apache Iceberg tables, we can create layers of logical views that encapsulate cleanup, validation, and business logic and organize these into folders for each business unit. This effectively organizes your data into data marts or data products, as you can see in Figure 14-3.

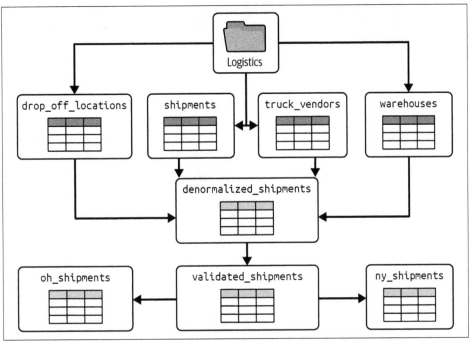

Figure 14-3. An example of the structure of a virtual data mart or data product in Dremio

Create a Reflection to Accelerate Our Dashboard

For many datasets, this will be performant enough without further action for a dashboard, but if you are working with a really large dataset to fuel a dashboard, you may want to create an aggregate reflection to ensure performance. For example, if you were creating a dashboard of Ohio shipments based on the oh_shipments view shown in Figure 14-3, you could enable an aggregate reflection on that table with a few clicks on the Dremio UI or through a simple SQL query:

```
ALTER TABLE arctic.logistics.oh_shipments
  CREATE AGGREGATE REFLECTION oh_shipments_agg
  USING
  DIMENSIONS (shipper_id, destination_city, shipping_method)
  MEASURES (shipment_id (COUNT), total_cost (SUM), delivery_time (AVG))
  LOCALSORT BY (shipper_id, destination_city);
```

This will create a reflection that is optimized for the particular dimensions and measures needed for the dashboard we are creating and the Apache Iceberg table containing pre-computed aggregates called oh_shipments_agg. Although our analysts need to be aware of the existence of this reflection, Dremio will swap out oh_shipments_agg anytime it sees aggregate queries coming in for oh_shipments across the same dimensions and measures. Also, since our source tables are Apache Iceberg tables, reflections can be incrementally applied, allowing the reflection to maintain near-real-time freshness.

Connect Our View to Our BI Tool

Many BI tools have Dremio integrations, but Tableau and Power BI in particular have integrations built into the Dremio UI. This means all you have to do is open your view (oh_shipments) in the Dremio UI and click the Tableau and Power BI buttons to immediately establish a live connection to Dremio for crafting your BI dashboard. You can see these buttons in the Dremio UI in Figure 14-4.

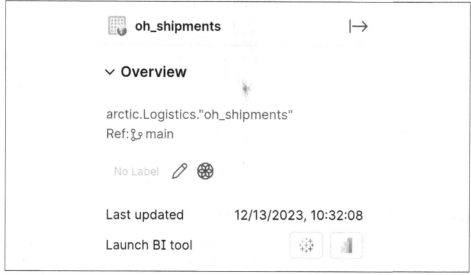

Figure 14-4. BI tool integration in Dremio

Benefits of Running BI Workloads on the Data Lake

By combining the power of Apache Iceberg and Dremio, we've created performant BI dashboards directly from the data lakehouse. This saved us the storage and compute costs of having to move that data into a data warehouse and create and maintain BI extracts and cubes while maintaining a simple and self-service model for our end users. The Apache Iceberg ecosystem is filled with tools that make different use cases such as this easy and scalable while working with only a single copy of your data in one place, the data lakehouse.

Implementing Change Data Capture with Apache Iceberg

CDC is an integral process in the analytics landscape. At its core, CDC is about capturing and tracking changes in the source data. This enables downstream systems to synchronize with the most recent data version efficiently and progressively. In traditional batch processing, databases and data warehouses would often be updated in bulk, potentially missing out on real-time insights and often leading to resource-intensive operations. This approach commonly resulted in outdated views of data, delays in decision making, and inefficient use of storage and computational resources. By focusing on incremental changes—whether they involve inserts, updates, or deletions—CDC ensures that data systems remain synchronized without needing to repeatedly process extensive static data. Figure 14-5 depicts a visual representation of what capturing CDC data looks like at a high level.

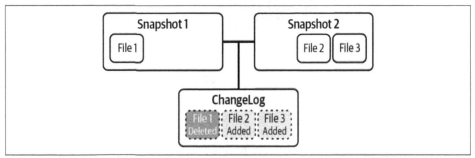

Figure 14-5. An illustration of capturing changes between snapshots

Imagine GreenMart, a retail company with fluctuating stock levels and changing prices in a dynamic retail environment. The company aims to gain real-time stock availability insights to meet customer demands and share these insights with stakeholders such as store managers through its BI reporting system. However, the challenge is maintaining updated BI reports without overloading the system by recalculating aggregates for each change, given the high transaction volume. To address these issues and manage its extensive data, GreenMart seeks a flexible data architecture supporting scalable storage and compute. The company requires schema evolution, ACID-based transactions (INSERT, UPDATE, MERGE INTO, DELETE), rollback capabilities, and CDC. A possible solution for its needs could involve using a cloud data lake storage system such as Amazon S3 in conjunction with Apache Iceberg as the table format.

One approach to address this problem involves creating two Iceberg tables, inventory and inventory_summary, within an S3 data lake. The inventory table will house data from operational systems such as databases and CRMs for analytical purposes, while the inventory_summary table will store aggregated and transformed data for BI reporting. All updates from the transactional systems will be stored in the data lake and subsequently applied to the inventory table through an ETL process utilizing Spark. Iceberg's CDC process will track any modifications to the inventory table, storing them in a change log view named inventory_changes. Using this change log view, only the altered data in the downstream aggregation table inventory_summary will be updated, eliminating the need to recalculate aggregates for the entire dataset with each change. This approach ensures that the BI reports consistently access the most up-to-date data.

Figure 14-6 demonstrates what this could look like visually. Next, let's see this in action.

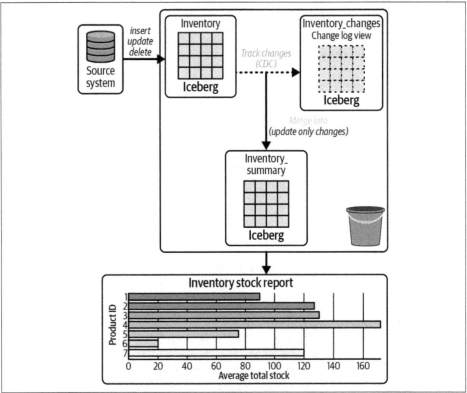

Figure 14-6. Using CDC data to update summary metrics for a BI dashboard

Create Apache Iceberg Tables

Let's create the first Iceberg table, inventory, and ingest some mock data:

```
spark.sql('''CREATE TABLE glue.test.inventory(
  product_id int,
  product_name string,
  stock_level int,
  price int,
  last_updated date) USING iceberg''')
```

```
spark.sql('''INSERT INTO glue.test.inventory VALUES (1, 'Pasta-thin', 60, 45,
'3/25/2023'),
(2, 'Bread-white', 55, 6, '3/10/2023'),
(3, 'Eggs-nonorg', 100, 8, '3/12/2023'),
(4, 'Sausage-pork', 72, 25, '3/29/2023'),
(5, 'Coffee-vanilla', 30, 45, '3/12/2023'),
(6, 'Maple Syrup', 20, 85, '3/29/2023'),
(7, 'Protein Bar', 120, 5, '3/15/2023')
''')
```

Let's query the table to make sure all the data is in there correctly:

```
spark.sql("SELECT * FROM glue.test.inventory").toPandas()
```

The results should look like this:

product_id	product_name	stock_level	price	last_updated
1	Pasta	50	35	3/24/2023
6	Maple Syrup	20	85	3/29/2023
7	Protein Bar	120	5	3/15/2023
2	Bread-brown	87	8	3/25/2023
3	Eggs-organic	30	11	3/26/2023
4	Sausage-chicken	100	20	3/24/2023
1	Pasta-thin	60	45	3/25/2023
5	Coffee-arabica	45	60	3/18/2023
2	Bread-white	55	6	3/10/2023
3	Eggs-nonorg	100	8	3/12/2023
4	Sausage-pork	72	25	3/29/2023

Now let's create the second Iceberg table, `inventory_summary`, which is a transformed dataset with aggregated values. This table is the primary source of data for the downstream BI reports that would help store managers get insights about the stock levels in a particular store:

```
spark.sql('''CREATE TABLE glue.test.inventory_summary(
    product_id string,
    total_stock string,
    avg_price string) USING iceberg''')

spark.sql('''INSERT INTO glue.test.inventory_summary
SELECT
```

```
    product_id,
    SUM(stock_level) AS total_stock,
    AVG(price) AS avg_price
FROM glue.test.inventory_new
GROUP BY product_id;
''')
```

Let's query the table to make sure we got the right data:

```
spark.sql("SELECT * FROM glue.test.inventory_summary").toPandas()
```

The results should look like this:

product_id	total_stock	avg_price
1	110.0	40.0
2	142.0	7.0
6	20.0	85.0
3	130.0	13.5
4	172.0	22.5
5	75.0	52.5
7	120.0	5.0

Apply Updates from Operational Systems

Now, to apply all the updates from the operational databases to the Iceberg tables, we will run a Spark-based ETL job. Iceberg allows you to do row-level updates with transactional guarantees. Here's a simple query to simulate a possible update to our inventory data:

```
spark.sql('''UPDATE glue.test.inventory
SET stock_level = stock_level - 15
WHERE product_name = 'Bread-white' ''')
```

 Capturing the changes from the operational source system and loading them into the data lake is not within the scope of this use case. We have assumed that the changes are made available as a file in the S3 data lake and are then applied to the affected records using the UPDATE command in Iceberg.

If we now query the inventory table, we should see the updated stock levels:

```
spark.sql("SELECT * FROM glue.test.inventory").toPandas()
```

Notice how the `Pasta` and `Bread-white` items have reduced in stock:

product_id	product_name	stock_level	price	last_updated
1	Pasta	30.0	35	3/24/2023
6	Maple Syrup	20	85	3/29/2023
2	Bread-white	40.0	6	3/10/2023
2	Bread-brown	87	8	3/25/2023
1	Pasta-thin	60	45	3/25/2023
7	Protein Bar	120	5	3/15/2023
3	Eggs-organic	30	11	3/26/2023
4	Sausage-chicken	100	20	3/24/2023
5	Coffee-arabica	45	60	3/18/2023
3	Eggs-nonorg	100	8	3/12/2023
4	Sausage-pork	72	25	3/29/2023

Create the Change Log View to Capture Changes

Next, we'll create a change log view to capture alterations in the `inventory_summary` table and update it efficiently based solely on changes, avoiding full recomputation. We'll leverage Iceberg's built-in Spark procedure, `create_changelog_view()`, to execute this task. To capture changes, we have two options: use start and end snapshot IDs or use start and end timestamps. In this example, we'll use specific snapshots as our reference points, with the start occurring after the initial `inventory` table record ingestion and the end following the ETL job execution. To obtain these snapshot IDs, we'll query the default `history` metadata table provided by Apache Iceberg:

```
spark.sql("SELECT * FROM glue.test.inventory.history").toPandas()
```

Let's assume that from inspecting our history table we've determined the target snapshot IDs are 4816648710583642722 and 2557325773776943708 (this may be different for you in practice). Now let's run the procedure:

```
spark.sql("""CALL
glue.system.create_changelog_view(
    table => 'glue.test.inventory',
    options => map(
    'start-snapshot-id',
    '4816648710583642722',
        'end-snapshot-id',
```

```
        '2557325773776943708'
    ))""" )
```

This procedure creates a change log view called `inventory_changes` that allows us to see the changes made to the table between the first and second snapshots specified. Let's query all the changes and see what this change log looks like:

```
spark.sql("SELECT * FROM inventory_changes").toPandas()
```

The results of querying the change log should look like this:

product_id	...	...	...	last_updated	_change_type	_change_ordinal	_commit_snapshot_id
2	...	...	...	3/10/2023	INSERT	0	2557325773776943708
2	...	...	...	3/10/2023	DELETE	0	2557325773776943708
1	...	...	...	3/24/2023	DELETE	1	2959510555509473926
1	...	...	...	3/24/2023	INSERT	1	2959510555509473926

Merge Changed Data in the Aggregated Table

The last step involves updating the downstream aggregated `inventory_summary` table, utilized by BI reports to extract store stock-level insights. Crucially, we aim to avoid recalculating aggregates for the entire dataset with every update. Instead, we focus on making only the essential adjustments when a product's stock level changes. This approach ensures computational and time efficiency, guaranteeing that BI reports consistently access the latest data without burdening the system with constant full recalculations.

In the following code, we'll first create a view from our change log data that is made up of the aggregated changes. We can then merge those aggregated updates into our `inventory_summary` table to have an updated summary table for our BI dashboard:

```
## Create the Aggregated View
spark.sql("""
    CREATE OR REPLACE TEMPORARY VIEW aggregated_changes AS
    SELECT
        product_id,
        SUM(CASE
            WHEN _change_type = 'INSERT' THEN stock_level
            WHEN _change_type = 'DELETE' THEN -stock_level
            ELSE 0 END) AS total_stock_change,
        AVG(price) AS new_avg_price
    FROM
        inventory_changes
    GROUP BY
        product_id
""")
```

```
## Merge the Aggregated View into our Inventory Summary
spark.sql("""
    MERGE INTO glue.test.inventory_summary AS target
    USING aggregated_changes AS source
    ON target.product_id = source.product_id
    WHEN MATCHED THEN
        UPDATE SET
            target.total_stock = target.total_stock + source.total_stock_change
    WHEN NOT MATCHED THEN
        INSERT (product_id, total_stock, avg_price)
        VALUES (source.product_id, source.total_stock_change,
source.new_avg_price)
    """)
```

Note that in a production environment, these operations for CDC would typically be automated and continuously monitored for optimal performance and reliability. Automation tools, such as Apache Airflow or cron jobs, could be employed to schedule and execute the CDC tasks at regular intervals, ensuring that data is updated in near-real time. Monitoring and alerting mechanisms would also be integral, with systems in place to log detailed operations and send notifications in case of failures or anomalies. This setup ensures timely data updates and quick issue resolution and maintains data integrity and consistency across the ecosystem.

Let's query the aggregated table now to see the changes:

```
spark.sql("SELECT * FROM glue.test.inventory_summary").toPandas()
```

As you can see, the records for product_ids 1 and 2 have changed and reflect the updates made to the underlying source table:

product_id	total_stock	avg_price
1	90.0	40.0
2	127.0	7.0
6	20.0	85.0
3	130.0	13.5
4	172.0	22.5
5	75.0	52.5

The BI report that works off the inventory summary used to monitor stock levels is now also updated, as shown in Figure 14-7.

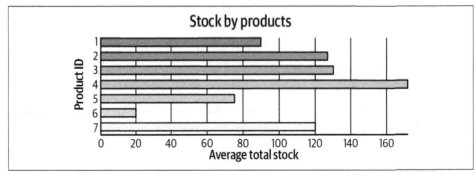

Figure 14-7. The updated BI dashboard reflecting updates to inventory summary

Using Apache Iceberg's change log view, we've addressed a critical issue for Green-Mart, offering several advantages. This approach delivers speed and efficiency by computing only the differences, leading to reduced processing time and cost savings. It ensures near-real-time reports for analysts, granting access to up-to-date inventory insights, product popularity, and restocking needs. Moreover, as GreenMart grows and its inventory data expands, this approach ensures scalable and efficient data processing.

Conclusion

In this chapter, we walked through a range of analytical use cases with Apache Iceberg as the table format on top of data lakes. From ensuring high-quality data to building BI dashboards and capturing changes, we've explored how to practically implement these critical applications.

With that, we have reached the end of our exploration of the Apache Iceberg table format, and you can now build effective data platforms.

Index

Amazon S3, 247-248
GCS, 254
HDFS, 246
encryption zones, 246
entries metadata table, 202-204
equality delete files, 34, 87, 89
ETL (extract, transform, load) jobs, 13,
158-160, 298
execute (SparkActions), 69
EXPIRE SNAPSHOTS (Dremio), 154
expire_snapshots, 93, 141
expiring snapshots to save on storage, 93-94
Expressions library, 72
extension module (Spark SQL), 130-133
extract, transform, load (ETL) jobs, 13,
158-160, 298

F

Facebook, and Hive development, 17
fanout writer option, streaming data, 223
file formats
    Iceberg's agnosticism, 31
    OLAP workloads, 5
file size and row group size (Parquet), 71
file-level security, 244-256
files metadata table, 189-192
files versus directories as basis for table format,
    19, 21
filter (SparkActions), 70, 89
filter rows query (Spark), 134
filtering rows (Dremio), 150
fixed versus variable costs in reading data, 68
Flink (see Apache Flink)
Flink SQL Client, 165-173
FlinkSink.forRowData() API, 232
FlinkSource class (Java), 231

G

GlueContext object, 161
GlueContext.write_data_frame.from_catalog(),
    161
Google Cloud Storage (GCS), 254-256
governance and security (see security and gov-
    ernance)

H

Hadoop
    catalog, 100-102, 120, 166

ecosystem, 10
Hadoop Common libraries (Flink), 164
Hadoop Distributed File System (HDFS), 5, 10,
    101, 245-246
hash function, bloom filters, 97
hash write distribution, 95, 97
headless warehouse (Tabular), 264
hidden partitions, 25, 47, 84-85, 169
Hints pattern, streaming data, 229
historical data snapshots, 15
history metadata table, 184-186, 299
Hive framework, 10, 17-19
    catalog, 102, 167
    migrating tables to Iceberg, 272-274
Hive Metastore, 17, 42, 103, 120
HudiToIcebergMigrationActionsProvider, 275

I

IAM (identity and access management), 244,
    249-250, 255
Iceberg (see Apache Iceberg)
iceberg-catalog-migrator procedure, 109-110
iceberg-delta-lake module, 274
iceberg-hudi module, 275
iceberg-spark-runtime package, 118
identifier fields, setting or dropping (Spark),
    132
identity and access management (IAM), 244,
    249-250, 255
immutability
    datafiles and COW versus MOR, 87
    snapshots and time-travel queries, 26
in-place migration, 270-271
INSERT INTO, 50
    Dremio, 152
    Flink, 172, 232
    setting sort order with, 78
    Spark SQL, 137
INSERT INTO SELECT, rewriting data into
    Iceberg, 278
INSERT OVERWRITE
    Flink, 172, 232
    Spark SQL, 138-140
inserting the query, writing queries, 50-53
INVOKER (Trino), 260
isolation of changes with branches, 207-213
isolation of database systems, multitable trans-
    actions, 213

J

JAR files, adding to Spark, 118
Java (Flink), 163, 174-178
Java API, batch reads with Flink, 231
Java Database Connectivity (JDBC), 107
JobManager (Flink), 165

K

Kafka Connect, 235-239
kafka-connect-iceberg module, 238
Key Management Service (KMS) (AWS), 247
Key Management System (KMS) (GCS), 255

L

logs and logging
    metadata_log_entries metadata table,
        186-187
    for security, 245

M

machine learning (ML), 3
    data warehouse limitations, 9
manifest files, 23, 35
    all_manifests metadata table, 198-200
    reading process, 59-60, 63
    rewriting, 92, 142, 155
    schema of, 36
    writing process, 51, 56
manifest lists, 23, 36-38
    reading process, 58, 63
    writing process, 51, 56
manifests metadata table, 192-194
MapReduce, 10, 17
massively parallel processing (MPP) systems, 7,
    95-96
Maven project, creating Flink job, 174-176
Maven-based packages, 118, 178
MAX()
    aggregation queries, 135
    Dremio, 151
max-concurrent-file-group-rewrites (SparkAc-
    tions), 70
max-file-group-size-bytes (SparkActions), 70
MERGE INTO, 54-56
    CDC implementation use case, 300-302
    Dremio, 54, 153, 281
    Flink, 173
    Spark SQL, 54, 138

merge-on-read (MOR), 32, 55, 87-91
metadata files, 38-40
    reading process, 58, 63
    writing process, 48-49, 50-52, 55-56
metadata layer, 22-23, 35
    (see also catalogs)
    architecture, 35-41
    files (see metadata files)
    manifests (see manifest files)
    partition evolution role of, 85
    partition field changes as metadata-only,
        132
    reads and writes, 46
metadata pointer, 42
metadata tables, 61, 184-206
    all_data_files, 196-198
    all_manifests, 198-200
    entries, 202-204
    files, 189-192
    Flink SQL access to, 171
    history, 184-186, 299
    manifests, 192-194
    metadata_log_entries, 186-187
    partitions, 194-195, 205
    refs, 200-202
    snapshots, 187-189
    using in conjunction, 204-206
metadata tags, object storage, 96
metadata_log_entries metadata table, 186-187
metrics collection, 91
MFA (multifactor authentication), 244
microbatching (Spark), 223
Microsoft SQL Server, 4
migrate
    between Iceberg catalogs, 109
    Hive tables to Iceberg, 86, 273
migrating between Iceberg catalogs, 102,
    108-113
migrating to Apache Iceberg, 269-282
    from Apache Hudi, 275
    from Delta Lake, 274-275
    from Hive tables, 272-274
    individual datafiles, 276-277
    planning considerations, 270-272
    by rewriting data, 277-282
ML (see machine learning)
model decay, data warehouse limitations, 9
modifying column attributes (ALTER TABLE),
    129, 149

About the Authors

Tomer Shiran is the founder and chief product officer of Dremio, an open data lakehouse platform that enables companies to run analytics in the cloud without the cost, complexity, and lock-in of data warehouses. As the company's founding CEO, Tomer built a world-class organization that has raised more than $400 million and now serves hundreds of the world's largest enterprises, including three of the Fortune 5. Prior to Dremio, Tomer was the fourth employee and VP at MapR, a big data analytics pioneer. He also held numerous product management and engineering roles at Microsoft and IBM Research, founded several websites that have served millions of users and hundreds of thousands of paying customers, and is a successful author and presenter on a wide range of industry topics. He holds an MS in computer engineering from Carnegie Mellon University and a BS in computer science from Technion–Israel Institute of Technology.

Jason Hughes is the director of technical advocacy at Dremio. Previously at Dremio he has been a product director, technical director, and senior solutions architect. He has been working in technology and data for more than a decade, including roles as tech lead for the field at Dremio, the pre-sales and post-sales lead for Presto and QueryGrid for the Americas at Teradata, and the development, deployment, and management lead of a custom CRM system for multiple auto dealerships. He is passionate about making customers and individuals successful and self-sufficient. When he's not working, he's usually taking his dog to the dog park, playing hockey, or cooking (when he feels like it). Jason lives in San Diego, California.

Alex Merced is a developer advocate for Dremio and has worked as a developer and instructor for companies such as GenEd Systems, Crossfield Digital, CampusGuard, and General Assembly. Alex is passionate about technology and has published tech content on outlets such as blogs, videos, and his podcasts *Datanation* and *Web Dev 101*. He has also spoken at many large industry conferences, such as Data Council, Data Day Texas, Subsurface, OSA Con, and more. Alex has contributed to various libraries in the JavaScript and Python worlds including SencilloDB, CoquitoJS, dremio-simple-query, and more.

Colophon

The animal on the cover of *Apache Iceberg: The Definitive Guide* is a type of seabird known as a whiskered tern (*Chlidonias hybrida*).

Whiskered terns are small-to-medium buoyant birds with a relatively short, slightly forked tail. Breeding adults have a black crown and nape as well as white cheeks and a white undertail. Their upperparts are medium gray, and their underparts are darker slate. Their bills and legs are red. Nonbreeding adults are much paler, with a dark-flecked pale crown, a dark patch behind the eye and down the nape, and a black bill.

Whiskered terns have a wide-ranging habitat. They can be found across southern Europe and Asia, southeastern Africa and Madagascar, and Australia. They live in freshwater wetlands, freshwater swamps, brackish lakes, irrigated cropland, artificial fish ponds, and a variety of other wetlands. Their diet reflects their habitat, consisting of small fish, amphibians, small crustaceans, and insects.

At one point, the global population of whiskered terns was estimated between 300,000 and 1,500,000. Their prevalence across the globe marks them as a species of least concern on endangered species lists. However, many of the animals on O'Reilly covers are endangered; all of them are important to the world.

The cover illustration is by Karen Montgomery, based on a black-and-white engraving from *British Birds*. The series design is by Edie Freedman, Ellie Volckhausen, and Karen Montgomery. The cover fonts are Gilroy Semibold and Guardian Sans. The text font is Adobe Minion Pro; the heading font is Adobe Myriad Condensed; and the code font is Dalton Maag's Ubuntu Mono.

Printed in the USA
CPSIA information can be obtained
at www.ICGtesting.com
JSHW052125270524
63872JS00009B/93

9 781098 148621